Latin American Monographs

Second Series

Military Reform and Society in New Granada, 1773–1808

22

Center for Latin American Studies
University of Florida

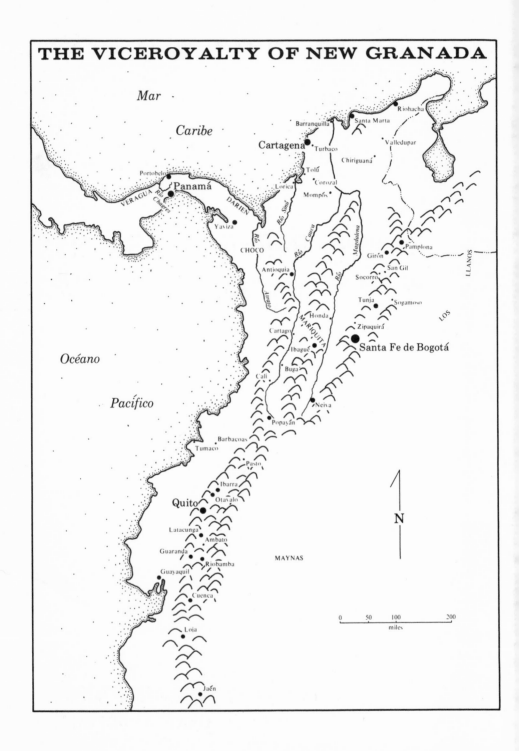

Military Reform and Society in New Granada, 1773–1808

Allan J. Kuethe

A University of Florida Book

The University Presses of Florida

Gainesville—1978

Latin American Monographs–Second Series

Committee on Publications

W. W. McPherson, *Chairman*
Graduate Research Professor
of Agricultural Economics

Paul L. Doughty
Professor of Anthropology

R. W. Bradbury
Professor Emeritus
of Economics

Lyle N. McAlister
Professor of History

Raymond E. Crist
Graduate Research Professor
of Geography

Felicity M. Trueblood
Assistant Professor of
Latin American Studies
and History

A University of Florida Book
sponsored by the
Center for Latin American Studies

The University Presses of Florida is the
scholarly publishing agency for the State
University System of Florida.

Library of Congress Cataloging in Publication Data

Kuethe, Allan J   1940–
     Military reform and society in New Granada, 1773–1808.

     (Latin American monographs; 2d ser., 22)
     "A University of Florida book."
     Bibliography: p.
     1.   Spain.   Ejército—Colonial forces—History.
2.   Colombia—History, Military.   3.   Colombia—History—
To 1810.   I.   Title.   II.   Series: Florida.   University,
Gainesville.   Center for Latin American Studies.   Latin
American monographs; 2d ser., 22.
UA789.K83   355.3'1'0946   77–21908
ISBN 0–8130–0570–1

Typography by Chapman's Phototypesetting
Fullerton, California

Printed by Rose Printing Company
Tallahassee, Florida

for my parents
Margaret and Raymond Kuethe

Acknowledgments

THOSE WHO have contributed to the appearance of this book have my deepest gratitude. From the University of Florida, I owe special thanks to Lyle N. McAlister, who suggested the possibility of this study to me as a dissertation and served as a constant source of inspiration, and to David Bushnell, who provided many helpful insights and imparted to me his enthusiasm for Colombian history. I also wish to thank J. León Helguera of Vanderbilt University for his criticism of the manuscript during its early stages and the late John Phelan of the University of Wisconsin for the ideas that he shared with me about the Comuneros. I am particularly indebted to Brian Blakeley of Texas Tech University for his incisive suggestions on style. To the staffs of the Archivo General de Indias, the Archivo General de Simancas, the Archivo Nacional de Colombia, the Archivo Central del Cauca, and the Archivo Nacional de Ecuador, I am deeply grateful for their gracious courtesy and cooperation. I appreciate the financial support provided by the College of Arts and Sciences and the Graduate School of Texas Tech University. Finally, my heartfelt thanks go to my wife, Lourdes, who supported and aided my work with patient understanding from the beginning research to the final editing.

Contents

Introduction

As a consequence of its stunning defeat in the Seven Years' War, the Spanish monarchy under Charles III (1759–88) initiated a far-reaching reorganization of its American empire. Until that conflict, the new Bourbon dynasty had been satisfied simply to repair and to revitalize the old Hapsburg military, economic, and administrative system that it inherited in 1700. The serious reverses suffered at the hands of the British and the anticipation of renewed hostilities, however, prompted the government of Charles III to undertake comprehensive reforms to strengthen its colonial domains.[1] This reorganization featured well-known programs designed to stimulate economic growth, to increase public revenues, and to promote effective administration. Specifically, the monarchy relaxed trade restrictions within the empire, which culminated in an edict of "free trade" in 1778; organized special technical missions and guilds to modernize mining methods; tightened revenue collection; created new government monopolies while expanding others; expelled the Jesuits; introduced the intendant system of provincial administration; and established a number of new captaincies general and one new viceroyalty, that in Río de la Plata. A final aspect of the colonial reorganization was an empire-wide military reform intended to enhance American defense capability and self-reliance. The course of that military reform in the Viceroyalty of New Granada, and its

1. Arthur S. Aiton, "Spanish Colonial Reorganization under the Family Compact."

impact upon the colonial social and political structure, is the subject of the present study.

The establishment of the Viceroyalty of New Granada in 1739 fixed the jurisdiction of the viceroy, as captain general of Santa Fe de Bogotá, over most of the territory which now comprises Colombia, Ecuador, Panama, and Venezuela.[2] The viceroy's authority extended from the Province of Veragua, bordering the Captaincy General of Guatemala in the north, to the Province of Mainas on the Amazon River in the south, and from the Presidency of Quito in the west, to the Province of Guayana across the Orinoco River on the Brazilian frontier. Within these perimeters, only Caracas was independent of the viceroy's command. When Caracas was elevated to the rank of a captaincy general in 1777, the three eastern provinces of Guayana, Cumaná, and Maracaibo, as well as the islands of Margarita and Trinidad, were detached from Santa Fe de Bogotá and joined to the new military jurisdiction. Thereafter, the Captaincy General of Santa Fe de Bogotá remained territorially stable until just before the end of the colonial period, when the southern provinces of Mainas, Quijos, and Guayaquil were transferred to the Viceroyalty of Lima. In the following text the administrative division "New Granada" will be taken to exclude the Captaincy General of Caracas, because, despite nominal subordination to Santa Fe de Bogotá, it was in effect a separate military jurisdiction after 1777.

Of the four American viceroyalties, New Granada has benefited the least from in-depth historical investigation. Enough information is available, nevertheless, to indicate that, as a rule, the Bourbon reforms made only a moderate, although far from negligible, impact in New Granada. The Granadine counterparts of the well-known missions of José de Gálvez and José Antonio de Areche, which laid the foundations for fiscal and administrative reform in New Spain and Peru respectively, were those of Juan Gutiérrez de Piñeres in New Granada and José García de León y Pizarro in the Presidency of Quito. The catastrophic Comunero Rebellion of 1781, however, confronted the reform efforts of Gutiérrez and for an instant even threatened to topple the regime in Santa Fe de Bogotá. As a consequence, although some progress was made in the improvement of tax collection and in the advancement of royal monopolies sought by Gutiérrez, plans to introduce the intendant system of administration did not materialize except for a short-lived experiment in the Province of Cuenca.[3]

Nor did endeavors to modernize silver mining methods in New Granada bear appreciable results. Juan José de Elhuyar, the older brother of the better

2. The crown had earlier experimented with a viceroyalty for New Granada from 1717 to 1723. María Teresa Garrido Conde, *La primera creación del Virreinato de Nueva Granada (1717–1723)*.

3. Luis Navarro García, *Intendencias en Indias*, pp. 49, 122; Antonio Caballero y Góngora, "Relación del estado del Nuevo Reino de Granada . . . 1789," in *Relaciones de mando: Memorias presentadas por los gobernantes del Nuevo Reino de Granada*, ed. by E. Posada and P. M. Ibáñez (hereafter cited as *Relaciones de mando*), pp. 256–57.

known Fausto who later headed the mining reform in New Spain, led a technical mission in 1785 to the Province of Mariquita, where he was later joined by a cadre of German scientists. This mission, however, was handicapped by the misfortune of having departed Europe prior to the discovery of the more advanced Born method of amalgamation. Also plagued by a poor location and by a lack of political support, it collapsed in 1795.[4]

The consequences in New Granada of the relaxation of trade restrictions were less clear-cut. On the negative side, the policy of "free trade" perpetuated serious recessions in the Quito textile industry and the Panamanian interoceanic commercial complex, which had dated from the opening of the more economical Cape Horn route to licensed vessels early in the century.[5] On the positive side, a minor diversification of exports did evolve by the end of the colonial period through the marketing of small quantities of cotton, *quina* (medicinal bark), indigo, and dyewood. Moreover, a substantial expansion developed in cacao production, chiefly from Guayaquil, but also to a lesser extent from the Cúcuta district. The preponderant export, nevertheless, continued as always to be gold.[6] Consequently, while substantial repercussions were felt in the Presidency of Quito and in Panama, the effect of relaxed trade restrictions upon most of New Granada was modest at best.

In some instances, however, colonial reorganization did produce definite changes. For one thing, the Jesuits, as in the rest of the empire, were successfully removed in 1767.[7] Also, tobacco and *aguardiente* monopolies became major sources of royal income and, along with an overall rise in customs taxes, they accounted in large measure for the noteworthy growth of public revenues from roughly 950,000 pesos in 1772 (territories later transferred to Caracas not included) to just over 3 million at the close of the colonial period nearly forty years later.[8] Nevertheless, the overall effect of the Bourbon reforms in New

4. Arthur P. Whitaker, "The Elhuyar Mining Missions and the Enlightenment," pp. 573–85; José Ezpeleta, "Relación del estado del Nuevo Reino de Granada . . . 1796," and Pedro Mendinueta, "Relación del estado del Nuevo Reino de Granada . . . 1803," both in *Relaciones de mando*, pp. 343–46, 500–502.

5. Pedro Messía de la Cerda, "Relación del estado del Virreinato de Santafé . . . 1772," in *Relaciones de mando*, p. 108; Francisco Antonio Moreno y Escandón "Estado del Virreinato de Santafé, Nuevo Reino de Granada . . . 1772," p. 588; Manuel Guirior, "Relación del estado del Nuevo Reino de Granada . . . 1776," in *Relaciones de mando*, pp. 148–49; Francisco Silvestre, *Descripción del Reyno de Santa Fe de Bogotá, escrita en 1789*, pp. 44–45.

6. Messía de la Cerda, in *Relaciones de mando*, pp. 105–6; Mendinueta, in *Relaciones de mando*, pp. 507–8; Luis Eduardo Nieto Arteta, *Economía y cultura en la historia de Colombia*, pp. 22–23; Luis Ospina Vásquez, *Industria y protección en Colombia, 1810–1930*, pp. 38–39.

7. The expulsion of the Jesuits from New Granada is one of the Bourbon reforms that has not been neglected. See Charles J. Fleener, "The Expulsion of the Jesuits from the Viceroyalty of New Granada, 1767" (Ph.D. diss.); Juan Manuel Pacheco, "La expulsión de la Compañía de Jesús del Nuevo Reino de Granada en 1767."

8. Moreno y Escandón, "Estado . . . 1772," pp. 603–5; José Manuel Restrepo, *Historia de la revolución de la República de Colombia en la América meridional*, 1: xxxi; John P. Harrison, "The Evolution of the Colombian Tobacco Trade, to 1875," pp. 164–66.

Granada was clearly not comparable to their impact in the other three vice-royalties.

The military aspect of the Bourbon reforms in the Spanish Empire has received excellent although limited analysis. The principal work to date, *The "Fuero Militar" in New Spain*, was completed by Lyle N. McAlister in 1957. McAlister found that, although the military reform did indeed revitalize and strengthen the defense system of New Spain through an expansion of the regular army and the creation of a new, disciplined militia, its chief significance lay, in the long run, in its unexpectedly disruptive impact upon social and political institutions. The expanded privileges of the reformed army placed the military beyond the effective reach of civilian authority and shaped a tradition of military elitism which, he concluded, became the foundation for a praetorian tradition in independent Mexico.

> During the closing decades of Spanish dominion, the army, thus created, acquired prestige and power as the defender of the nation in the face of almost constant threats of war and invasion. By the very nature of its functions and constitution it was also a class apart and so regarded itself. The possession of special privileges enhanced its sense of uniqueness and superiority, and at the same time rendered it virtually immune from civil authority. Unfortunately, power and privilege were not accompanied by a commensurate sense of responsibility. A large proportion of officers and men regarded military service as an opportunity for the advancement of personal interests rather than as a civic obligation. Until the abdication of Ferdinand VII in 1808, the troublemaking potential of the military was held in check by a long tradition of loyalty to the crown. However, as the prestige of the monarchy declined in the following years, this limitation was removed and the army emerged as an autonomous and irresponsible institution. It was this army, under the banner of the Three Guarantees, that consummated independence and behind a façade of republican institutions made itself master of Mexico.[9]

Just how far the McAlister thesis can be extended to the rest of the empire remains to be seen, but recent research on various aspects of the colonial period strongly suggests that diversity within the colonial experience was the rule rather than the exception.[10] In the case of the military reform, Leon Campbell found that the impact of military privileges was considerably more subdued in Peru than in New Spain.[11] And for New Spain itself, Christon Archer has

9. McAlister, *The "Fuero Militar" in New Spain, 1764–1800*, pp. 1–15.
10. For example, see Lewis Hanke, "A Modest Proposal for a Moratorium on Grand Generalizations: Some Thoughts on the Black Legend."
11. Campbell, "The Military Reform in the Viceroyalty of Peru, 1762–1800" (Ph.D. diss.). See also Campbell, "The Changing Racial and Administrative Structure of the Peruvian Military under the Later Bourbons."

convincingly demonstrated that militia service, despite expanded corporate privileges, was far from an unmixed blessing, especially for enlisted men who frequently suffered severe hardships when mobilized for garrison duty.[12] Moreover, McAlister limited the focus of his pioneering study almost solely to the issue of military privilege. He did not attempt either to relate directly the military reorganization to other Bourbon reforms or to explore in his social analysis the relationship between military privileges and the highly explosive sociopolitical rivalry between the Spanish and native-born, which contributed significantly to the Wars for Independence.

Certainly, McAlister's conclusions cannot be extended to New Granada without substantial modifications. The processes he identified in New Spain were, in fact, present in New Granada, but they were not destined to produce the same results. Military reform, which included an appreciable strengthening of the regular army and the establishment of a disciplined militia complete with full military privileges, worked as in New Spain to convert the armed forces into an elite element in the colonial community and, as a consequence, encouraged arrogant and irresponsible military behavior. The long-run impact of the reformed army upon existing political institutions and the colonial heritage was, however, modest at best.

The crucial factor in shaping the history of the military reform in New Granada was the use of the army—apart from its accepted responsibilities for external defense—as a controversial instrument to sustain royal authority in areas of domestic policy. The enlightened regime of Charles III, at the same time that it reduced its dependence upon the Church and expelled the Society of Jesus from America, embraced the military to underpin its reform program in New Granada. It also employed its troops in costly, wasteful frontier campaigns that drained the treasury of newly acquired revenues and by so doing eventually undermined and weakened much of the impetus for reform. The political role of the army provoked widespread hostility and even resistance from local creole elites, especially those from the interior provinces who, because the new Bourbon political and fiscal rigor threatened their traditional independence and vested interests, were at best dubious beneficiaries of the colonial reorganization. As a consequence, a successful marriage never emerged between the military corporation and the creole aristocracy of those vital interior provinces, and an enduring elitist military tradition failed to take root in New Granada.

The reformed military, nevertheless, functioned in its own right as a dynamic catalyst for social change in the colonial community, particularly in the coastal areas where its role as defender of the colony won it general acceptance. Most significant, the disciplined militia, through its privileged corpo-

12. Archer, "The Key to the Kingdom: The Defense of Veracruz, 1780–1810," and "To Serve the King: Military Recruitment in Late Colonial Mexico."

rate constitution, offered its members rights and immunities not available in civilian life. These rights were an important vehicle for social improvement, especially for the humble Negro and mulatto populations of the lowlands. On another level, the acquisition of militia officerships worked to validate claims to social excellence for those of uncertain status and often acted to reinforce individual power and influence within local communities. Finally, the expanded regular army offered career opportunities for the younger sons of creole families who lacked other alternatives to sustain a respectable social position.

The impact of the military reform, however, varied considerably from region to region in New Granada. The provinces were so diverse and the gulf between coast and uplands so vast that the reform never developed a unitary character. Rather, its history in New Granada was the cumulative story of individual provinces, each with its own characteristics and peculiar experiences. When pieced together, nevertheless, the history of the military reform in New Granada provides an invaluable insight into the fortunes of the royal administration as it first attempted to strengthen and reform the viceroyalty, and, finally, in the twilight of the colonial period, as it struggled to preserve the colony from the revolutionary forces sweeping the western world.[13]

13. A census taken in 1778 calculated the population of New Granada at slightly under 1,300,000 inhabitants. "Padron general del Virreynato del Nuevo Reino de Granada, 1778" (hereafter cited as "Padron general, 1778"), AGI, Estado, legajo 54.

1. Early Military Reform in Cartagena and Panama

As PART OF THE ATTEMPT to strengthen its American empire in the aftermath of the Seven Years' War, the Spanish monarchy began a reorganization of the army of the Viceroyalty of New Granda in 1773. Initially emphasizing the most strategic portions of New Granada, this reform first embraced the Caribbean coastal provinces of Cartagena and Panama. A few years later the crown reorganized the defenses of Guayaquil on the Pacific and those of inland Popayán, but it did not significantly extend the reform into the interior of the viceroyalty until the 1780s. Largely due to weak local leadership, the important beginnings in Cartagena and Panama produced more failures than successes, a pattern destined to plague the early history of the military reform. Yet, it was on the coast that the reformed military, despite its apparent weaknesses, first asserted itself as the powerful, revitalized institution that would dominate the closing decades of eighteenth-century New Granada.

At the time the Spanish government acted in New Granada, it had already completed extensive, pioneering experiments in military reform. The disastrous reverses inflicted upon the empire by the British at Havana and Manila during the Seven Years' War had exposed the perilously weak, flabby condition of Spain's defenses. Motivated by a fervent desire for revenge, as well as by the fear that the British would in all likelihood seek further advantage, and prodded by its French ally under the Family Compact, the government of

Charles III undertook an extensive reassessment of its military strategy.[1] Concluding that a far-reaching reorganization of its colonial defenses was imperative, the monarchy dispatched the able Conde de Ricla to Cuba as captain general in 1763 to repossess Havana under the terms of the Treaty of Paris and to reform immediately the island's military forces. To serve as Ricla's chief assistant and inspector general of the army of Cuba, the crown selected Field Marshal Alejandro O'Reilly, an officer of brilliant record, who commanded the respect and trust both of the French government and of his own.[2] Ricla's and O'Reilly's military experiments in Cuba not only proved important for that island, but they served as a pilot project for the whole empire as well.

The Conde de Ricla's instructions commanded troop reform at two levels. First, the regular or veteran (these terms may be used synonymously) army, which had been vanquished in 1762, was to be rebuilt and strengthened. Second, and more far-reaching, the militia of Cuba was to be remodeled along lines already developed in Spain, something which Ricla himself originally had recommended to the crown.[3] Because of poor health, however, Ricla conceded to O'Reilly the primary responsibility for the actual reshaping of Cuba's defenses.[4] The latter ably exploited the opportunity to establish a personal reputation, which later led to his appointment as inspector general of the army of America.

Changes in the regular army were quite modest and much less significant than those for the militia. The regular army of the empire possessed two basic types of units. One operated on a *fijo* or fixed basis. During the reign of Philip V (1700–1746) these units usually had been established in battalion or regiment size in the principal ports and strongpoints of the empire.[5] Permanently garrisoned in specific locations, they recruited principally in America, although sometimes they received European replacements.[6] Problems arose, however, because most strategic points lay along tropical coasts where disease, among other factors, constantly drained effective troop levels. To compensate for local manpower deficiencies, a second type of unit, the Spanish-based bat-

---

1. Aiton, "Spanish Colonial Reorganization." The only serious consideration inhibiting Spain from reopening the struggle with Great Britain was the fear of further defeat. Unsigned *dictámenes* (opinions), San Ildefonso, October 4, 1775, and September 27, 1776; dictámen of the Conde de Ricla, January 17, 1777, and of José de Gálvez, El Pardo, February 3, 1777, all in AGS: GM, legajo 7311.

2. Aiton, pp. 276–80; for a recent description of this mission to Cuba, see Bibiano Torres Ramírez, "Alejandro O'Reilly en Cuba," or Torres Ramírez, *Alejandro O'Reilly en las Indias*, pp. 17–48.

3. Secret instruction to Ricla, Buen Retiro, March 29, 1763, AGI: Santo Domingo, legajo 1211.

4. Torres Ramírez, *Alejandro O'Reilly*, p. 21.

5. The dates for the establishment of many of the military units of America can be found in *Estado militar de España*.

6. The fijo regiment of Cuba traditionally recruited in the Canary Islands. *Expediente* (file) on recruitment in the Canary Islands, 1754–63, AGI: Santo Domingo, legajo 2116.

talion, was deployed in America during wartime or crisis, as well as at the more vulnerable positions during peacetime. Although expensive, these rotating battalions placed fresh European troops in key trouble spots and rendered invaluable assistance. To upgrade the quality of the Cuban defenses, Alejandro O'Reilly injected new officers and personnel into existing fijo units and developed a formalized system for rotating the supplementary Spanish battalions.[7]

In reforming the militia of Cuba, O'Reilly formulated policies of great significance, which were later extended to the Viceroyalty of New Granada. The primary difficulty with depending too much on regular troops, especially on an empire-wide basis, had been the prohibitive expense occasioned both by the vast American coastline and by the relatively limited, if expanding, resource base. A more realistic alternative was the establishment of a large, well-trained reserve, which could reinforce fewer, strategically placed regular units.[8] Earlier, in 1734, the government of Philip V had created this kind of an instrument in Spain when it converted the provincial militia to what was called a "disciplined" footing. Under this system, the royal authorities standardized militia battalions and regiments; assigned them cadres of regular officers and enlisted men; developed a systematic training program; provided arms, uniforms, and other essential equipment; and, to enhance motivation, granted militiamen extensive military corporate privileges.[9] This scheme exposed much of the Spanish citizenry to military service in the hope that a capable reserve force could be readily assembled to supplement the regular army. O'Reilly's mission was to extend that system to America.

The American militia had never been converted to a disciplined footing. Although many provinces maintained a militia, these establishments were usually more shadow than substance. The largest tactical units were seldom more than separate companies; they were woefully deficient in leadership, equipment, and training; and, as demonstrated at Havana, they counted for little in battle. A second but rarer type of volunteer force was the "urban" militia. Urban units were normally sponsored by municipalities or guilds, and they were called into sevice only when their immediate locality was threatened.[10] Once the disciplined militia system was introduced into America, the military reformers commonly lumped the older, non-disciplined provincial militia with the urban militia in order to distinguish it from its reformed counterpart, a usage sanctioned by law in 1791 (see chapter 7).

7. Secret instruction to Ricla, Buen Retiro, March 29, 1763; royal order, San Ildefonso, October 1764, AGI: Santo Domingo, legajo 2078; O'Reilly to Secretary of the Indies Julián de Arriaga, Havana, July 1763, AGI: Santo Domingo, legajo 2117; idem, Havana, July 28, 1764, AGI: Santo Domingo, legajo 2118.
8. General discourse, by Ricla, Madrid, January 20, 1763, AGI: Santo Domingo, legajo 2116.
9. Félix Colón y Larriátegui Ximénez de Embún, *Juzgados militares de España y sus Indias . . .* , 2: 469, 562; Lyle N. McAlister, "The Reorganization of the Army of New Spain, 1763–1766," p. 4.
10. McAlister, "Reorganization," pp. 4–6; Colón, *Juzgados militares*, 2: 562.

During 1763 and 1764, O'Reilly toured Cuba and in accordance with his instructions he replaced the existing militia with new, "disciplined" units.[11] After he completed this work, the crown ordered O'Reilly to Puerto Rico, where he continued his reorganization of the defense system.[12] When recalled to Spain in 1765, he codified his accomplishments in a *Reglamento para las milicias de infantería, y caballería de la Isla de Cuba*, first drafted in 1764 but not officially promulgated until 1769. This legislation was supplemented by a *reglamento* (regulation) issued for Puerto Rico in 1765.[13] While preserving the system originally developed in Spain, these codes contained important American adjustments and could, therefore, serve as models for attempts at reform in other colonies. After a brief return to America for a special tour of duty in Louisiana, where he also created a disciplined militia, the crown rewarded O'Reilly for his valuable services by appointing him inspector general of the army of America.[14] Meanwhile, in 1764, a separate commission under Lieutenant General Juan de Villalba y Angulo undertook a similar mission to New Spain, although Villalba elected largely to produce his own policies rather than to adopt those developed by O'Reilly in Cuba.[15]

In New Granada, the years immediately following the Seven Years' War witnessed a heightened concern with defense problems, but this concern produced no major institutional departures. On one level, a burst of activity developed in the repair and construction of fixed coastal fortifications.[16] On another level, the crown attempted to alleviate manpower problems by employing Spanish battalions. Thus, from 1766 to 1773 at least two rotating battalions served in the viceroyalty at all times.[17] It was not until 1771 that Alejandro O'Reilly, fresh from his return to Spain from Louisiana, and now inspector general of the army of America, directed his attention toward a structural reorganization of the army of New Granada.

11. Ricla to Arriaga, Havana, April 9, 1764, AGI: Santo Domingo, legajo 1509.

12. Torres Ramírez, *Alejandro O'Reilly*, pp. 55–94; Ricardo Torres Reyes, "El Mariscal O'Reilly y las defensas de San Juan, 1765–1777."

13. The original draft of the Cuban reglamento (hereafter cited as *Reglamento . . . de Cuba*) can be found in AGI: Santo Domingo, legajo 2118; the published work is in AGI: Indiferente, legajo 1885; for a copy of the Puerto Rican reglamento, see AGI: Santa Fe, legajo 1007.

14. Jack D. L. Holmes, *Honor and Fidelity: The Louisiana Infantry Regiment and the Louisiana Militia Companies, 1766–1821*, pp. 17–21; royal orders, August 25, November 21, 1770, AGI: Indiferente, legajo 1885.

15. McAlister, "Reorganization." Before the reform reached New Granada, a military reorganization had also taken place in Santo Domingo, Río de la Plata, and Peru. Troop report for America, Madrid, January 8, 1771, AGI: Indiferente, legajo 1885.

16. Royal order, December 16, 1765, AGI: Quito, legajo 573; expediente on the fortification of the Plaza de Panama, 1764–71, AGI: Panama, legajo 359; Enrique Marco Dorta, *Cartagena de Indias: Puerto y plaza fuerte*, pp. 293–302.

17. These battalions included two from the Regiment of the Queen, which served in Panama and Quito from 1766 to 1769. They were replaced by one battalion each from the regiments of Murcia and Naples; a third battalion, this from the Regiment of Savoy, was sent to Cartagena in 1771. Governor Blasco Orosco to Messía de la Cerda, Portobelo, April 25, 1769, ANC: MM,

New Granada's defense system was based upon a series of coastal strong-holds and fortified cities. The most important were Santa Marta, Cartagena, Portobelo, Panama, and Guayaquil. With the exception of a small number of companies stationed in the interior, the regular army of the viceroyalty had traditionally been deployed in these coastal bases. This army, however, was pitifully small, and in 1771, when O'Reilly focused his attention on the defenses of New Granada, it amounted to only one infantry battalion and twelve and one-half separate infantry, cavalry, and artillery companies, not including units located in those provinces later transferred to Caracas (see Table 1). The militia, moreover, which was scattered at random among the various provinces and municipalities, lacked any real value due to extreme deficiencies in organization, leadership, training, and equipment. Cartagena, with one infantry battalion and two artillery companies, possessed the largest veteran garrison in New Granada. On the other extreme, Panama, despite its strategic significance, had a fixed garrison of only one artillery company. Both strongholds depended heavily upon Spanish-based forces.

Administrative responsibility for the fortifications and fixed garrisons of New Granada was largely divided among the three important regional military jurisdictions, the commandancies general of Cartagena, Panama, and Quito, each of which eventually played a major role in the evolution of the military reform. The commandancies general of Cartagena and Panama dated from the second establishment of the viceroyalty in 1739, while Quito reached that status just after the Seven Years' War.[18] The office of commandant general pertained to the governor of the province from which each of these jurisdictions derived its name; in Quito this functionary was also the president of the royal *audiencia* (high court). In addition to their immediate governorships, the commandants general also exercised military responsibilities in neighboring provinces. The Commandancy General of Cartagena extended east to include Santa Marta and Riohacha; Panama encompassed Veragua, Portobelo, and Darién; and Quito consisted of the seven governorships and seven *corregimientos* dependent upon that region's audiencia.[19]

It is difficult to define the precise responsibilities of the commandants gen-

vol. 92, fols. 750–57; Governor Manuel de Agreda to Messía de la Cerda, Portobelo, April 25, 1769, ANC: MM, vol. 64, fols. 108–11; Governor Nicolás de Castro to Messía de la Cerda, Panama, May 3, 1769, ANC: MM, vol. 90, fols. 825–26; Governor Vicente de Olazinegui to Messía de la Cerda, Panama, August 1, 1769, ANC: MM, fols. 948 52; idem, Panama, September 10, 1771, ANC: MM, vol. 92, fols. 527–29; Governor Gregorio de la Sierra to Messía de la Cerda, Cartagena, October 11, 1771, ANC: MM, vol. 89, fols. 225–38.

18. Royal cédula, August 20, 1739, in *Ximénez de Quesada* 4 (August 1968): 241–49; Silvestre, *Descripción*, pp. 17–18; expediente on the command of the troops of Quito, 1779, AGI: Quito, legajo 573.

19. Governorships: Quito, Guayaquil, Popayán, Cuenca, Mainas, Quijós y Macas, Jaén de Bracamoros; corregimientos: Quito, Loja y Zamora, Riobamba, Chimbo or Guaranda, Ibarra, Tacunga, Otavalo.

eral to their outlying provinces. These relationships were vague and varied considerably from one region to the next. Moreover, much depended upon individual administrations and problems. The commandant general of Cartagena exercised authority in Santa Marta and Riohacha mainly in matters of common defense involving his own governorship. The governor of Santa Marta had an independent troop allotment of two and one-half companies and sometimes provided detachments for use in Riohacha. In matters of local concern, he normally bypassed Cartagena, communicating directly with the viceregal capital, Santa Fe de Bogotá. In the Commandancy General of Quito, the governors of Guayaquil and Popayán, who each commanded one company, enjoyed prerogatives similar to those of the governor of Santa Marta. However, the remaining provinces of that jurisdiction were directly dependent on Quito for their troops and equipment. Likewise, the provinces of Veragua, Portobelo, and Darién obtained their military outlays through Panama. Nevertheless, the officials ruling the dependent provinces within the jurisdictions of Panama and Quito, although more directly tied to their respective commandants general than their counterparts with independent troop allotments, often bypassed these officers in purely local affairs. Not until the 1790s did the functions of the commandants general become more clearly defined.

The importance of these regional jurisdictions is, to a large degree, a reflection of the difficult nature of New Granada's geography. New Granada was a large land of towering mountains, deep valleys, and tropical coasts and lowlands. Communication among the various regions was painfully slow. Because of the impassable jungles that covered the Chocó region, Panama could only be reached by sea from the rest of New Granada. Depending upon weather conditions and the season of the year, it took roughly a month to journey from Cartagena, the main port on the Caribbean coast, up the Magdalena River to Honda, the interior river port, although theoretically the mail could make it in half that time. From Honda it took another eight days to reach Santa Fe by land.[20] From Santa Fe, the effort to reach Quito in the southwest, or even Popayán, was immense. While estimates of the time varied with the luck and endurance of the individual, even a good traveler was unlikely to reach Quito in less than two or two and one-half months.[21] As a consequence of these communication difficulties, therefore, the regional commandants general often asserted considerable local autonomy, while frequently mistrusting the distant central authority.

As a result of the geographically enforced decentralization of institutional

20. Antonio Ybot León, *La arteria histórica del Nuevo Reino de Granada* (*Cartagena-Sante Fe, 1538–1798*), pp. 38, 169–70, 217–20.
21. Abel-Romeo Castillo, *Los gobernadores de Guayaquil del siglo XVIII*, p. 95.

life, the history of the military reform in New Granada cannot be understood in terms of a unitary viceregal experience. There was no attempt at wholesale reform as in the smaller jurisdictions of Cuba and Puerto Rico or even as had been executed in New Spain by the Villalba mission. The military reform in New Granada evolved on a clearly regional, piecemeal basis, with local authority asserting substantial initiative, influence, and power. The New Granada reform was the sum of the varied experiences of the several regions and their respective subdivisions.

O'Reilly first attempted military reform in the strategic coastal provinces of Cartagena and Panama. In mid-1771 he prompted the crown to order a census of able-bodied men, an action which amounted to the first step in the planning of a disciplined militia, and shortly thereafter, he won authorization to proceed with the formulation of concrete plans for the raising of such a militia, including the selection of officer cadres. He also gained approval for a substantial enlargement of the regular army. By October 1772, preparations were complete.[22] The reform began with a royal order of November 24, 1772, which commanded the expansion of Cartagena's fixed infantry complement from one to two battalions; a second decree of January 11, 1773, created a fixed battalion for Panama.[23] Orders for the establishment of a disciplined militia came on February 12, 1773, for Panama and on March 18, 1773, for Cartagena.[24]

Cartagena and Panama, although possessing similar climates and a shared sense of strategic importance, differed in a number of significant ways. During the early colonial period the Isthmus of Panama had enjoyed immense prominence as the legal crossing for commerce destined for Peru and the South American Pacific coast. However, with the decline of the galleon system under the Bourbons and the transition to a widespread use of registered ships that could sail directly around Cape Horn, transisthmian commerce ground to a near halt.[25] As a result, Spain demoted Panama from the seat of an audiencia to a mere military governorship in 1751, although at the rank of a commandancy general.[26] As the economy withered, the population stagnated in number and vitality. By 1778 the Governorship of Panama proper possessed

22. Expedientes on the formation of the disciplined militia of Cartagena and the establishment of the Fixed Regiment of Cartagena, 1771–73, AGI: Santa Fe, legajo 1007; letter jacket, Arriaga to O'Reilly, June 1, 1771, AGI: Panama, legajo 359.

23. Quiroga to Secretary of the Viceroy Pedro de Ureta, Cartagena, February 8, 1773, ANC: MM, vol. 85, fols. 865–67; Governor Nicolás Quijano to Guirior, Panama, June 10, 1773, ANC: MM, vol. 90, fols. 1044–49.

24. Royal order, February 12, 1773, ANC: MM, vol. 98, fol. 539; royal order, March 18, 1773, ANC: MM, vol. 87, fols. 790–94.

25. Jorge Juan and Antonio de Ulloa, *A Voyage to South America*, pp. 55–58, 72–77; Silvestre, *Descripción*, pp. 44–45; description of Portobelo, January 25, 1753, AGI: Panama, legajo 356.

26. Clarence H. Haring, *The Spanish Empire in America*, p. 316.

only 37,631 pacified and free inhabitants; Veragua, 18,747; Portobelo, 1,479; and Darién, 1,093.[27]

Despite its economic decline, the Commandancy General of Panama retained military significance because of its strategic location. Both ports, Panama on the Pacific side of the isthmus and Portobelo on the Caribbean, were fortified as was the entrance to the Chagres River, the main transportation artery for interoceanic crossings. Nevertheless, its defenses normally languished in a deficient state. In the War of Jenkins' Ear, an English attack under the command of Admiral Edward Vernon, which immediately followed the outbreak of hostilities, caught Portobelo so completely by surprise that its handful of defenders managed no real resistance. Apparently planning to return later, Vernon destroyed Portobelo's fortifications and abandoned the city in favor of more challenging conquests.[28] Spain quickly dispatched the rotating Infantry Battalion of Granada to Portobelo, which proved sufficient to deter further attacks, and in 1741 converted it into a fixed battalion.[29] Initially, Spain hoped to sustain this unit at ten companies, but the small local population provided few recruits, and the tropical climate inflicted a terrible attrition on troop levels. The crown soon officially reduced the battalion to only seven companies, but in the long run even these could not be sustained.[30] When Spain entered the Seven Years' War, the unit possessed little more than 100 men, so again Spain dispatched European rotating battalions to the isthmus and, in the peace that followed, continued to rely on them.[31] Finally, in 1769, the fixed battalion completely disintegrated.[32] Thereafter, with the exception of a local artillery company, the enfeebled commandancy general depended entirely upon rotating troops until O'Reilly reestablished Panama's battalion in 1773.

In contrast to Panama, Cartagena experienced modest growth during this same period. Located near the mouth of the Magdalena River, it was the principal Caribbean port of New Granada. Because of its immense, magnificent bay, Cartagena had served during the era of the convoy system as the shelter

27. "Padrón general, 1778", AGI: Estado, legajo 54.

28. James Ferguson King, ed., "Admiral Vernon at Portobelo: 1739"; description of Portobelo, January 25, 1753.

29. President Dionisio Martínez de la Vega to Spain, Panama, August 26, 1741, AGI: Santa Fe, legajo 940; President Dionisio de Alsedo y Herrera to Spain, Panama, March 28, 1744, AGI: Panama, legajo 356.

30. Royal order, July 14, 1751, AGI: Panama, legajo 356.

31. Governor Manuel de Montiano to Viceroy José de Solís, Panama, May 15, 1759, ANC: MM, vol. 103, fols. 709–12; royal order, December 8, 1762, ANC: MM, vol. 83, fols. 316–22; Orosco to Messía de la Cerda, Panama, August 27, 1766, ANC: MM, vol. 92, fols. 750–57; Agreda to Messía de la Cerda, Portobelo, April 25, 1769; Castro to Messía de la Cerda, Panama, May 3, 1769; Olazinegui to Messía de la Cerda, Panama, August 1, 1769; idem, Panama, September 10, 1771.

32. Olazinegui to Messía de la Cerda, Panama, August 1, 1769.

for the fleet destined for Portobelo, and it was the first legal landing point for purposes of commerce, with merchants coming from as far away as Popayán and Quito.[33] The liberalization of commercial regulations, climaxed by the 1778 edict of free trade, affected Cartagena positively although moderately, as the port continued to serve as a depot for manufactured consumer goods moving up the Magdalena for the interior of the viceroyalty in exchange for agricultural products, brazilwood, precious metals, and emeralds.[34] In 1795, in recognition of its commercial significance, the crown established a *consulado* (merchant guild) in Cartagena.[35] Demographically, the city contained a relatively large and commercially oriented population of slightly under 10,000 freemen.[36]

The inland portions of the province, although substantial in area and population, remained underdeveloped except for the river port of Mompós. Most of the rural population lived by ranching and subsistence agriculture; others provided the city with necessities, usually by small boats traveling along the coast or through nearby swamps and rivers. Significantly, however, the agricultural output of the province was insufficient to meet local urban needs, and consequently the city of Cartagena depended upon interior agriculture for much of its supply and in later decades upon direct imports from the United States.[37] At the time of O'Reilly's reform, the population of Cartagena Province, including the city, totaled some 108,756 freemen.[38]

Militarily, Cartagena ranked among Spain's most important strongholds in America. Its massive system of fortifications, naval facilities, and strategic location made it the key to the coast of northern South America. Along with the lesser stronghold of Santa Marta to the east, Cartagena protected the Magdalena River Valley, the principal transportation and invasion route into the interior of the viceroyalty. So important was this defensive complex that between 1771 and 1777 the government spent over a million pesos simply to construct a dike closing an unwanted opening in the bay at Boca Grande.[39] The office of governor and commandant general of Cartagena rated as one of the most prestigious in the viceroyalty and was normally filled by a man holding the rank of brigadier general. It carried a salary that on occasion surpassed

33. Juan and Ulloa, *A Voyage to South America*, pp. 41–45.

34. Moreno y Escandón, "Estado . . . 1772," p. 588; Ybot León, *La arteria histórica*, pp. 43, 195–96.

35. Robert S. Smith, "The Consulado in Santa Fe de Bogotá," p. 446.

36. Moreno y Escandón, "Estado . . . 1772," p. 581.

37. Juan and Ulloa, *A Voyage to South America*, pp. 35, 45; Ybot León, *La arteria histórica*, pp. 195–96; defense plan of Agustín Crame, Cartagena, December 29, 1778, ANC: MM, vol. 41, fols. 405–54; Militia Colonel Juan Fernández de Moure to Governor Juan Pimienta, Cartagena, May 16, 1778, AGI: Santa Fe, legajo 948.

38. "Padrón general, 1778."

39. The most exhaustive publication on Cartagena's fortifications is Marco Dorta, *Cartagena de Indias*; for a description of the construction of the dike, see pp. 273–76, 297–301; or see Silvestre, *Descripción*, p. 64.

even that of the president of Quito.[40] In one instance, a governor moved directly from Cartagena to serve as interim viceroy.[41]

In spite of the significance of the city, the garrison of Cartagena could hardly be described as impressive under the early Bourbons, although it was better sustained than Panama's. In 1736, the government of Philip V established a fixed battalion of ten companies in Cartagena.[42] This unit, usually known as the "Fijo," did assist in the successful defense against the English invasion under Admiral Vernon in 1741, but that victory proved to be more a credit to marines and rotating units hurried to Cartagena from Spain than a testimony to local preparedness. A scandalous troop mutiny in 1745 over wages, during which the viceroy himself was temporarily taken captive, dispelled any possible illusions about the dependability of the garrison.[43] During the Seven Years' War, Spain again had to resort to rotating troops to reinforce Cartagena, and she occasionally deployed them there following the peace.[44] O'Reilly hoped to reduce significantly Cartagena's dependence upon outside support.

To equip the new militia O'Reilly prepared supplies of guns, uniforms, and other material for transport to New Granada. This equipment was sufficient for four battalions for Cartagena and three battalions and twelve separate companies for Panama. To train the militia, the inspector general recruited cadres of veteran officers, some of whom had earlier worked with him in Cuba. These cadres were insufficient for the entire undertaking, however, so he authorized the local authorities to recruit additional officers from the fixed veteran units as necessary. Cementing institutional continuity with the Cuban and Puerto Rican reforms, the crown ordered both provinces to act under the policies earlier promulgated in the reglamento for the militia of Cuba as well as that for Puerto Rico.[45] The supplies and personnel for the new militia, along with a number of copies of the Cuban reglamento, arrived in New Granada in late 1773.[46] For the regular army, O'Reilly specified that the new fixed battalions would be formed out of recruits from the European rotating battalions cur-

40. The salary of the governor of Cartagena, for example, was 7,500 pesos in 1790 compared to 6,435 for the president of Quito. However, additional emoluments arising from special assignments or qualifications could alter these figures. The salary of President José García Pizarro, 1778–84, for example, exceeded 10,000 pesos a year. Relación of salaries in Ezpeleta to Minister of the Indies Antonio Valdés, Santa Fe, May 19, 1790, AGI: Santa Fe, legajo 561; Oidor Fernando Cuadrado to Viceroy Francisco Gil y Lemos, Quito, June 18, 1789, AGI: Quito, legajo 271.

41. This man was Juan Pimienta, who briefly served as viceroy following the resignation of Manuel Antonio Flores in 1782.

42. Royal order, November 30, 1736, AGI: Santa Fe, legajo 938.

43. Allan J. Kuethe, "La batalla de Cartagena de 1741: Nuevas perspectivas."

44. Royal order, December 8, 1762; de la Sierra to Messía de la Cerda, Cartagena, October 11, 1771.

45. Royal order, February 12, 1773; expediente on the formation of the disciplined militia of Cartagena, 1771–73.

46. Governor Roque de Quiroga to Guirior, Cartagena, June 11, 1773, ANC: MM, vol. 87, fols. 784–95; Guirior to Quiroga, Santa Fe, January 30, 1774, ANC: MM, vol. 56, fols. 784–87.

rently serving in New Granada.[47] In order to attract officers, a promotion of one rank was awarded to men who transferred to the new units.[48]

Because his initial reform was limited to only two coastal provinces, O'Reilly entrusted its execution to existing colonial authorities rather than a special high-ranking mission, such as his own in Cuba or Villalba's in New Spain. Under the general supervision of Viceroy Manuel Guirior (1772–76), Commandant General Roque de Quiroga conducted the reorganization in Cartagena while Commandant General Nicolás Quijano directed it in Panama. For the reform of the regular army, the new responsibilities of the commandants general were consistent with their traditional functions as supraprovincial commanders, just below the level of the viceroy in the chain of command. In the sphere of disciplined militia leadership, the commandants general assumed the duty of inspector, the most powerful militia post below the viceregal level. This function permitted the commandants general to control officer appointments, to conduct inspections, to serve as intermediaries in correspondence between the commanders of the various units and the viceroy, and to maintain a general supervision over militia affairs. The employment of the individual commandants general for the implementation of the reform provided direct supervision uninhibited by the geographical separation of Cartagena and Panama, but it also signaled, when combined with the limitation of the initial reform to just Cartagena and Panama, the beginnings of a localized, piecemeal approach to the problem of New Granada's defenses.

The decision to proceed without a special mission, although sound in principle, proved to be a weak point in the execution of the early reform, largely because of the uncertain character of the local leadership. Manuel Guirior, lieutenant general of the royal armada and viceroy since 1772, although occasionally capable of vision and some leadership, lacked the overall strength and drive demanded by the reform. Remembered for his relaxed, urbane disposition and his love for courtly diversion, he was not a man terribly concerned about administrative details. He asserted little actual control over the conduct of the reform, permitting matters largely to follow their own course at the provincial level.[49]

The weak character of provincial leadership at this same time, however, did not justify Guirior's restrained posture. As during most of the reform period, Cartagena and, especially, Panama were plagued by a devastatingly high mortality rate among governors, attributable to a combination of old age and an unhealthy climate. As a result of the death of Governor Gregorio de la Sierra

47. Expediente on the establishment of the Fixed Regiment of Cartagena, 1771–73; Quiroga to Ureta, Cartagena, February 8, 1773; Quijano to Guirior, Panama, June 10, 1773.

48. O'Reilly to Arriaga, Madrid, November 20, 1772, AGI: Santa Fe, legajo 1007.

49. Vicente Palacio Atard, "Areche y Guirior: Observaciones sobre el fracaso de una visita al Perú," p. 294; José Manuel Pérez Ayala, "Aspectos desconocidos de la vida del Virrey don Manuel de Guirior, co-fundador de la Biblioteca Nacional de Bogotá," pp. 170–82.

in mid-1772, Roque de Quiroga succeeded to the governorship of Cartagena on an interim basis from his position as lieutenant governor (*teniente de Rey*).[50] Although a distinguished soldier, Quiroga merely held the rank of colonel, and because he functioned only on an interim basis, he lacked any real mandate of his own.[51] In Panama during this same period, acting governor Nicolás Quijano, lieutenant colonel of infantry and commander of the Second Battalion of the Regiment of Naples, found himself in an even more precarious position than Quiroga. Following the deaths of Governor Vicente Olazinegui and Lieutenant Governor Nicolás de Castro in 1772, he succeeded to the military governorship as the senior military officer of the province. The *cabildo* (municipal council) of Panama, however, successfully challenged his authority in the civil realm.[52] Thus, when the military reform reached Panama, the authority of the governorship was divided and Quijano was hardly in an effective position to assert much power in supervising the actions of the military reformers. The next regular governor of Panama, Colonel Pedro Carbonell, did not take possession of his office until mid-1775.[53]

The commandants general rapidly effected the comparatively easy expansion of the regular army. In accordance with their royal instructions, they formed the new units out of recruits drawn from the European battalions currently deployed in the viceroyalty. The Infantry Battalion of Savoy provided personnel for Cartagena's new battalion, the battalions of Murcia and Naples for Panama's.[54] Moreover, a new unit pertaining to the Royal Corps of Artillery replaced the tenth company of Cartagena's original battalion, an artillery company, which disbanded.[55] The remainder of the three European battalions then returned to Spain.[56] This expansion tripled the strength of the regular fixed contingent in the two commandancies general, thereby substantially enhancing their self-reliance (see Table 4). Although later complications necessitated further deployments of Spanish troops in the viceroyalty, the newly strengthened local army bore the main burden of defense after 1773.

The formation of a disciplined militia was a more tedious, difficult task. Recruits were usually selected by lottery from census rolls compiled by the local authorities that listed those aged fifteen to forty-five. In Spain potential recruits were subdivided into five categories, defined by the severity of the hardship

50. Messía de la Cerda to Arriaga, Santa Fe, June 15, 1772, AGI: Santa Fe, legajo 1010.
51. Service records, plana mayor, Plaza de Cartagena, 1776, AGI: Santa Fe, legajo 1156.
52. Expediente on the succession to the governorship of Panama, 1773, AGI: Panama, legajo 256.
53. Carbonell to Arriaga, Panama, July 1, 1775, AGI: Panama, legajo 257.
54. Colonel José Bernet to Guirior, Cartagena, May 11, 1773, ANC: MM, vol. 87, fols. 739–45; Quijano to Guirior, Panama, June 10, 1773.
55. Quiroga to Guirior, July 11, 1773, ANC: MM, vol. 71, fols. 237–44.
56. Quiroga to Ureta, Cartagena, June 11, 1773, ANC: MM, vol. 84, fols. 916–23; Quiroga to Guirior, Cartagena, June 24, 1773, ANC: MM, vol. 87, fols. 764–68; Quijano to Guirior, Panama, June 10, 1773.

their possible absence would cause their families and other dependents.[57] In Cuba, however, undoubtedly because of the smaller population, O'Reilly did not bother with such amenities, and there is no evidence that anyone in New Granada did either. Nevertheless, the Cuban reglamento exempted men from a number of vital occupations, including the clergy, medical personnel, school teachers, certain kinds of students, lawyers, scribes, notaries, tax collectors, and a number of other public functionaries.[58] Beyond these exemptions, however, recruitment appears to have been generally indiscriminate.

The fundamental objective of disciplined militia policy was to develop through a combination of quality leadership, regular training, and a sense of corporate pride, a militarily capable citizenry which in time of crisis could share the burden of defense. The command structure consisted of a delicate balance between regular and volunteer personnel. Command was entrusted to volunteers, but proper discipline and training was insured by placing veterans in places where they could effectively enhance quality service. At the head of each battalion was a *plana mayor* (command and staff group) comprised of a colonel, who was a militia volunteer; a *sargento mayor*, who was a veteran plans and training officer; an *ayudante*, who was also a veteran and charged with assisting the sargento mayor in the conduct of his duties; and a group of non-commissioned officers and other personnel. The veteran positions of sargento mayor and ayudante were functions, not ranks, and men who in the regular army held the offices of captain, lieutenant, or first sergeant normally performed them. At the company level, the captain was a volunteer, but as with the command and staff group, the second in command, the lieutenant, was a veteran. A man who held the rank of corporal or cadet in the regular army would usually discharge the latter function. In addition, the militia was provided with a cadre of veteran enlisted men, who served as sergeants and corporals in the companies and handled basic instruction (see Table 3).[59]

Among the veteran personnel which Spain provided for New Granada's militia were two special militia commanders, Félix Martínez Malo for Panama and José Pérez Dávila for Cartagena. Each acted as special technical assistant to the commandant general, and during the formative years of the militia, they assumed duties normally reserved for colonels.[60] Both men enjoyed O'Reilly's confidence. Pérez Dávila, a captain of the Regiment of Navarre, had served under O'Reilly in Cuba as a militia battalion commander; Martínez Malo was a seasoned captain from the Regiment of Spain.[61]

57. *Real declaración sobre puntos esenciales de la ordenanza de milicias provinciales de España* . . . , títulos 2–3.

58. *Reglamento . . . de Cuba*, chap. 2, arts. 25–32.

59. Ibid, chaps. 1–3.

60. Quiroga to Guirior, Cartagena, June 11, 1773; idem, Panama, November 20, 1773, ANC: MM, vol. 90, fols. 645–62.

61. Expediente on the formation of the disciplined militia of Cartagena, 1771–73; expediente on the promotion of Félix Martínez Malo, 1778, AGI: Panama, legajo 253.

Although initially subjected to a more intensive training, disciplined militia units ordinarily drilled once a week. The authorities commonly scheduled these sessions after Sunday Mass in the local communities, even in those cases where companies were attached to battalions. The supervision of the weekly drills was the responsibility of the veteran enlisted men, although all company-level officers were obliged to assist once a month. Periodically, battalions and regiments were required to conduct full-unit maneuvers, including a bi-monthly firing practice, which the veteran members of the command and staff groups were obliged to attend. The colonel, who was a volunteer, was not formally bound to assist at drills of any level, although he was encouraged to do so as frequently as possible.[62] It was almost a year after the initiating orders, however, before the new units of Cartagena and Panama emerged in semi-finished form prepared for drilling.[63]

It is difficult to reach firm conclusions about the reorganization of the Panamanian militia because the records of early work there are somewhat fragmentary, reflecting uncertain political conditions and geographic isolation. Based on preliminary militia census reports, the decree of February 12 had ordered the creation of three battalions and twelve separate companies of infantry. Quijano, with the assistance of Special Commander Martínez Malo, attempted to execute that order, and a year later, the acting governor reported that the initial establishment was complete, with all of the new militia based in the Governorship of Panama except for six companies formed in Portobelo and along the Chagres River. However, most of these units were seriously under-strength from the start, especially the separate companies. Under the Puerto Rican reglamento, which constituted the rule for separate companies, they should have consisted of 100 men each.[64] Most had only from forty to seventy.[65] Moreover, when Colonel Pedro Carbonell took possession of the governorship in mid-1775, he found that the supplies and equipment destined for Panama from Spain had not yet arrived, a factor which had seriously impaired the training of the new units.[66]

Although the militia continued to exist on paper during the remainder of the decade, it did not develop into the kind of auxiliary force that O'Reilly had envisioned. Part of the problem was that Governor Carbonell, who promised to bring steady, able leadership to Panama, soon became a new dimension in that province's unhappy political history. Shortly after his arrival, he entered into a damaging jurisdictional dispute with Félix de Soto, the local director of the

62. *Reglamento . . . de Cuba*, chaps. 2–3.
63. Quijano to Guirior, Panama, November 20, 1773, ANC: MM, vol. 90, fols. 645–62; Commander José Pérez Dávila to Ureta, Cartagena, March 1774, ANC: MM, vol. 88, fol. 73.
64. "Reglamento para las milicias de la isla de San Juan de Puerto Rico," February 19, 1765, estado 2, AGI: Santa Fe, legajo 1007.
65. Quijano to Arriaga, Panama, February 6, 1774, AGI: Panama, legajo 260.
66. Carbonell to Arriaga, Panama, August 10, 1775, AGI: Panama, legajo 260.

aguardiente monopoly. The incident eventually led to the intervention of Regent-Visitor Juan Gutiérrez de Piñeres, the recall of Carbonell in 1779, and his disgrace and imprisonment. Although Carbonell was later exonerated, eventually becoming captain general of Caracas, while De Soto was incarcerated for corruption, the chain of leadership had again been broken.[67]

Against this backdrop of political paralysis the militia languished. By 1779, when war broke out with England, a number of the separate companies had completely disintegrated, and the man who replaced Carbonell, Colonel Ramón Carvajal, found the remainder in disarray.[68] Yet under the pressures of war, Governor and Commandant General Carvajal was able to use the militia structure to produce a force that through partial mobilization could and did sustain the troop level of the regular army.[69] Thus, when the war ended in 1783 and the first decade of the reform in Panama drew to a close, it would have been impossible to classify the reform as anything approaching a success; yet it was not a complete failure either.

The results of the early reform in Cartagena were also less than fully successful, largely because of an indiscriminate proliferation of new units. In raising the militia, Special Commander José Pérez Dávila enjoyed greater latitude than had Martínez Malo in Panama. Dávila's freedom developed because dying Governor Gregorio de la Sierra had just managed to begin the census of able-bodied men ordered during his administration, and Roque de Quiroga had not accomplished anything significant either by the time he received the order of March 18 to form a disciplined militia.[70] Thus, when formulating their plans for the reorganization in Cartagena, the authorities in Spain had little solid data available, and as a consequence their instructions to the local authorities were necessarily vague. Relying largely upon the judgment of the officers in the field, O'Reilly placed no specific limitation on the size of the militia; he simply ordered Quiroga and Pérez Dávila to proceed one battalion at a time, limiting the militia to a size that could be adequately supported. In Spain he made provisions for four battalions, which, as long-run events would demonstrate, was a reasonable estimate.[71]

Prior to the arrival of Special Commander Pérez Dávila, Governor Quiroga, proceeding slowly, began to organize a disciplined militia in the area around the city of Cartagena. When the special commander arrived in late 1773, Quiroga stepped aside, permitting him to have virtually a free hand, and the tempo of the reform quickly changed. Pérez Dávila was an aggressive officer, who was deter-

67. Expediente, the cause of Carbonell, 1778–1803, AGI: Panama, legajo 257; Carbonell to Gálvez, Cartagena, September 28, 1781, and idem, Málaga, July 9, 1784, AGI: Panama, legajo 257.

68. Carvajal to Gálvez, Panama, August 22, 1782, AGI: Panama, legajo 260.

69. Carvajal to Gálvez, Panama, June 15, 1782, AGI: Panama, legajo 260.

70. Quiroga to Arriaga, Cartagena, July 15, 1773, AGI: Santa Fe, legajo 1007; Pérez Dávila to Arriaga, Cartagena, December 7, 1773, AGI: Santa Fe, legajo 1007.

71. Expediente on the formation of the disciplined militia of Cartagena, 1771–73.

mined to convert the opening O'Reilly had given him into a personal opportunity. Building upon Quiroga's work, he raised a massive militia of two battalions and fifty-eight separate companies of infantry, two cavalry companies, and two companies and a brigade of artillery.[72] Of these, the two battalions and a separate company of infantry, and the two artillery companies, were from the city of Cartagena and its immediate surroundings; twenty-eight infantry companies and the artillery brigade were raised in the outlying district (*partido*) of Lorica; sixteen infantry companies and the two cavalry companies came from Barranquilla; and thirteen infantry companies were from Mompós (see Table 4). On paper, this force was over twice as large as Panama's, and, indeed, greater than the entire militia of the viceroyalty during the later phases of the reform.

Pérez Dávila's extravagant militia was the consequence of ineffective supervision and leadership by Guirior and Quiroga and was far beyond what Cartagena could effectively sustain, either financially or in terms of human resources. For example, it would have taken over 300 regulars to have staffed the veteran positions specified by the reglamento, or nearly one-fourth of the regular army. Under these circumstances, the special commander could not have realistically hoped to make his establishment meet disciplined militia standards.

Pérez Dávila's motives for overexpanding the militia structure are unclear. He may simply have been unable to distinguish between quality and quantity, despite the crown's insistence on the former. A more probable explanation, however, is that in the largely rural backlands, where company proliferation was the greatest, Pérez Dávila used his position for self-enrichment by selling officerships to eager buyers who sought the prestige, but not the responsibility, of officership. Some men appear to have acquired officerships in order to tighten their grip on the lower classes through the enlistment of peasant soldiers and a subsequent exploitation of them for personal profit. Juan Pimienta, who became the next regular governor in May 1774, just after the special commander had completed his reorganization, strongly hinted at corruption in later criticisms of the early reform, but no formal charges or investigation ever arose.[73] This kind of abuse would normally have been restrained by the established system for promotion and appointment, which prescribed that the names of three candidates, together with a description of each man's qualifications, be offered for each position by the commanding officer, along with his recommendation for appointment. Pérez Dávila had submitted only one candidate per militia position, with no discussion of the nominee's qualifications, and neither Quiroga nor Guirior objected as the list moved through their hands.[74] Pérez Dávila declared the militia ready for drilling in early 1774, and as a reward for what appeared to

72. Pérez Dávila to Arriaga, Cartagena, March 21, 1774, AGI: Santa Fe, legajo 1007; Quiroga to Guirior, Cartagena, June 11, 1773.
73. Expediente on the reorganization of the militia of Cartagena, 1778–83 (hereafter cited as Expediente, militia of Cartagena), AGI: Santa Fe, legajo 948.
74. Officer proposals, Cartagena, 1774–76, AGI: Santa Fe, legajo 1007.

be a highly ambitious, successful execution of his orders, he was promoted to lieutenant governor of Panama in 1777.[75]

When Viceroy Manuel Flores descended to the coast in 1779 to assume personal command of Cartagena during the war with England, he found much of the militia badly under strength, without uniforms, and poorly trained. Many soldiers had been enlisted indiscriminately, without any regard for dependents or occupation. He was able to mobilize parts of the two battalions of the city of Cartagena to reinforce the Fijo, which proved of some value, but beyond that the militia proved more fictitious than real. When Flores attempted to relieve the city's battalions in 1781 by calling upon the separate companies of the backlands, he was shocked to find that men had been enlisted on the spot to fill company quotas or to replace men whose names had appeared previously on company lists. Some of these companies apparently had had no real membership beneath the officer level. In other instances, company captains who had enlisted laborers from their holdings declined to lose their services by sending them off as replacements for the regular army. Other officers simply accepted bribes to exempt their men from duty. Apparently the veteran cadres assigned to these units, which included a plana mayor for each of the three districts, had been content to collect their salaries without seriously attempting to discharge their responsibilities.[76]

To aggravate matters further, the militia of the city of Cartagena, although of some use, was itself badly under strength, but for a different reason. In 1775, at the petition of Viceroy Guirior, the crown established a *matrícula de mar*, or navy register, in Cartagena. Designed to organize crews for an expansion of the coast guard, this was the first appearance of that institution in America. The matrícula possessed exclusive claim to those vassals who earned their livings from the sea, and, in particular, sailors and fishermen. The coast guard enjoyed corporate privileges similar to those of the militia, and significantly, these privileges included a monopoly over maritime occupations. As a result, those wishing to continue earning their livelihoods from the sea had to register, a factor which worked greatly against militia recruitment. Furthermore, because of a relatively easy training schedule, people from other professions, including silversmiths, masons, cobblers, tailors, painters, grocers, and small farmers, who should have pertained to the militia, were lured from the once full militia companies into the coast guard. By 1781 the matrícula could claim over three thousand men, which

75. Royal order, June 17, 1777, ANC: MM, vol. 56, fols. 933–37; expediente, militia commander v. the lieutenant governor of Panama, 1779, ANC: MM, vol. 40, fols. 669–87.

76. One exception was the militia of Mompós which was directed by Captain Ramón García de León y Pizarro acting as sargento mayor; Lieutenant Colonel Anastasio Zejudo reported it to be the best trained in the province. García Pizarro later became governor of Guayaquil. See the report of Zejudo, Cartagena, September 15, 1779; the representation of Fernández de Moure, Cartagena, July 28, 1781; and Flores to Gálvez, unsigned, Cartagena, December 29, 1781, all in AGI: Santa Fe, legajo 948.

represented a considerable drain on local manpower. The militia leadership vigorously protested this competition, especially when the authorities interpreted the boundary of the matrícula de mar to encompass even those who fished the swamps around Cartagena and those who transported foodstuffs to the city by boat from the nearby farms. However, Viceroy Flores, who like Guirior was a navy man, had given no satisfaction to the militia on this point, and he was, therefore, partly responsible himself for the depleted condition of the units of the city of Cartagena when war broke out.[77]

Lieutenant Colonel Anastasio Zejudo, whom Flores had commissioned to inspect the militia in 1779, had warned him of its deplorable condition, but various attempts to rectify the situation had little effect. Part of the difficulty was that Governor Juan Pimienta, who had begun efforts of his own to deal with the problem, became seriously ill in 1780, and the weak Roque de Quiroga once again assumed the acting governorship. Moreover, Flores himself suffered an emotional and physical collapse in 1781. Hence, Cartagena's militia, except perhaps for those undermanned units immediately around the city, proved to be a largely useless drain on the treasury. Viceroy Flores, Governor Pimienta, and Colonel Zejudo all urged a thorough reorganization of the Cartagena militia once the war had ended.[78]

77. Angel O'Dogherty, "La matrícula de mar en el reinado de Carlos III"; expediente, militia of Cartagena.

78. Report of Zejudo, Cartagena, September 15, 1779; report on the militia of Cartagena, Pimienta, March 26, 1778, ANC: MM, vol. 40, fols. 152–65.

2. The "Fuero Militar" and Officer Recruitment in Cartagena and Panama

THE NEW DISCIPLINED MILITIA, despite its failure to emerge as a satisfactory reserve force, quickly displayed signs of becoming an elite political and social institution in New Granada. This status derived from extensive corporate privileges, designed to convey honor and prestige, which the crown bestowed upon the new militia to underscore the significance the government attached to the reform and to insure the militia's success in meeting its military objectives. The regular army had traditionally enjoyed broad corporate privileges, but Spain had not formerly viewed the American militia as important enough to be so honored. However, during the reorganization of the American defense system, most military authorities regarded the granting of some form of privilege to the militia as absolutely essential for promoting morale and instilling a love of duty—without which, they argued, no amount of veteran advisors, equipment, or training could be effective. O'Reilly had generously bestowed extensive privileges upon the Cuban militia he had raised, and the crown had codified his action in the Cuban reglamento, which was now policy in New Granada. The impact of military privileges upon existing social and political institutions in New Granada would soon threaten to overshadow the role of the army as defender of the colony.

Military corporate privileges consisted in part of *preeminencias*, or special prerogatives, which included immunities from certain municipal taxes, levies, and responsibilities, as well as exemptions from the obligation to quarter

25

troops and from the payment of prison cell fees.[1] More important was the highly prized *fuero de guerra militar*, a judicial prerogative that conveyed the right to present causes before military tribunals rather than before royal, or ordinary, tribunals. The fuero de guerra militar, or simply the "fuero militar" as it was commonly known, dated as a distinct legal code from the sixteenth century and subsequently developed into a complex body of law. By the eighteenth century, it consisted of two subdivisions, the *fuero militar privilegiado* for special corps, including the artillery, engineers, and provincial militia, and the *fuero de guerra ordinario* for the regular army. As codified by the *Ordenanzas de S.M. para el régimen, disciplina, subordinación, y servicio de sus exércitos . . .* of 1768, the definitive statement on regular army policy, the judicial privileges granted to veteran troops encompassed both civil and criminal causes for officers, men, and their families and other dependents. The fuero militar privilegiado as defined for the provincial militia of Spain did the same for officers, but it conceded only the criminal fuero to enlisted men unless they were mobilized, in which case they also enjoyed full privileges.[2]

The military fuero was only one of some thirty-four privileged jurisdictions operating within the colonial community. Others enjoying special fueros included the church and its subdivisions; the universities; artisan and mining guilds; various commercial corporations; and the matrícula de mar. "Such privileged *fueros* or jurisdictions were the juridical expression of a society in which the state was regarded not as a community of citizens enjoying equal rights and responsibilities, but as a structure built of classes and corporations, each with a unique and peculiar function to perform."[3] In this sense, the fuero militar conveyed prestige and distinction, and like other fueros it set the holder above and apart from the remainder of society in varying degrees. This status provided a strong incentive to lure men into military service and to insure a continuing commitment to duty.

Before the reform, military privileges had only minor influence in New Granada. The regular army, for its part, was small, largely confined to the coast, and by the nature of its duties was isolated from daily community life. As for the militia, it was of even less consequence; only officers could exercise the fuero—and that was not always certain—while the enlisted men enjoyed no immunities unless mobilized.[4] The reform profoundly altered this situa-

1. *Reglamento . . . de Cuba*, chap. 2, art. 40, chap. 4, arts. 2, 6–7.
2. McAlister, The *"Fuero Militar,"* pp. 6–8. (See this work for a complete description of the fuero de guerra militar and its workings.)
3. Ibid., pp. 5–6. For an excellent analysis of the theory and nature of Spanish colonial society, see Lyle N. McAlister, "Social Structure and Social Change in New Spain."
4. Expediente, judicial dispute in Mompós, 1757, ANC: Competencias Bolívar and Panama, vol. 2, fols. 137–42; expediente, judicial dispute in Cartagena, 1763, ANC: MM, vol. 93, fols. 558–74; expediente, judicial dispute in Santa Marta, 1777, ANC: MM, vol. 76, fols. 294–314.

tion by increasing the size of the regular army, and therefore the number of people exercising the fuero militar, and, more important, by creating a large disciplined militia entitled to more comprehensive judicial privileges than its predecessor. In fact, the fuero granted to the reorganized militia in New Granada was more extensive than that granted to its disciplined counterpart in Spain, for the Cuban reglamento, as structured by the zealous O'Reilly, conceded the full fuero, both civil and criminal, to all the membership, including enlisted personnel.[5] Furthermore, by a special concession of April 15, 1771, the crown accented the status of the officers and sergeants functioning under the Cuban reglamento by making their fuero "active"; that is, not only did their privilege apply when they were defendants but also when they were plaintiffs.[6] By contrast, the fuero militar of the disciplined militia of Spain, and also that of the empire's regular army, appears to have been regarded as only passive.[7]

To process military causes under the Cuban reglamento, the provincial governor or his deputy acted as the court of first instance in cases pertaining to military jurisdiction, and appeals went to the captain general. In outlying regions where neither of these officers was accessible, the highest ranking unit commander performed this duty.[8] However, while military authorities could hear most actions, there were a number of instances, known as cases of *desafuero*, over which ordinary justice or other privileged jurisdictions retained competency. These cases included resistance to ordinary justice or the abuse of its officers, crimes committed prior to enlistment, sedition, gambling, defrauding the royal treasury, counterfeiting, smuggling, the succession to entailed estates, and the execution of contracts negotiated before enlistment.[9] Initially, the Cuban reglamento did not enumerate these exceptions, but Spain remedied that omission by an amendment of April 15, 1771.[10] On the other hand, the failure to invoke the fuero when entitled to it could be a serious offense.[11]

The implantation of privileges of this magnitude, enjoyed by so many, severely strained existing political and social institutions. Politically, by exempting large portions of the most active citizenry from ordinary justice, the fuero militar tended to undermine the authority of the cabildos, or municipal governments. Socially, many of those excepted as members of the new military organization came from the lower classes. This circumstance worked to sub-

5. *Reglamento . . . de Cuba*, chap. 10, art. 1.
6. José María Zamora y Coronado, *Biblioteca de legislación ultramarina en forma de diccionario alfabético . . .*, 3: 325–26.
7. McAlister, *The "Fuero Militar,"* pp. 7–8.
8. *Reglamento . . . de Cuba*, chap. 10, arts. 1–5.
9. Colón y Larriátegui Ximénez de Embún, *Juzgados militares*, 1: 24–136.
10. Expediente, judicial dispute in Panama, 1774, ANC: MM, vol. 79, fols. 672–92.
11. *Reglamento . . . de Cuba*, chap. 11, art. 22.

vert the traditional order of society, because the fuero removed militiamen from the authority of the cabildos—normally comprised of members of the creole aristocracy—and placed them under officers who might be inclined to regard military interests first and social origins second. Indeed, those pleading cases often sought, and sometimes received, preferential treatment at the hands of military justices who were more concerned with promoting the *esprit de corps* of their units than with dispensing impartial justice. These factors were additionally important because reformed militia units tended to exist in the principal population and administrative centers, where the institutional impact of their status was greatest. Furthermore, because the militiamen were in effect citizen soldiers, they carried the influence of military privileges with them into daily community life. Consequently, as the military reform entered the provinces of Cartagena and Panama, local authorities resented, and at times bitterly contested, the intrusion of military privileges into their jurisdictions. The most visible consequence of this confrontation was a series of civil-military conflicts, which raged throughout the early period of the reform.

During the first years of the miltary reorganization, the most sensitive point in the emerging crisis over military privileges was the status of black militiamen.[12] During the formation of the disciplined militia, Pérez Dávila and Martínez Malo had enlisted large numbers of free blacks and mulattoes into what were euphemistically called *pardo* and *moreno* companies. The latter term referred to the free offspring of purely Negro parents; the former encompassed the various types of mulattoes.[13] For all intents and purposes, however, the same laws applied to both kinds of units, and most colonial officials ignored the distinction, referring to both as pardos, a policy that shall be observed in this work as well.[14] Nearly half of the disciplined militia of Panama and Cartagena was of the pardo category; the total included three battalions, one from Cartagena and two from Panama, as well as twenty-one separate companies and a brigade (see Table 4).

Given the demography of the coastal areas, the enlistment of pardos was more a matter of necessity than of choice. Originally, colonists had imported large numbers of Negro slaves as agricultural workers, domestic servants, and laborers for the mines. The government itself had increased the Negro population by employing significant numbers of slaves for the construction of the massive fortification complex at Cartagena.[15] Because manumission was a

12. For a detailed discussion, see Allan J. Kuethe, "The Status of the Free Pardo in the Disciplined Militia of New Granada."

13. For fuller definitions, see Gonzalo Aguirre Beltrán, *La población negra de México, 1519–1810*, p. 173.

14. Pardos received slightly higher salaries than morenos. *Reglamento . . . de Cuba*, relaciones 9–11.

15. Aquiles Escalante, *El negro en Colombia*, pp. 121–31; James Ferguson King, "Negro History in Continental Spanish America," p. 12.

relatively simple process in the Spanish Empire, many blacks soon won the status of freemen, and eventually far outnumbered slaves.[16] One fairly reliable authority places the number of free Negroes and mulattoes in New Granada in 1810 at 182,000, compared to merely 78,000 slaves.[17] This free population remained largely clustered in the tropical lowlands and in some places comprised a majority of the inhabitants. Moreover, miscegenation, a common feature of the colonial social scene, had reached an advanced stage by the end of the eighteenth century, with few people clearly able to claim the more prestigious white social position.[18] Given these circumstances, the military reformers could ill afford to ignore the black and mulatto populations.

Policies regarding the Indian further contributed to the importance of the pardo. Socially, the Indian constituted what amounted to a separate estate in the empire. Legally, he was in effect a perpetual minor and, as an expression of this status, was barred from service in the military.[19] A question arose on this point in New Granada, however, when Pérez Dávila, Cartagena's special commander, enlisted Indians in Turbaco, a small town near the provincial capital. He based his action on a special provision in the Cuban reglamento which allowed the enlistment of Indians to complete the white battalions of Cuba and Bayamo. Upon hearing of Pérez Dávila's action, Commandant General Roque de Quiroga became concerned, because he suspected that such recruitment was inconsistent with "the privileges and exemptions conceded to this group of people." Finding nothing in the regulations specifically prohibiting the practice, but believing that the Cuban example was an exception due to extenuating local circumstances rather than a precedent, he asked Viceroy Manuel Guirior for a ruling. Guirior confirmed Quiroga's suspicions and ordered the immediate termination of Indian enlistment.[20]

Although prized as a laborer and accepted as a soldier, the Negro held a most unfavorable place in the colonial social structure. Colonists credited him with few redeeming qualities and commonly condemned him as stupid, degenerate, and untrustworthy.[21] The "taint" of Negro blood, or the suspicion of illegitimate parentage, placed a man in the lowest estate of society, the *castas* (literally

16. James Ferguson King, "Negro Slavery in New Granada," pp. 311–12; Alexander von Humbolt and Aimé Bonpland, *Personal Narrative of Travels to the Equinoctial Region of America during the Years 1799–1804*, 3: 280–81; William Frederick Sharp, "Forsaken but for Gold: An Economic Study of Slavery and Mining in the Colombian Chocó, 1680–1810" (Ph.D. diss.), chaps. 8, 9.

17. Restrepo, *Historia de la revolución*, 1: xx. See also T. Lynn Smith, "The Racial Composition of the Population of Colombia," p. 215.

18. Escalante, *El negro en Colombia*, pp. 133–39. See also Juan and Ulloa, *A Voyage to South America*, pp. 26–29, 51, 70.

19. Angel Rosenblat, *La población indígena y el mestizaje en America*, 2: 147.

20. Quiroga to Guirior, Cartagena, January 10, 1774, and reply, Santa Fe, February 15, 1774, both in ANC: MM, vol. 88, fols. 1–4. Guirior's ruling conformed to policy in New Spain, where Indians also were not permitted to enter the military. McAlister, *The "Fuero Militar,"* p. 2.

21. Escalante, *El negro en Colombia*, pp. 107–8, 139.

"castes"), where for all intents and purposes he lived under a separate legal code with harsher punishments and tighter controls. Colonial law went so far as to impose limitations on his form of dress and his right to possess horses. He paid tribute and found himself barred from entering most honorable professions.[22]

In the strategic Caribbean, however, military reformers keenly appreciated the crucial role that the Negro would have to play in any successful defense system. Thus, O'Reilly, when organizing the disciplined militia of Cuba, not only recruited significant numbers of pardos, but in order to increase morale, loyalty, and dignity, he extended the fuero militar to pardo militiamen on the same basis as for whites. This concession was a significant instance where a functional corporation cut across the stratified classes in Spanish society, granting an equal juridical status to both whites and pardos, at least so far as their relations with the outside world were concerned. Under this parity of privilege, both white and black soldiers presented their causes before the same tribunals and enjoyed the same immunities from ordinary justice.[23]

Some evidence suggests that the social tolerance displayed in the military reform may have stemmed partly from the egalitarian spirit of the Enlightenment, which, during the closing decades of the century, brought about some improvement in the status of those with Negro parentage. In 1784, for example, the monarchy ordered a halt to slave branding, and in 1789 it furthered this humanitarian spirit through the promulgation of a new code intended to improve the treatment of slaves. Moreover, a 1795 *cédula* formalized the fee structure and the legal procedure to be used by mulatto subjects petitioning for a dispensation from the stigma of slave ancestry and, thus, for the acquisition of the rights of whites.[24] Yet the apparent willingness to smooth over social differences, while enlightened in tone, was principally a response to demographic reality. In the Province of Cartagena, members of the white estate were not only few in number but also widely scattered. The 1778 census, for example, recorded only 6,860 white males, excluding clergymen.[25]

The extensive miscegenation in coastal New Granada, combined with the judicial parity, gave rise to still another intriguing development—the creation of companies "of all colors." These were integrated units formed in those areas where no single social grouping was sufficient to permit the establishment of

22. Irene Diggs, "Color in Colonial Spanish America," pp. 403, 418; William Dusenberry, "Discrimination Aspects of Legislation in Colonial Mexico"; Edgar F. Love, "Negro Resistance to Spanish Rule in Colonial Mexico," pp. 90–92; John Tate Lanning, "Legitimacy and Limpieza de Sangre in the Practice of Medicine in the Spanish Empire"; J. Vicens Vives, *Historia de España y América*, 4:432.

23. Herbert S. Klein, "The Colored Militia of Cuba: 1568–1868"; Kuethe, "Status," pp. 110–11.

24. Rosenblat, *La población indígena*, 2: 159–60; James Ferguson King, "The Case of José Ponciano de Ayarza: A Document on *Gracias al Sacar.*"

25. "Padrón general, 1778," AGI: Estado, legajo 54.

a full company. As indicated earlier, evidence strongly indicates that the reformers were indifferent to marital status when forming the new units; this indiscriminate attitude often applied to race as well. Fortunately, a number of company rosters are available for analysis, and they reveal that the term "all colors" must be taken literally. These units contained varying mixtures of men listed as morenos, pardos, *tercerones* (quadroons), *cuarterones* (octeroons), *zambos* (of Indian and Negro parents), mestizos, whites, and even an occasional Indian, although as indicated earlier this class legally could not serve in the militia.[26]

A word of caution is in order concerning the classification *blanco*, or white, for it cannot be presumed that all members of that group derived from purely white racial stock. Companies labeled as "white" could fill out their enlistment quotas with mestizos and cuarterones, although both groups also could and did serve in pardo units.[27] Moreover, culture was important in determining social status. Those who behaved like Spaniards were usually taken for Spaniards and, as indicated earlier, if they possessed sufficient wealth they could purchase a certificate of whiteness in Spain.[28] As Viceroy Pedro Mendinueta (1797–1803) commented some years later, "those enlisted in the militia [of Cartagena] are at best from the ones known as local whites [*blancos de la tierra*], who in reality are mulattoes [but] somewhat closer to our race, and in that contingency only the circumstance of engaging in labors less demanding than those of agriculture lightens the color [*hace disimular el color*]."[29]

So blurred were racial distinctions in New Granada that in some instances the military leadership itself differed concerning the proper classification of companies. Governor Juan Pimienta, for example, labeled five of the companies of Mompós as white, two as pardo, and six as all colors, while Lieutenant Colonel Anastasio Zejudo classified five as white, three as pardo, one as zambo-moreno, and four as all colors. Even greater variation occurred in the companies of Lorica, where Governor Pimienta pronounced nine companies as white and nineteen as all colors; Zejudo found eleven companies white, four zambo, two pardo, one pardo-zambo, two cuarterón, one moreno, and seven all colors![30]

The critical question regarding the status of the pardo within the military corporation was whether, in the interest of achieving military objectives, the

26. Militia membership rolls, Cartagena, 1780, ANC: MM, vol. 14, fols. 173–210, vol. 17, fols. 260–310. The term *cuarterón* cannot be literally translated to quadroon in New Granada; it meant octoroon. See Juan and Ulloa, *A Voyage to South America*, p. 27.

27. Militia membership rolls, Cartagena, 1780.

28. Aguirre Beltrán, *La población negra*, pp. 250–51; McAlister, "Social Structure," pp. 355, 366–69; King, "Case of José Ponciano."

29. Mendinueta to Secretary of State and War Juan Manuel Alvérez, Santa Fe, June 19, 1798, AGS: GM, legajo 7069.

30. Report on the militia of Cartagena by Pimienta, March 26, 1778, ANC: MM, vol. 40, fols. 152–65, and report of Zejudo, September 15, 1779, AGI: Santa Fe, legajo 948.

white leadership would uphold pardo privileges against cabildo opposition or whether social loyalties and affiliations from civilian stratified society would penetrate the military corporation. Coastal cabildos chafed at the prospect of losing authority over much of the pardo population, which they viewed as inherently vicious and untrustworthy. Moreover, pardo overreaction to the newly acquired immunities exacerbated the crisis. Long subject to the control of the superior classes, men of color, once freed from the restraints of ordinary justice, responded with pent-up resentment and boldly defied and harassed local magistrates. To the cabildos this development placed a special, alarming emphasis on what was already an obvious erosion of their authority, and they challenged the issue of pardo and military privilege at every opportunity. Yet throughout the history of the reform, military objectives normally prevailed over civilian social allegiances. From company captains to the viceroys as captains general, military officers typically reacted first as loyal members of the military corporation and willingly defended even the lowliest soldier from civilian authority. An illuminating illustration of this tendency occurred in the Province of Cartagena, where a catastrophic clash between military and ordinary justice shattered the tranquility of the province during the first years of the reform. This conflict is particularly interesting because it illustrates the fear with which local magistrates regarded pardo privileges and immunities, as well as the high-handed manner with which the military quite typically responded to civil interference—all in the good interest of corporate pride and integrity—and consequently subverted the credibility of royal justice.[31]

The dispute arose on August 7, 1773, when *Alcalde Ordinario* (Municipal Magistrate) José Díaz de Escandón dispatched *Alguacil* (Constable) José García de Olea to arrest a militiaman from the Second Pardo Artillery Company for indebtedness. The case was in fact an instance of desafuero, because the militiaman had incurred the liability prior to his acquisition of the fuero. Alcalde Díaz, however, chose not to invoke the desafuero but rather acted on the basis that the accused had no fuero at all. Consequently, Díaz did not fulfill the courtesy of informing the man's senior officer, Domingo Esquiaqui, commander of the Royal Artillery Corps, before dispatching the alguacil.

Alcalde Díaz' conduct in the case might have been due to confusion, although that is unlikely. The artillery companies were not part of Dávila's original special mission in reorganizing the province's militia, but rather they were administratively set apart from the infantry and mounted units, being directly attached to the Royal Corps of Artillery. Thus, the fuero of these companies was not an explicit part of the reorganization, and furthermore, no one had ever bothered to define it. On the other hand, the crown, which

31. The records of the dispute can be found in ANC: MM, vol. 10, fols. 750–54; vol. 12, fols. 329–37, 354; vol. 28, fols. 282–335; vol. 30, fols. 199–201; vol. 59, fols. 37–38; vol. 65, fols. 391–93; and vol. 87, fols. 620–22.

had approved the formation of these companies, obviously intended that they, as the rest of the new militia, should enjoy full privileges, and this appears to have been a widely held assumption. Alcalde Díaz, a justice himself, probably knew this, although he seems to have lacked formal legal training. If he were truly in doubt, which is the most that can be assumed, a simple inquiry could have resolved the problem, since prosecution for indebtedness was not an urgent matter. In effect, it appears that the alcalde was taking advantage of the existing ambiguity, where the pardo fuero was most vulnerable, to bring the whole question of pardo privileges under review. In subsequent correspondence with the viceroy, he expressed a very real fear that the pardo community, from which he had experienced abuse, was getting out of control. As he described it, the pardos armed with the fuero militar "ridicule and mock the royal justices with manifest contempt and shameless disdain for their esteemed authority and prestige." Presumably, a successful arrest would demonstrate that the alcalde remained an authority to be reckoned with in the community, even though subsequent military court action might extract the man from his custody. And, in any case, such action would bring the pardo question before the viceregal authorities.

At the time of his apprehension, the militiaman realized that ordinary justice was violating his fuero and accordingly sought military protection. He shrewdly persuaded arresting officer García to allow him consultation, first with his pardo captain, then with Commander Esquiaqui, for the alleged purpose of procuring the funds required to satisfy the debt. García, who was less than astute throughout the entire episode, was apparently unaware that he was being led into a trap. When confronted with this invasion of his jurisdiction, Commander Esquiaqui took immediate and decisive action. He separated the alguacil from his prisoner and sent the latter to obtain his uniform so that ordinary justices would not dare tamper with him. He then gave García a lengthy lecture on the fuero militar, and directed him to relate to Alcalde Díaz what had happened, with specific instructions to inform him that he had no jurisdiction in the case.

Whether or not the prisoner in question was entitled to the fuero militar, the action of Commander Esquiaqui constituted the illicit removal of a prisoner from ordinary jurisdiction. The proper procedure was an appeal to higher authority, not the extrication of a prisoner under what was at least implied physical threat. Because the boundary between ordinary and military jurisdictions was not always clear to those administering justice—a problem frequently arising from ambiguities existing within the regulatory texts themselves and from what often appears to have been an inability to understand them, or even in some instances to read them—the crown had prescribed procedures to be followed in case of error or doubt. If ordinary justices apprehended a man possessing the military fuero, he was to inform the justices of his privilege, and they in turn were to correct the error by transferring the action to military authorities. If the justices refused, the illegally arrested individual was responsible for notifying his superior officers so that appropriate legal measures might be taken to place him under military custody. Appeal in such cases could be launched to the captain general and from there to the *Consejo Supremo de Guerra*, the supreme military court in Spain. Pending the outcome of such appeals, the defendant was to remain in military custody. Yet if ordinary justice refused to cooperate, it was still not legitimate to employ remedial force. Instead, the violation was to be noted in the appeal so that the viceroy could correct the mistake. To avert direct jurisdictional clashes, the reglamento sternly admonished the militia leadership to insure that their men displayed no disrespect for ordinary justice. On the contrary, they were to accord its officials honor, respect, and full cooperation in the pursuit of their duties.[32] However, despite the good intentions of the crown, such ideals seldom materialized in practice, and this instance was no exception.

Commander Esquiaqui, whose ambition would award him the rank of lieutenant colonel within a year, was a tough young officer, who had devoted his entire career to the Royal Artillery Corps. Along with a company of regulars, he had been assigned to New Granada in 1770 to develop an artillery corps, and he had promptly raised two militia companies, which later became part of the new disciplined militia establishment.[33] Like the military leadership as a whole, Esquiaqui regarded military privileges as the basis for building sound corporate pride and a corresponding dedication to duty, both essential for promoting a functional militia. He therefore believed that the fuero must resolutely be defended, especially since it appeared that the alcalde was openly challenging it. Moreover, at this time the pardo companies were responding well to training and already constituted a valuable asset for Cartagena's artillery defenses. If the leadership did not resolutely defend the membership's corporate rights, Esquiaqui feared that their zeal might correspondingly diminish.

Additional blunders by García soon further complicated the affair. Rather than proceeding directly to the alcalde's residence to inform him of the artillery commander's intervention, García first went to the militiaman's shop, perhaps hoping to persuade him to report to the alcalde. García intimated that he did not understand the commander's lecture, which was probably true, but it is also likely that he desired to produce the prisoner as ordered. The artilleryman, however, confounded him by directing a companion, who by curious coincidence happened to have a copy of the reglamento, to read aloud the

32. *Reglamento . . . de Cuba*, chap. 2, art. 24; chap. 4, art. 1; and chap. 11, arts. 17, 20.
33. He was thirty-eight at this time. Service record, December 1794, ANC: MM, vol. 56, fols. 582–84; de la Sierra to Messía de Cerda, Cartagena, October 11, 1771, ANC: MM, vol. 89, fols. 225–38; royal order, March 31, 1773, AGI: Santa Fe, legajo 945.

section on the fuero. That was more than the unhappy alguacil could bear, so he abandoned the effort and somewhat belatedly set out alone for the alcalde's residence. By the time García arrived, Díaz had already begun his afternoon *siesta*, which the alguacil prudently chose not to interrupt. Instead, he departed, not returning until evening. Meanwhile, the artilleryman returned to his commander's residence in uniform to await word from the alcalde, but after several hours Esquiaqui gave him leave to return home.

When Alguacil García finally ceased vacillating and appeared at the residence of Alcalde Díaz, he feared punishment for having permitted a prisoner to elude him. Consequently, he exaggerated the events of the day to obscure his blunders. The main features of García's story were that the pardo captain had intercepted him in the street and had forced him by threat to proceed with the prisoner to Commander Esquiaqui's home. He further asserted that Esquiaqui, when denying the jurisdiction of ordinary justice, had also promised corporal punishment in the event of further meddling in military affairs. The precise validity of these most serious allegations cannot be determined, because García in this instance, and in the furor of subsequent events, gave three different versions of his conversation with Esquiaqui, all of them under oath. Later investigations proved conclusively that García's explanation of how the prisoner came to arrive at the commander's residence was false, but the threat of reprisals for any further interference could have been and in all likelihood was true.

Alcalde Díaz was outraged. He dispatched García, a deputy alguacil, and the cabildo's *escribano*, along with a corporal and four men from the fixed regiment, to make the arrest, uniform or no uniform. This time, it was successfully accomplished but not before the artilleryman in a loud voice fearlessly boasted that the arresting officers had no jurisdiction and that his commander had proven that fact by extricating him from ordinary justice that morning. Indeed, upon the request of those present he twice repeated the incriminating statement. The following morning Alcalde Díaz informed Governor and Commandant General Roque de Quiroga of the incident and charged Commander Esquiaqui with interfering in the administration of justice, violently seizing a prisoner, and intimidating royal officials. Esquiaqui, who was unaware that the man had been re-arrested until he failed to appear that day for Sunday drill, also filed a spirited complaint. However, when informed that he had been accused of employing force, he denied the charge, contending that he had behaved urbanely throughout the entire incident.

To resolve the affair, Quiroga summoned Alguacil García. Upon questioning, again under oath, the blundering peace officer changed his story completely. He admitted that he had been peacefully persuaded to go to the commander's home and now testified that Esquiaqui's message contained no threat whatever. Esquiaqui had still illegally removed a prisoner, but the languid Quiroga urged Díaz to drop the matter in the interest of harmony. He also imprisoned the alguacil for perjury, but he hinted to Díaz that he would release him as soon as the furor had subsided. To Díaz, it now appeared that he, as alcalde, was being victimized by a military conspiracy to frustrate ordinary justice, and he was probably correct. He believed that Quiroga had intimidated the alguacil into changing his testimony in order to conceal Esquiaqui's flagrant abuse of authority, and that the commandant general was merely compounding the offense. However, Alcalde Díaz was unable to act because Quiroga possessed the key prisoner, García, who had knowledge of those who could be called upon to act as witnesses. Hence, when the mail left for Santa Fe several days later, Díaz had not succeeded in compiling testimony to sustain his charges. He did, however, send a communication to Viceroy Guirior, stating his intentions and complaining of his frustration at the hands of Quiroga. The commandant general also sent a report, expressing consternation that Díaz would not accept his judgment and asking that the viceroy personally inform him of the artillery companies' fuero. Finally, Esquiaqui filed a statement denying misconduct and warning that unless the integrity of the fuero were upheld his work with the artillery companies would become useless.

During the following month, Díaz compiled a massive collection of testimony which, if not precisely proving that a pronounced threat had been made against ordinary justice, did at least demonstrate that Esquiaqui had violated the code of procedure. Díaz' case included a sworn statement by García, who confirmed that he had reached the commander's house peacefully, but who now reasserted that a threat of physical violence had indeed been made. The most important information contained, however, was that Quiroga was wantonly suppressing evidence. Of several examples, the most flagrant was a sudden inaccessibility of the military personnel who had assisted with the second arrest and had heard the artilleryman's loud boasts concerning his extrication. In spite of numerous written requests by Díaz for access to these men, Quiroga stalled. And, although the corporal finally testified, the other four men never did appear.

Presumably, Governor Roque de Quiroga, who possessed both civil and military authority, would have been the ideal figure to mediate the dispute and perhaps soothe the alcalde's ruffled feelings and injured pride. However, not only in this instance, but generally, when military governors found themselves confronted by such circumstances, they reacted first as members of the military corporation. Hence, Alcalde Díaz stood alone and frustrated, while public knowledge of the affront to his authority exacerbated the growing crisis in local government.

Viceroy Guirior did very little to help the alcalde, and, in the final analysis, he probably did more harm than good to the prestige of ordinary justice.

Despite his knowledge that Díaz was gathering evidence to demonstrate a need for corrective measures against the local military leadership and of a second communication complaining that Quiroga was still obstructing the investigation, Guirior ruled on the matter before he had seen the alcalde's case. In his decision, Guirior acted directly against no one. On the one hand, he reminded the military authorities of the respect due ordinary justice; but, he also rigorously sustained Quiroga and Esquiaqui's position that the artillery companies did indeed possess the fuero militar. More important, he maintained silence on the specific plight of Alcalde Díaz and the high-handed actions of Quiroga and Esquiaqui; and, thereby, the abuse of ordinary justice at the hands of the military went unpunished. Eventually, O'Reilly and the crown upheld Guirior's decison on the fuero of the artillery companies, but no action was taken to rectify the damage that had been done to the cabildo of Cartagena, a matter which was not even significant enough to reach Spain.[34]

This confrontation between civil and military authorities in Cartagena was typical of the general coastal experience. In both Panama and the district of Natá, extensive feuding, chiefly stemming from the pardo question, erupted in 1774 between the militia and the cabildos. As a result the deputy governor of Panama, Joaquín Cabrejo, a civilian, petitioned Santa Fe on behalf of ordinary justice, asking for a clarification of the cases of desafuero, and particularly for a firm statement emphasizing the occurrence of desafuero in instances of abuse of royal justice. As at Cartagena, the cabildo complained of recurrent humiliations, chiefly at the hands of unruly pardos. However, although clarifying the items of desafuero, the viceregency vacillated, again declining to act decisively.[35]

Although ambiguities regarding judicial boundaries contributed to this rash of jurisdictional conflicts, in all likelihood a spirit of patience, prudence, good will, and cooperation could easily have forestalled most of the controversies. Under the circumstances, however, the exercise of such laudable virtues was precluded, and both sides approached the problem with pride, jealousy, and emotion. Indeed, to assume that in most confrontations the embattled participants were seriously concerned with either the letter or the spirit of the law would be taking far too much for granted. Rather, the more immediate concern of winning whatever prestige might accrue from a momentary advantage over the rival jurisdiction all too often obscured the cause of justice.

The fundamental arguments recurred with monotony. Ordinary justices contended that the exemption of so many individuals from their authority diminished their power, and they complained that they were humiliated by

34. O'Reilly to Arriaga, Madrid, April 22, 1774, AGI: Santa Fe, legajo 945.
35. Expedientes, judicial disputes in Panama, 1774, ANC: MM, vol. 79, fols. 672–92 and vol. 90, fols. 336–38.

the contempt and arrogance displayed by the immune lower classes, as well as by a general military disregard and disrespect for the dignity of their offices. Conversely, the military jealously defended its fuero as just compensation for the highest order of service to the state and regarded any incursion by ordinary justice into its domain as a menace to the promotion of pride and dedication to duty. The result was a withering of respect for justice, an undermining of the prestige and credibility of local government, and the establishment of the military as a dominant force in the provinces of Cartagena and Panama.

Significantly, however, while the military proved willing to uphold pardo privileges in its struggle to establish military prerogatives, in its own affairs it carried liabilities associated with the pardo status in the stratified society into the military corporation. The assumption that men of Negro parentage were inherently inferior and less trustworthy than their white counterparts remained. The most visible consequence of this attitude was a limitation of the authority delegated to pardos in the command system of pardo battalions. Under the Cuban reglamento, these battalions were equipped with a dual command and staff group, including one of white regulars, the other of volunteer men of color, which was an extension of unit segregation. The head of the pardo section was entitled the "commander," and he was assisted by standard-bearers, a drum major, and other non-commissioned personnel. A subinspector, who held the militia post of ayudante mayor, headed the white command and staff group. He was accompanied by four men of the militia position of lieutenant, who served as ayudantes. Since the militia operated on a segregated basis, no veteran personnel integrated the company ranks; rather, a number of pardo volunteer officers were maintained on permanent salary to handle the same sort of duties performed by veterans in white companies. In addition, the white staff and command group contained a number of noncommissioned officers, *garzones*, to provide the necessary technical advice. In contrast to pardo units, those with the all-color designation, when consolidated into regiments in the following decade, operated with only a white command and staff group, in the same manner as the white units.[36]

In pardo units the title of commander for the colored chief amounted to more pretense than reality. Supreme authority actually rested with the subinspector, who was responsible for supervising the training, discipline, and general conduct of the battalion. All were to obey him when he performed these comprehensive duties, including the pardo commander. However, the reglamento cautioned the subinspector that the pardo commander's authority was to be considered equal to that of the other battalion heads. Furthermore,

36. Troop inspection reports, Regiments of All Colors of Santa Marta and Riohacha, August 4, 1784, and Regiment of All Colors of Mompós, December 31, 1793, in ANC: MM, vol. 11, fol. 463, and vol. 99, fol. 445.

the pardo commander had the power to arrest any battalion soldier or officer who did not comply with his commands. Here the precise lines of authority were very nebulous. It is inconceivable that the commander would have dared to arrest a subinspector or, for that matter, any other white official. In any event, such a confrontation was extremely unlikely because the supreme duties of subinspection, the key loophole, were so broadly defined. Moreover, since the regulations specifically labeled the remainder of the white officers and non-commissioned personnel as the subinspector's assistants for the execution of his duties, they were, for all practical purposes, beyond the reach of pardo authority. In effect, the pardo commander was commander of pardos, and no more.[37]

Militia practice also drew important distinctions between pardos and whites in personal relations. An illuminating example was the requirement that pardo officers, by penalty of their undistinguished birth, had to remove their hats in the presence of white officers, as did white enlisted men. This policy had developed in Cuba, where José Pérez Dávila had served as subinspector of pardos. He brought the practice to Cartagena during his mission there and, after consultation with Cartagena's leadership, Viceroy Guirior ordered its observance in Panama. This practice remained a sore point between the two classes of troops, but all pardo efforts to escape this symbol of social inferiority failed.[38] Thus, while military privilege elevated the pardo in colonial society, distinctions of birth remained intact inside the military organization.

Although in the early years of the reform disruptive pardo privileges were the most sensational dimension of the status of the emerging military corporation, a subtler and ultimately more important drama was unfolding on another level. This was the question of relating the military organization to the upper stratum of society, or what in a general sense can be called the white estate. In hierarchical colonial society, anyone who was not an Indian or relegated to the castas—and who was therefore free from the juridical and political limitations imposed upon these groups—belonged to the white estate. This class included vassals of European origin, Americans who were ethnic Europeans, and legitimate mestizos who were free from the "taint" of Negro blood and who had adopted Spanish culture. As the conquering race, the Spaniard and his creole descendants enjoyed a distinguished social reputation, which was reflected by a superior status in colonial law, and which frequently led to the pretense of nobility. He was exempt from tribute, received lighter punishments than the humble castas, suffered no special restraints upon his person, and had access to reputable professions, government offices, and public honors.[39]

37. *Reglamento . . . de Cuba*, chap. 1, art. 13; chap. 2, arts. 13, 22, 34; chap. 4, art. 13.
38. Expediente, the militia commander v. the lieutenant governor of Panama, 1779, ANC: MM, vol. 40, fols. 669–87.
39. McAlister, "Social Structure," pp. 354–59; Rosenblat, *La población indígena*, 2: 133–68.

Despite the unifying characteristics of the white estate, important distinctions appeared within its membership. Fundamentally, the creole, at least partly because of the presumed corrupting influence of the American environment, suffered discrimination at the hands of the European, who believed him dull and lacking in virtue and enterprise. He sometime might even find himself compelled to establish his *limpieza de sangre* (purity of blood) before the audiencia to eliminate the suspicion of any taint upon the honor of his lineage.[40] Yet within the creole class there existed an elite, including the *beneméritos de Indias*, who were the descendants of the conquerors and early colonists; those who could claim *hidalguía*; and those who acquired, usually through purchase, legal titles of nobility or memberships in Spanish military orders. These marks of social quality assumed special significance when fortified by personal fortunes, usually in land, mining, or wholesale commerce, and when reflected by deeds of public generosity and governmental service.[41] On the other hand, the Spaniard, by nature of his birthplace, universally aspired to noble status and so classified himself; he probably could maintain this pretense unless he overtly engaged in a dishonorable occupation, such as one requiring manual labor.[42]

Tensions between creole and Spaniard in the Spanish empire and the favoritism accorded the latter in recruitment for high office are familiar themes in colonial history. Yet, largely through the purchase of public office, the creole elites of Mexico, Peru, and Chile were able to dominate their audiencias and bureaucracies under the early Bourbons. This situation changed abruptly under the enlightened despot, Charles III, and his tough minister of the Indies, José de Gálvez (1776–87). In order to regenerate the empire through far-reaching reforms, many of which threatened the vested interests of the entrenched creole aristocracy, the reformers turned to an anti-creole orientation in which they depended upon the Spanish-born to implement the policies of the government.[43] In New Granada, creoles never achieved numerical dominance on the Audiencia of Santa Fe de Bogotá under the early Bourbons. Indeed, only one native vassal, Juan de Ricaurte, acquired a judgeship.[44] The

40. Rosenblat, p. 26; Jaime Jaramillo Uribe, "Mestizaje y diferenciación social en el Nuevo Reino de Granada en la segunda mitad del siglo XVIII," pp. 27–30.

41. Richard Konetzke, "La formación de la nobleza en Indias," pp. 336–48; McAlister, "Social Structure," pp. 361–63.

42. Konetzke, "La formación," p. 356.

43. For the audiencia, see D. A. Brading, *Miners and Merchants in Bourbon Mexico, 1763–1810*, pp. 35–44; Leon G. Campbell, "A Colonial Establishment: Creole Domination of the Audiencia of Lima during the Late Eighteenth Century"; Mark A. Burkholder, "From Creole to Peninsular: The Transformation of the Audiencia of Lima"; Jacques A. Barbier, "Elite and Cadres in Bourbon Chile," pp. 430–33; Mark A. Burkholder and David S. Chandler, "Creole Appointments and the Sale of Audiencia Positions in the Spanish Empire under the Early Bourbons, 1701–1750." For provincial administration, see Brading, *Miners and Merchants*, p. 64, and J. R. Fisher, *Government and Society in Colonial Peru: The Intendant System, 1784–1814*, pp. 8–28, 36–38.

44. Jose María Restrepo Sáenz, *Biografías de los mandatarios y ministros de la Real Audiencia (1671–1819)*.

most probable cause for this phenomenon was the widespread poverty of the viceroyalty during the early century and the small number of creoles who could afford expensive posts.[45] The appointment of three *limeños* to the Audiencia of Santa Fe would seem to allay any suspicions about a systematic exclusion of creoles. After the accession of Charles III, however, and in spite of the increasing prosperity and development of the viceroyalty, few creoles achieved *oidor* (judge) status either, indicating a convergence of New Granada's experience with that of the other regions of the empire, where enlightened despotism depended principally upon Europeans to achieve its objectives. Further, during the ministry of José de Gálvez those oidores of the Santa Fe audiencia who over the years had established close contacts with the local creole elite through marriage or other means were quickly retired or transferred.[46]

One indispensable tool for the implementation of enlightened reforms was the military, which, in the final analysis, provided the power that underpinned royal initiatives. The military was reorganized and strengthened not only to defend the empire from foreign aggression but to maintain order and to support the government as well; in the long run, the latter proved the more compelling objective.[47] Thus, given the tension between the creole aristocracy and the enlightened despotism of the government of Charles III with its dependence upon Europeans, the relationship of the military to the social structure—and in particular to the various elements of the white estate—was a critical question, especially as the tensions generated by reform increased.

The creole, historically, was not a significant participant in the defense system. Rotating battalions, which shouldered much of the defense burden before the expansion of the veteran colonial army, were Spanish. Moreover, even the early Fijo of Cartagena, although mainly comprised of the native-born in the ranks, possessed a predominantly Spanish officer corps. The 1741 battle, in which the army of Cartagena defeated the British invasion under Admiral Edward Vernon, has frequently been characterized as a creole-Spanish victory. Yet close examination reveals that most of the fighting was done by marines and troops from the battalions of Aragón and Spain, while the Fijo played a secondary role. In any event, by conservative estimate, half of its officers were Spanish.[48] The first set of service records for the Fijo, year 1749, indicates a four-to-one Spanish-to-creole ratio, with most of the latter

45. The underdevelopment of New Granada and the poverty of its inhabitants are common themes in contemporary descriptions. For example, see Moreno y Escandón, "Estado . . . 1772," pp. 547–48, 554, 558, and Antonio Manso, "Relación hecha . . . como presidente de la audiencia del Nuevo Reino de Granada, sobre su estado y necesidades en el año de 1729," in *Relaciones de mando de los virreyes de la Nueva Granada: Memorias económicas,* ed. Gabriel Giraldo Jaramillo, pp. 21–30.

46. Restrepo Sáenz, *Biografías,* pp. 366–438; John L. Phelan, "El auge y la caída de los criollos en la Audiencia de Nueva Granada, 1700–1781," pp. 597–606.

47. Expediente on the establishment of the Fixed Regiment of Cartagena, 1771–73, AGI: Santa Fe, legajo 1007.

48. Kuethe, "La batalla de Cartagena."

serving in the lower levels.[49] This percentage remained stable up to the Seven Years' War, after which the gap gradually narrowed to just under a two-to-one margin on the eve of the reform, still a considerable edge in favor of Europeans. In the old Fixed Infantry Battalion of Panama, the difference was even more substantial. Spanish officers outnumbered creoles six to one in 1751, and although that margin eventually shrank too, Spaniards still held nearly a three-to-one superiority in the years following the Seven Years' War.[50]

There is a temptation to explain the preponderance of Spanish officers as either a systematic exclusion of the native-born or, perhaps, a manifestation of creole reluctance to enter the military. While there is probably some validity to both contentions, neither is adequate in itself because of built-in limitations on creole opportunity. The principal and most convenient source of experienced officers was the rotating battalions returning to Spain, from which officers could easily be recruited, usually with the incentive of a promotion of one rank. Thus, the battalions of Spain and Aragón, which returned to Europe in 1748, left behind in Cartagena a large number of young officers, a process repeated by other units after the Seven Years' War.[51] In Panama, the early fixed battalion was formed directly from the Battalion of Granada; there could hardly, therefore, have been many creole officers in it.[52] On the other hand, during the 1750s and 1760s young creoles began embracing military service in significant numbers as cadets. In Cartagena most of these men claimed noble status, which indicated a willingness to make the military a career by those sons of families who had to find outside outlets and support. In Panama, these cadets were nearly all sons of Spanish officers who had joined the fixed battalion and who obviously found the military one of the few honorable professions available on the isthmus.[53] Thus, while few openings existed for creoles in the early army, the monarchy did display a willingness to train creoles as officers, an opportunity that many sought.

The prereform militia provided, to some extent, an outlet for the creole's search for titles and honors to fortify his noble self-image, but it is difficult to establish solid conclusions concerning this phenomenon. Early records

49. Service records, Fixed Battalion of Cartagena, April 19, 1749, AGI: Santa Fe, legajo 940.

50. With non-Spanish Europeans and Africans placed with the Spanish, the service records of Cartagena produced the following Spanish-to-creole ratios in officer counts: 1749 (28 to 7); 1764 (27 to 8); 1765 (24 to 8); 1766 (20 to 9); 1767 (21 to 7); 1768 (20 to 10); 1769 (20 to 10); and 1770 (19 to 10). For Panama, the count was: 1751 (18 to 3); 1763 (16 to 3); 1764 (17 to 4); and 1765 (17 to 4). AGI: Santa Fe, legajos 940, 941, 944, and 1010, and AGI: Panama, legajos 356 and 357. As may be inferred from the above documentation, the military command produced service records at irregular intervals, depending upon personnel and occasion. See also Table 10.

51. Viceroy Sebastián Eslava to the Marqués de la Ensenada, Cartagena, September 16, 1749, AGI: Santa Fe, legajo 940; royal order, December 8, 1762, ANC: MM, vol. 83, fols. 316–22.

52. Report of Alsedo y Herrera, Panama, March 28, 1744, AGI: Panama, legajo 356.

53. Service records, Fixed Battalion of Cartagena, February 28, 1770, AGI: Santa Fe, legajo 944, and Fixed Battalion of Panama, April, 1764, AGI: Panama, legajo 357.

are fragmentary at best and provide only a few, limited glimpses into the militia's composition. Indeed, it is impossible even to estimate the size of the militia in New Granada at any one time. The absence of documents on the subject is in itself a commentary upon the lack of importance accorded to the militia, and the available records overwhelmingly support the contention that it was far more shadow than substance. The units lacked standard organization, rarely possessed adequate equipment, drilled only in emergencies, had few if any competent officers, and in general were of little value.[54] In some instances the fuero was granted to officers but usually only for criminal matters.[55] Despite the early militia's lack of significance, fragmentary evidence indicates that creoles sought officerships in it; indeed the lack of any real function or regular obligations probably enhanced its attractiveness to those seeking to validate their social reputation without incurring much corresponding responsibility or a full commitment to the military life.[56] This largely meaningless dabbling in the militia should not, however, detract from the general conclusion that the creole was not a significant participant in the colonial army prior to 1773.

The increased size of the reformed military placed new pressure upon the human resources of Panama and Cartagena and made the enlistment of significant numbers of creoles inevitable. In the ranks of the white militia there were various kinds of storekeepers, craftsmen, artisans, and small farmers who comprised the nucleus of the coastal creole population.[57] These people, it should be remembered, were in the main "blancos de la tierra," ethnic mulattoes who through occupational status and social reputation passed as white.

In Panama, which had only a small European population, creoles dominated the volunteer officer corps nearly four to one.[58] Presumably, as already indicated, creoles also dominated officerships in the backlands of Cartagena, because of the lack of Spanish-born competition, except for localities like the commercially oriented river port of Mompós. Unfortunately, it is impossible to conduct a full social analysis of these units because service records were never compiled for them. On the other hand, the authorities did maintain such records for the six companies of the white battalion which were raised

54. Governor Miguel de Gálvez to Messía de la Cerda, Neiva, March 19, 1766, ANC: MM, vol. 105, fols. 901–2; Governor Ignacio Nicolás Buenaventura to Messía de la Cerda, Ibagué, October 4, 1766, ANC: MM, fols. 903–28; Engineer Francisco Requena to Messía de la Cerda, Guayaquil, April 20, 1771, ANC: MM, vol. 100, fols. 328–33; and de la Sierra to Arriaga, Cartagena, April 30, 1771, AGI: Santa Fe, legajo 1007.

55. Expediente, judicial dispute in Mompós, 1757; expediente, judicial disputes in Cartagena, 1763 and 1767; expediente, judicial dispute in Santa Marta, 1777.

56. Nomination of Felipe Areche y Sarmiento for captain, militia of Quito, 1763, ANC: MM, vol. 25, fols. 52–53.

57. Expediente, militia of Cartagena, AGI: Santa Fe, legajo 948.

58. Service records, White Infantry Battalion of Natá, December 1780, ANC: MM, vol. 26, fols. 966–1011.

in the city of Cartagena itself. In this instance, Spanish volunteer officers outnumbered creoles two to one, which illustrates that when Europeans were available they bested creoles in the competition for commissions.[59] Moreover, the colonel chosen for the battalion in 1777, Juan Fernández de Moure, who commanded the unit for most of the remainder of the century, was a Galician.[60]

The preponderance of Spanish-born colonists over creoles in this unit was probably simply a result of the leadership's social values and not a direct attempt at this time to exclude creoles systematically. The reglamento admonished the militia leadership to select men of the highest social standing for officerships, especially for positions of command.[61] Since most of the Spaniards who were selected claimed nobility and since the authorities in charge of recruitment—Pérez Dávila, Quiroga, and Guirior—were all Europeans and hence likely to see validity to such a claim in America, the dominance of Spaniards is not surprising. On the other hand, there was a general creole willingness to serve in the militia. Seven of the battalion's ten cadets were young creoles, a pattern matched by already demonstrated trends in the regular army.[62] Thus, the native colonist, while experiencing some disappointments in competition with Spaniards, obviously entertained hopes of achieving an active role in the new colonial militia.

It should be noted in passing that the social standing of volunteer officers in white units could vary considerably. In militia service records, officers with an unimpeachable claim to the white status would probably pass as "noble" in *calidad* (social derivation). Other common ratings included *distinguida* (distinguished), *honrada* (honorable), *conocida* (known), *decente* (decent), and *buena* (good), but there was no precise definition for these terms because their significance depended upon the subjective evaluation of the officer who used them, normally the sargento mayor. Francisco Bassi, for example, who was ayudante mayor of dragoons in Guayaquil at the end of the century, rated his fellow officers as uniformly "distinguished," significantly included a number who had only managed a "good" in earlier times and one who seemingly tumbled from a "noble" status.[63]

Despite these ambiguities, descriptions such as "honorable," "known," "decent," and "good" certainly suggested a potentially flawed social standing; yet they were common enough in the white militia. In 1780, for example, fourteen of fifteen creole volunteers in the Battalion of White Infantry of Natá,

59. Service records, White Infantry Battalion of Cartagena, December 1776, AGI: Santa Fe, legajo 946.
60. Service records, White Infantry Regiment of Cartagena, June 1785, AGI: Santa Fe, legajo 1156.
61. *Reglamento . . . de Cuba*, chap. 6, arts. 2, 9.
62. Service records, White Infantry Battalion of Cartagena, December 1776.
63. For 1788, ANC: MM, vol. 47, fols. 10–34; for 1797, AGS: GM, legajo 7281.

Panama, were merely "decent," while the other rated "noble."[64] For such vassals, officerships in a white unit could cement whatever claims they might have had to the upper estate, apart from the additional advantage they acquired from the fuero militar. Presumably, much the same situation existed in the backlands of Cartagena, which like Panama had a blurred social structure. By contrast, the large European population in the city of Cartagena meant that the reformers could be more selective in recruiting officers. Of Cartagena's four creole officers, only one was a "blanco de la tierra."[65]

One important segment of the upper stratum of society, the merchant elite, did not fully share in the quest for militia offices. Instead, it stubbornly asserted a separate corporate identity. The wholesale merchants of Cartagena, most of whom were Spanish-born, consisted of dealers registered in the Consulado of Cádiz as well as provincial traders who were local residents. Although Cartagena did not yet possess a consulado of its own, the Cádiz guild maintained a deputy there with authority to convene commercial councils (*juntas de comercio*); the governor, acting in conjunction with two magistrates selected from the commercial community, sustained juridically the merchants' corporate identity.[66] When the militia was first organized in Cartagena, the merchants successfully petitioned Viceroy Manuel Guirior for an exemption from militia service for themselves and their apprentices. The viceroy based his decision on a vague precedent established in Spain concerning the lottery for the regular army.

A controversy over the issue erupted in 1778 when Viceroy Manuel Flores, acting upon a petition of Colonel Juan Fernández de Moure of the white battalion, temporarily suspended the merchant exemption pending consultation with the crown. The colonel, already injured by competition in recruitment from the matrícula de mar and short some 200 men in the six city companies, complained that Guirior's decision made it nearly impossible to sustain the militia at authorized strength or to find suitable candidates for officerships. In Cartagena, he argued, "the white men, and especially the Spaniards, have no other occupation than the mercantile profession. . . ."[67] In addition, he complained that the exempted merchants shielded others from recruitment by fraudulently claiming them as assistants.[68]

Various factors contributed to the Spanish merchants' hostility to militia service. Their most legitimate claim was that enlistment would impede the

64. Service records, White Infantry Battalion of Natá, December 1780.

65. Service records, White Infantry Battalion of Cartagena, December 1776.

66. Moreno y Escandón, "Estado . . . 1772," p. 580.

67. Moure to Pimienta, Cartagena, May 21, 1778, AGI: Santa Fe, legajo 948. Brading also found this pattern in New Spain. See *Miners and Merchants*, pp. 104–5.

68. Expediente, militia of Cartagena. The merchant community of New Spain shared this aversion to military service. See McAlister, *The "Fuero Militar*," pp. 31–39.

conduct of their businesses. This fear was especially valid for merchants registered in Cádiz, who were obliged to return periodically to Iberia. Moreover, militia service in the city of Cartagena was not a matter to be taken lightly. Not only might weekly drills become an annoyance but there was great physical danger in serving there, probably more so than anywhere else in New Granada—except possibly Panama—because of the relative frequency of militia service. It had been necessary, for example, to mobilize the old militia from time to time throughout the century because of war, and a number of companies saw action during the 1741 invasion.[69] A fear of hardship would prove justified in the present instance too, because during the war with England (1779–83), the mobilized militia suffered a heavy death rate due to epidemics in the garrison.[70] The well-established maritime merchant, therefore, might find little attraction to the militia; in contrast, the creole, in his perpetual search for status—and presumably also because of a degree of loyalty to his birthplace—seemed willing to take the risk where officership was involved.

In arguing for retention of their exemption, the merchants also revealed subtler preoccupations. Service in the militia conflicted with the integrity of their own functionally derived status in the hierarchical scheme of society. While lauding the role of the military as the defender of the nation, they viewed their own mission as equally vital and honorable. Furthermore, the qualities that made them suitable for the mercantile profession were not those that made good soldiers. In the words of their legal representatives, the burden of service would be too great for men "employed continuously at their desks with pen in hand from sunup to sundown . . . [because with] their bodies mortified by close-order drills and tactical maneuvers on holidays . . . even if by chance no other demands are made on work days, they awaken tired and fatigued, unfit for clerical labors, which in this extremely hot land demand physical stamina and agility, and an alert mind."[71] In short, military service, except in great emergency, was an incongruous function for those of the commercial occupation. This conviction was reinforced when, for want of more acceptable candidates, the militia leadership appointed a number of mere shopkeepers to officerships, one of whom could not even pretend to "nobility" despite a Spanish birthright.

The crown was caught in this controversy between its desire for a full, prestigious militia headed by recognized community leaders and its ambition to promote an expanding, healthy commerce. In October 1778, it promulgated the momentous edict of free trade, which threw open the ports of

69. Diary of Eslava, in Roberto Arrázola, comp., *Historial de Cartagena*, p. 333.
70. Flores to Gálvez, Cartagena, December 29, 1781, AGI: Santa Fe, legajo 948.
71. Petition of Francisco Joaquín Barrozo and Ramón de Garay on behalf of the Consulado of Cádiz, Cartagena, August 7, 1778, AGI: Santa Fe, legajo 948.

America and Spain to unrestricted trade within the empire, in order to invigorate commerce and to stimulate further economic regeneration. Consistent with this objective, it acted in November to resolve the militia controversy in Cartagena by exempting transient merchants from enlistment, although it limited each such merchant to only one nonincumbered assistant.[72] A year later the crown extended the exemption of Spanish merchants from military service to the whole empire.[73]

The merchant exemption represented at least a momentary setback for the prestige of the emerging military corporation. As a consequence, Colonel Juan Fernández de Moure aggressively asserted the fuero militar throughout the following decade in nearly endless litigation, much of it involving business contracts, in an attempt to assert the prestige and honor of those who accepted service in the colonial militia (see chapter 5). Wholesale merchants, however, remained on the exempted list for the remainder of the colonial period.[74]

The exemption that the government extended to transient merchants weakened Spanish domination of the militia officer corps, but not drastically at this time. Not all wealthy Spaniards, of course, qualified for the exemption, and among those who did, a number, such as Colonel Juan Fernández de Moure, served as a matter of choice. Additionally, the veteran advisors for the city and the province, who in effect controlled the militia by acting as sargentos mayores and company lieutenants, were overwhelmingly Spanish career officers.[75] These men, such as Domingo Esquiaqui, seldom exhibited sympathy for creole sensitivities, as in their support of pardo pretensions against the cabildos. Thus, as the regime of Charles III prepared to assert itself in New Granada, the disciplined militia of the Caribbean provinces seemed a trustworthy, if not particularly effective, instrument.

72. Expediente, militia of Cartagena; J. Muñoz Pérez, "La publicación del reglamento de comercio libre de Indias, de 1778."

73. Royal order, June 18, 1779, ANC: MM, vol. 71, fols. 532–34.

74. *Reglamento para las milicias disciplinadas de infantería y dragones del Nuevo Reyno de Granada, y provincias agregadas a este virreynato* (hereafter cited as *Reglamento . . . del Nuevo Reyno de Granada*), chap. 2, art. 24.

75. Service records, veteran officers of the disciplined militia of the Governorship of Cartagena, June 30, 1776, AGI: Santa Fe, legajo 1156.

3. Early Reform in Guayaquil and Popayán

FOLLOWING THE INITIAL reorganization in Panama and Cartagena, Viceroy Manuel Guirior extended the military reform to the Province of Guayaquil, and shortly thereafter his successor, Manuel Antonio Flores, acted in Popayán. This phase of the reform developed with very little direct royal assistance or direction and opened the way for a significant modification of militia policy by the viceroys in Santa Fe. Viceroy Flores, in particular, was a leader whose commitment to a rapid expansion of the military reorganization exceeded that of the crown, although for want of sufficient royal support he never fulfilled many of his aspirations. Yet by raising a disciplined militia in the inland Province of Popayán, Flores was able to test the new system in the cultural heartland of New Granada, where he experienced a foretaste of the bitter aristocratic hostility which would plague attempts to extend the inland militia during the following decade.

Both Guayaquil and Popayán pertained to the Commandancy General of Quito, which possessed only a small, recently created, fixed military establishment. In times past, the only regular garrison in the entire region was the guard of the Quito audiencia. Established with twenty-five men in 1755, that number had doubled by 1764.[1] This force soon had to be expanded and diver-

1. Royal orders, September 26, 1764, and June 26, 1765, ANC: MM, vol. 51, fol. 67, and vol. 100, fols. 23–24; expediente on the formation of the regular garrison of the Presidency of Quito, 1764–65, AGI: Quito, legajo 573.

sified, however, when it proved unable either to protect the audiencia or to maintain public order.

The first serious test of Bourbon authority in Quito came in mid-May 1765, when a massive popular uprising overthrew the existing organs of royal administration. This insurrection, usually known as the *Aguardiente* and *Aduana* Rebellion, resulted from the aggressive revenue policies of the regime of Charles III. Viceroy Messía de la Cerda had ordered a strict enforcement of the aguardiente monopoly, established shortly before the Seven Years' War, and had levied a tax called the "aduana" on the sale of foodstuffs in the city. To enforce this initiative, the viceroy had dispatched a special agent from the treasury in Santa Fe, Juan Díaz de Herrera.

As the new tax policy took effect, discontent mounted. Finally, with cries of "Death to *chapetones*" and "Down with bad government," the populace seized control of the city, forced the capitulation of the audiencia, and won the acceptance of its demands, including the suppression of the aguardiente monopoly and the aduana. Moreover, strong anti-Spanish antagonism surfaced during the rebellion, with the terms of the capitulation expelling all Spanish-born vassals from the city.[2] Significantly, the incident also sparked a series of secondary disorders in neighboring provinces, including serious incidents in the cities of Cali, Cartago, and Popayán of the Province of Popayán.[3] The government was unable to reassert its full authority in Quito until an expedition of 600 militiamen and regulars, originating in Panama and Peru, marched into the troubled city in September of the following year under the command of Juan Antonio Zelaya, governor of Guayaquil.[4] These spectacular, grave events were an early manifestation of the broad crisis of community which would accompany the struggle of Charles III to restructure the colonial empire and, in particular, to enhance revenue collection.

The rebellion in Quito seriously shook the faith of the crown in the docility and innocence of its vassals, and the government reacted by opting for a greater dependence on military force to support its dominion. Viceroy Pedro Messía de la Cerda expressed his thoughts on that subject in his *relación de mando* (terminal report) to Manuel Guirior in 1772: "let us recognize that the obedience of this kingdom's inhabitants has no other support, with the exception of the armed forces, than the free will and pleasure with which they accept directives; because, without their approval, there is no force, weapon, or authority which their superiors can use to gain respect and compliance; hence, command is very uncertain and the good success of measures taken is excessively tenuous; by the same token, this lack of confidence requires treading lightly and, at

2. Federico González Suárez, *Historia general de la República de Ecuador*, 5: 206–25.
3. Demetrio García Vásquez, *Revaluaciones históricas para la ciudad de Santiago de Cali*, 2: 318–19.
4. González Suárez, *Historia general*, 5: 225–26; Zelaya report, Quito, June 2, 1767, AGI: Quito, legajo 237.

times, without complete freedom, trying to accommodate circumstances; and, because of this situation, it follows that the enemy can be of two categories, disobedient vassals and rebellious barbarians. . . ." The viceroy went on to report that, as a result of the humiliating experience in Quito, he believed disloyal vassals were the gravest menace to the government.[5]

Shortly after the suppression of the disorders, Messía de la Cerda informed the president of Quito that he believed that a large fixed regular force in the troubled areas would preserve domestic peace and order.[6] Actually, in 1765, just before the rebellion, the viceroy had proposed the creation of a 200-man force for the commandancy general to be distributed among Quito, Cuenca, and Guayaquil. He took this action shortly after ordering Díaz de Herrera to Quito, because he anticipated disorders and believed that only armed forces could exact compliance to the royal will. Spain had approved this plan but too late to have any effect; now the plan had to be revised to cope with the difficulties that had surfaced in 1765.[7] Pending a final decision, troop detachments, numbering about 200 men and coming for the most part from the currently available European battalions, were employed from Panama.[8]

The first new fijo company was established in Guayaquil in 1767.[9] Four years later a fijo contingent of three companies was organized for the city of Quito, as well as one unit for Popayán.[10] All five units were infantry companies of fifty men each (see Table 1). The original plan had not entailed a regular garrison for Popayán, but the events of 1765 prompted a revised distribution. Upon viceregal recommendation, the crown placed the new units under the general command of the first president to take office after the restoration of royal authority, José Diguja (1767–78), who also took the title of commandant general, although, as explained earlier, the governors of Popayán and Guayaquil and their garrisons retained practical autonomy.[11] These troops for the Presidency of Quito represented an overt Bourbon embrace of military force to support royal authority and policies, an association which was destined to intensify as the conflicts generated by the reforms of Charles

5. Messía de la Cerda, in *Relaciones de mando*, p. 113.
6. Zelaya to Messía de la Cerda, Quito, April 3, 1767, ANC: MM, vol. 101, fols. 555–56.
7. Royal order, June 26, 1765, ANC: MM, vol. 51, fol. 67; expediente on the formation of the regular garrison of the Presidency of Quito, 1764–65.
8. Orosco to Messía de la Cerda, Panama, July 7, 1766, ANC: MM, vol. 92, fols. 750–57; Captain Francisco Antonio Fernández to Messía de la Cerda, Quito, June 3, 1767, ANC: MM, vol. 100, fols. 745–54.
9. Governor Francisco de Ugarte to Guirior, Guayaquil, August 2, 1773, ANE: Pres., vol. 194, fols. 51–62.
10. De la Sierra to Messía de la Cerda, Cartagena, February 11, 1771, ANC: MM, vol. 103, fols. 104–5; report of Subinspector General Joaquín de Cañavaral, Cartagena, May 9, 1793, ANC: MM, vol. 92, fols. 1019–35.
11. President and Regent-Visitor José García de León y Pizarro subsequently tried but failed to convert this office into a captaincy general. Expediente on the command of the troops of Quito, 1779, AGI: Quito, legajo 573.

III grew in the following decade. It is noteworthy that this increased reliance on the military coincided with the expulsion of the Society of Jesus in 1767, which removed a traditional, if "unenlightened," pillar of royal support and one which, as a matter of fact, had been instrumental in coping with the 1765 crisis in Quito.

During the period of the military reorganization, Guayaquil, the scene of the first militia reforms in the Presidency of Quito, experienced transformation into an expanding, highly commercialized seaport.[12] Guayaquil was the traditional shipbuilding center of the Pacific and the major supplier of lumber to Peru, but restrictive trade policies had long stifled her potential in cacao production. With the liberalization of trade practices under the Bourbons, the latter industry experienced dramatic growth, becoming a boom in the period following the Seven Years' War and making Guayaquil's cacao output in America second only to that of Caracas.[13] The province's free population reflected its increased prosperity, jumping from 28,289 in 1778 to over 50,000 bustling inhabitants by the end of the century.[14]

In social composition, Guayaquil Province closely resembled Cartagena, although the Spanish-born population was smaller, probably because this Pacific region had less direct contact and commerce with Spain. Castas or "libres," as they were sometimes known in New Granada, constituted more than half of the province's population, numbering 15,509 in 1778 compared to 3,722 whites; the remaining population included 8,985 Indians, 73 clerics, and 1,063 slaves.[15] The castas typically included not only free blacks but a preponderant percentage of mixed bloods because miscegenation had reached an advanced stage, similar to the Caribbean coastal region. A word of caution is again in order regarding the temptation to explain social status by purely racial criteria. As the German scientist Alexander von Humboldt remarked concerning his visit to the area just north of Guayaquil, "We were surprised in La Esmeralda to see many zambos and mulattoes and other people of color who, for vanity, called themselves Spanish and believed themselves white

12. Interesting contemporary descriptions can be found in Dionisio Alsedo y Herrera, *Compendio histórico de la provincia . . . de Guayaquil . . .* , and Alfredo Flores y Caamaño, ed., *Relación inédita de la ciudad y la provincia de Guayaquil*. For a carefully researched account of life in late colonial Guayaquil, see Michael T. Hamerly, "A Social and Economic History of the City and District of Guayaquil during the Late Colonial and Independence Periods" (Ph.D. diss.).

13. Dora León Borja and Ádám Szászdi Nagy, "El comercio del cacao de Guayaquil"; Eduardo Arcila Farías, *Comercio entre Venezuela y México en los siglos XVII y XVIII*, chap. 9.

14. "Padrón general, 1778," AGI: Estado, legajo 54; Governor Juan de Urbina to the Príncipe de la Paz [Manuel Godoy], Guayaquil, March 14, 1802, AGI: Quito, legajo 262.

15. "Padrón general, 1778." Because Spanish and creole vassals possessed the same legal status, census figures do not distinguish between them and it is therefore impossible to determine their exact percentages of the white population. Nevertheless, the documents for Guayaquil produced relatively few references to Europeans and permits the subjective conclusion that they played a lesser role in Guayaquil than in Cartagena.

because they were not as red as Indians."[16] The population of the city of Guayaquil itself numbered just under 5,000 freemen at the beginning of the reform. Including its dependent settlements of Samborondón, Baba, Daule, Puná, and Yaguache, the total population was 14,311, of which 1,624 were Indians, 1,995 white, and 10,692 libres.[17]

As Guayaquil grew in importance, the need to improve its defenses became critical. A royal order of December 8, 1762, transformed the province from a corregimiento into a governorship, and shortly thereafter the crown took steps to begin the fortification of the port and city.[18] Within this context, the creation of a fixed garrison in 1767, although definitely connected to the crisis of authority in the presidency, also related to Guayaquil's development as a seaport. The fixed company of 50 men, however, proved too small both to defend Guayaquil and to protect the royal monopolies; upon recommendation of Viceroy Flores, the crown therefore expanded it to 100 men in 1779.[19] Thus, when Viceroy Manuel Guirior extended the military reform to Guayaquil, he acted not only against a backdrop of increasing dependence upon the military as a guardian of domestic security but within the framework of the emergence of Guayaquil as a major center of Pacific commerce with important claims for external defense.

Guirior solicited royal approval for the establishment of a disciplined militia in Guayaquil on May 15, 1774, and the crown granted its authorization on August 26.[20] Nothing which approached careful planning preceded this action, nor did the decision specifically provide for supplying, equipping, or training the new units. Indeed, the striking characteristic of this phase of the reform was the casual attitude exhibited by both viceregal and royal authorities. Guirior had ordered Governor Francisco de Ugarte (1772–79) to formulate recruitment rolls but was unable to advance an overall troop plan.[21] In its order, Spain instructed the viceroy to adopt the system employed in Cartagena but said nothing about the means of reaching that goal, apparently hoping that Guirior would independently procure the necessary resources. As a consequence, Guirior acted largely on his own during the important formative period of the militia of Guayaquil.

16. In Rosenblat, La población indígena, 2: 137.
17. "Padrón del número de almas con distinción de sexos, estados, clases, y castas que havitan en los pueblos más immediatos a la plaza de Guayaquil," Guayaquil, January 1, 1782, AGI: Quito, legajo 574; Castillo, Los gobernadores, pp. 72–77.
18. Royal orders, December 8, 1762, and December 16, 1765, AGI: Quito, legajos 237 and 573.
19. Flores to Gálvez, Santa Fe, November 15, 1778, and royal order, March 14, 1779, both in AGI: Quito, legajos 237 and 573.
20. Royal order, August 26, 1774, ANC: MM, vol. 97, fols. 807–8; Guirior to Arriaga, Santa Fe, December 15, 1775, ANC: MM, vol. 10, fols. 812–20.
21. Expediente on the complaints of Ugarte, the governor of Guayaquil, 1774–75, ANC: MM, vol. 108, fols. 727–46.

In conducting the reform in Guayaquil, Viceroy Guirior altered militia policy in three fundamental ways. He greatly reduced the size of the veteran cadres; he modified the system of inspection; and he openly sold volunteer officerships in order to equip the new units. All of these measures were practical compromises between the Cuban reglamento and local conditions, but they also worked to dilute the quality of militia organization and ultimately jeopardized the reputation of the disciplined militia as a worthwhile component of the defense system. The crown never officially sanctioned Guirior's innovations, but, as a practical matter, those areas of New Granada which were caught up in the reform during the 1780s adopted practices much closer to those of Guayaquil than to those of Cartagena and Panama.

The most radical innovation was a reduction in the size of the veteran cadres. With the viceroyalty left to its own resources, the major difficulty in honoring the letter of the law stemmed from an inability to provide the specified number of veteran advisors. A complete veteran cadre for a militia infantry battalion, for example, would contain eighteen corporals, nine first sergeants, and nine lieutenants, personnel which in the cases of Cartagena and Panana were recruited from veteran sergeants, corporals, and enlisted men. In addition, each battalion's command and staff group required two men of the veteran officer category, or at least first sergeants, to act as sargento mayor and ayudante. The provision of such cadres meant a manpower loss in the regular army of almost a half company for each new militia battalion. If the various provinces of New Granada were each to establish several battalions of disciplined militia in rapid succession, the veteran units would soon be totally depleted, not to mention the Guayaquil garrison, which at this time numbered only fifty men.

The corollary to this personnel problem, to the extent that the regular army replaced the veteran personnel assigned to militia units, was rising costs. On a unit basis, the expense of supporting the salaried personnel of one complete white militia battalion was 11,952 pesos a year.[22] The payroll of Cartagena's disciplined militia, for example, presented an annual expense of roughly 51,000 pesos.[23] Moreover, units were supposed to be equipped. While the obligation for providing uniforms rested with the local communities, the royal treasury assumed official responsibility for defraying the cost of arms and salaries. However, New Granada, which was always a poor source of royal revenue, found the treasury especially depleted at this time because of the huge expenditures being lavished upon the new dike under construction in Cartagena's bay (see chapter 1). This construction burden had a particularly harsh impact in the Presidency of Quito, where a large share of the revenue

22. *Reglamento . . . de Cuba*, relacion 8.
23. Report on the militia of Cartagena by Pimienta, March 26, 1778, ANC: MM, vol. 40, fols. 152–65.

collections was especially earmarked for that project. The outflow of currency from Quito surpassed 700,000 pesos during the eleven-year administration of President José Diguja (1767–78) and topped the million mark for the four-year rule of the vigorous tax collector, José García de León y Pizarro (1778–84).[24] Thus, not only were general revenues largely exhausted, but the very areas to undertake militia reform next were among those most seriously disadvantaged.

Provided with no practical alternatives, Guirior limited the veteran cadre for the Guayaquil militia to only a first sergeant, who would act as ayudante, and two corporals, all three of whom were selected from the veteran garrison of Panama.[25] Guirior hoped to employ the regulars for an intensive instruction of volunteer officers, who would themselves become capable of providing suitable training to their troops; the veterans could then continue to serve in a general advisory capacity as personal assistants to the militia commander.[26] In subsequent years, this hope proved illusionary, because the militia of Guayaquil and others modeled after it did not reach the standards of disciplined militia. Yet, in one respect Guirior's action pointed toward the future, because the size of the veteran cadres envisioned in the plans of O'Reilly was in fact excessive. By the end of the decade top officers such as Anastasio Zejudo recommended the elimination of the veteran lieutenants, and this became standard practice during the 1780s.[27]

In his attempt to economize, Guirior also was willing to combine regular army offices with militia positions. On March 17, 1775, he commissioned Captain Víctor Salcedo y Somodevilla of Guayaquil's fixed company to function as special commander in raising Guayaquil's disciplined militia.[28] Salcedo's dual function, at one time acting as both captain of the regular company and commander of militia, represented a departure from practice both in Cartagena and Panama, where the special commanders sent from Spain were employed solely in militia duty. Yet, in the absence of a general reform commission in New Granada or specific assistance from Spain, this was a realistic move, although one destined to cause considerable difficulty.

Commander Salcedo y Somodevilla functioned in much the same way as his counterparts in Cartagena and Panama, but he soon found himself embroiled in a violent struggle with the local governor, Francisco de Ugarte, which had important consequences for the military reform in Guayaquil.

24. González Suárez, *Historia general*, 5:295.

25. Guirior to Arriaga, Santa Fe, December 15, 1775. All things equal, it would have been more feasible to have selected these men from the Fixed Infantry Regiment of Cartagena since it was larger; however, at this time the fixed unit's services were actively engaged in an Indian war in Riohacha (see chapter 6).

26. Militia Commander Víctor Salcedo y Somodevilla to Guirior, Guayaquil, June 2, 1775, ANC: MM, vol. 51, fols. 55–56; Guirior to Arriaga, Santa Fe, December 15, 1775.

27. Zejudo to Caballero y Góngora, Santa Fe, May 4, 1783, AGS: GM, legajo 7089.

28. Guirior to Salcedo y Somodevilla, March 17, 1775, ANC: MM, vol. 100, fols. 187–93.

Governor Ugarte, one of the few remaining heroes of the 1741 defense of Cartagena, was a gruff, belligerent old navy officer, who had transferred to the regular army with the rank of colonel. Wielding an autocratic disposition and an extraordinarily violent temper, he was in constant conflict with other authorities during his tenure as governor, although in fairness to Ugarte not all the difficulty was his own doing. Following the transfer of Governor Juan Antonio Zelaya to Popayán and prior to Ugarte's arrival in January 1772, Guayaquil had suffered extensive strife because of the rival pretensions of Captain Francisco Gómez Miró of the Fixed Infantry Company of Guayaquil and Deputy Governor (*Teniente de Gobernador*) Juan Miguel Pérez de Villamar to the vacant governorship. Their struggle of nearly a year alienated Guayaquil's military establishment from the civilian aristocracy, and it seriously disrupted city life until Viceroy Messía de la Cerda ruled in favor of the deputy governor, pending the arrival of Ugarte. This difficult political situation demanded astute leadership, but Ugarte was unsuited temperamentally to meet the challenge. His abrasive, despotic manner and the offensively corrupt conduct of his administration quickly alienated much of the respectable citizenry, while his personal dislike of Captain Miró and his henchman, Lieutenant Ruiz Romero, prevented Ugarte's establishment of ties with the local military.[29]

When Captain Gómez Miró died in 1774, Governor Ugarte attempted to placate the community and undercut his remaining military opposition by blocking the promotion of Lieutenant Romero, who was next in line for the captainship, but whose abusive behavior during the earlier strife had earned him the intense enmity of Guayaquil's creole aristocracy. Ugarte appealed to Guirior for the appointment of an outsider, and the viceroy complied by selecting Salcedo from the staff of Cartagena.[30] The appointment, however, developed into more than Ugarte had anticipated, because Salcedo, in addition to the captainship, also obtained appointment to command the reorganization of the militia. The governor had assumed that he, as a colonel and a war hero, would personally be selected. As a consequence, the internal turmoil of the Guayaquil colony entered a new phase, one directly involving the militia.

The appointment of Salcedo as commander of militia was by all indications an afterthought on the part of Guirior, who had originally intended to vest the governor with direct responsibility. The viceroy had, however, become dissatisfied with Ugarte's slow rate of progress on preliminary work, which he attributed to the governor's other extensive duties, and as a consequence he elected to delegate the burden to the captain.[31] Guirior was also probably aware that Ugarte was old and in poor health. Salcedo, for his part, was an

29. Castillo, *Los gobernadores*, pp. 115–43.
30. Ibid., pp. 144–45, 153–55.
31. Ugarte to Guirior, Guayaquil, July 19, 1775, ANC: MM, vol. 110, fols. 353–62.

ambitious but brash young officer, who seemed to benefit politically from a brother who held the title of count and who resided in the royal court; regarding the task at hand, he had the important qualification of having witnessed the implementation of the reform in Cartagena.[32] Salcedo had begun his military career as a cadet in the Regiment of Savoy, had advanced to second lieutenant three years later, and had been promoted to lieutenant upon his incorporation into the Fixed Regiment of Cartagena in May 1773. He was only twenty-two years of age when in late 1774 Guirior appointed him captain of the Fixed Company of Guayaquil.[33]

Governor Ugarte was outraged to discover that he had been denied first-hand participation in the conduct of the reform, although actually he could still act in the higher capacity of inspector. Salcedo aggravated this hostility by working independently of the unpleasant governor whenever possible, a snub which led the latter to conclude, probably correctly, that his military authority was being undermined.[34] Moreover, Salcedo exacerbated matters by siding with Ugarte's enemies in the province's numerous local disputes. A vendetta ensued, which included public insults, charges and countercharges of misconduct, threatened resignations by both parties, and even the momentary imprisonment of Salcedo by the governor.[35] Despite this harassment, however, by mid-1775 the special commander reported the formation of two infantry battalions, one pardo, the other white; one regiment of dragoons; and three artillery companies.[36]

In one important sense, Governor Ugarte's tactics proved valuable to Captain Salcedo. As the personal enemy of the unpopular governor, the militia commander could appeal to the frightened, alienated aristocracy by offering them the militia as a rival source of power. Indeed, the striking, and largely unique, characteristic of the Guayaquil reform was the intimate connection between the established colonial elite and the militia. Nearly all the captains of the white battalion and the regiment of dragoons and many second lieutenants were either sons of men who had been on the cabildo or had themselves served at one time or another. Many were or became alcaldes ordinarios; others served as *regidores* (councilors) or in lesser positions. Still other officers held deputy governorships or pertained to the revenue administration. Significantly, of the

32. Guirior to Arriaga, Santa Fe, December 15, 1775; President Luis Muñoz de Guzmán to the Secretary of State and War, the Conde del Campo de Alange, Quito, January 18, 1792, AGI: Quito, legajo 249.

33. Service record, Salcedo y Somodevilla, July 19, 1776, ANC: MM, vol. 107, fol. 189.

34. Ugarte to Guirior, Guayaquil, April 19, June 2, and July 19, 1775, ANC: MM, vol. 105, fols. 302–12, vol. 58, fols. 205–9, and vol. 110, fols. 353–62, respectively.

35. Ibid.; Salcedo y Somodevilla to Guirior, Guayaquil, November 19, 1774, April 19, October 5, and December 2, 1775, ANC: MM, vol. 106, fols. 699–701, vol. 101, fols. 233–35, and vol. 107, fols. 135–36, and fols. 742–43, respectively; Castillo, *Los gobernadores*, pp 153–55.

36. Salcedo y Somodevilla to Guirior, Guayaquil, June 2, 1775; Guirior to Arriaga, Santa Fe, December 15, 1775, AGI, Quito, legajo 574.

nine men who acquired the original captainships in the white infantry battalion (Damián Arteta, Miguel Antonio Anzuátegui, Ignacio Novoa, Ignacio Arteta, Vicente Sereno del Castillo, José Millán, Miguel Alejandro Montero de Puga, Jacinto Sumalbe, and Francisco Maruri), six either had been, were, or would become alcaldes ordinarios of Guayaquil; one was a regidor *perpetuo*, one a deputy governor, and the other simply a creole "noble." In the regiment of dragoons, which is more difficult to appraise because much of it was based in outlying settlements, there were at least three captains who became alcaldes ordinarios and one who was the son of an alcalde; there was one who served as *alférez real* and another who was *procurador general*.[37] Although some of these men were Spaniards, most seem to have been natives of Guayaquil.[38]

In addition to its political value, militia officership provided an attractive vehicle for the status-conscious creole seeking titles and honors and, unlike service in the more strategic centers such as Cartagena, it had the great advantage of involving very little personal risk. Nor, for that matter, did the military as an arm of the government pose a serious threat to the independent, creole style of life. The regular army in Guayaquil was small and, unlike Cartagena and Panama where the larger garrisons exercised great autonomy, it easily could be absorbed into the existing power structure. Moreover, the position of Captain Salcedo, as commander of both the regular garrison and the disciplined militia, facilitated a marriage between the creole community and the military establishment. As long as the creole aristocracy embraced the military by seeking militia officerships, they smothered its independent identity and had little to fear from it. Finally, the extreme isolation of Guayaquil greatly reduced the possibility that the administration in Bogotá might actually employ the military to enforce distasteful policies. Guayaquil was, in any event, one of those regions benefiting most from the reforms of Charles III, and hence

37. Reflective of the haphazard character of early militia organization in Guayaquil, there is a paucity of records providing solid data for social analysis. The first set of service records, for example, does not appear until 1788 for the regiment of dragoons and 1797 for the infantry. Much can be learned from officer proposals, however, which in some instances contain valuable candidate descriptions, although in other cases, only the names of candidates were advanced. Yet a comparison of the officer corps with the cabildo rosters—many of which can be found in Castillo, *Los gobernadores*—is often helpful. Moreover, there was a degree of continuity between the original officer corps and those of the late 1780s and the 1790s when service records were kept. Officer proposals Guayaquil militia, 1775–79, AGI: Quito, legajo 574, and in ANC: MM, vol. 101, fols. 571–72, vol. 105, fols. 313–26, and vol. 106, fols. 790–96; service records, Squadron of Militia Dragoons, Guayaquil, 1788, ANC: MM, vol. 47, fols. 10–34, and Regiment of Militia Infantry, Guayaquil, 1797, AGS: GM, legajo 7281.

38. Salcedo y Somodevilla to Guirior, Guayaquil, October 1, 1775, ANC: MM, vol. 107, fols. 742–43. Miguel Agustín de Olmedo was one noteworthy Spanish militiaman. Although not an original officer, he soon became a captain in the white infantry battalion. Born in Málaga, Olmedo reached Guayaquil as part of the force sent to quell the 1765 disorders. He is best known as the father of the famous poet José Joaquín Olmedo. Castillo, *Los gobernadores*, pp. 94, 200; officer proposals, Guayaquil, 1776, AGI: Quito, legajo 574.

less mistrust of royal intentions existed there than in the less favored portions of the viceroyalty.

Guirior's third significant change in militia policy involved the outfitting of the units. The price of officerships, at least for the rank of captain and above, was the cost of uniforming a company and, frequently, the surreptitious purchase of the good will of Captain Salcedo. Despite the prohibition of such practices in the Cuban reglamento, Guirior with knowledge of the crown encouraged the exchange of officerships for contributions to the expense of providing uniforms as the most effective method of clothing the new units.[39] The outflow of revenues to Cartagena had weakened the ability of the municipality to bear the cost, and the danger of imposing any new taxation had already been made far too evident in the Presidency of Quito. Moreover, the new-found prosperity of the Guayaquil business community provided a throng of vassals, many of whom had served in the previous militia, who were eager to acquire the status of officership.

If one may believe Governor Ugarte, who admittedly is a poor source, but whose testimony was corroborated by his successor, Ramón García de León y Pizarro, Special Commander Salcedo managed to extract fair sums for himself from these transactions and, in return, did not carefully enforce company enlistment levels and, hence, uniform costs.[40] Indeed, the pressure for officership was sufficient to induce Salcedo later to create an additional six separate companies, five of them white, although there obviously were not enough white vassals to fill them, or, for that matter, most of the other units he had created.[41] The census taken in 1782 for the city of Guayaquil and its immediate dependencies, where Salcedo organized the militia, showed 1,995 whites, counting men, women and children. With a full complement, Salcedo's white militia, including a regiment of dragoons at 600 men, a battalion of infantry at 800, five separate infantry companies at 50 each, and an artillery company of 50, should have totaled 1,700 men, in addition to over 100 officers and staff! Indeed, the 1778 census counted only 3,722 whites in the entire province, including the remote backlands.

One conspicuous and informative example of the close connection that developed among the business community, the local government, and the militia in Guayaquil is the Arteta family, which was among Guayaquil's most distinguished families through both ancestry and wealth. The Artetas provided three officers, all of whom also served terms as alcaldes ordinarios during

39. Salcedo y Somodevilla to Guirior, Guayaquil, June 2, 1775; Guirior to Arriaga, Santa Fe, December 15, 1775; Reglamento . . . de Cuba, chap. 2, art. 1.
40. Ugarte to Guirior, Guayaquil, June 2, 1775; informe, Ugarte, Babahoyo, October 1, 1776, AGI: Quito, legajo 237; informe, R. García Pizarro, Guayaquil, January 1, 1782, AGI: Quito, legajo 574.
41. Officer proposals, separate infantry companies, Guayaquil, September 19, 1776, AGI: Quito, legajo 574.

the first years of the militia. Ignacio served first as a captain in the white infantry battalion, then as lieutenant colonel of dragoons before his death in 1777; Damián became captain of grenadiers in the infantry battalion; and Pedro, who held a doctorate in theology from the Universidad Pontífica of Quito, served as an infantry captain and on a number of occasions stubbornly confronted Governor Ugarte. Pedro was related to dragoon colonel José Antonio Cossío Argüelles, who also served at least twice as alcalde. Further, Ana Arteta, presumably a sister, was the wife of Ignacio Novoa, an infantry captain who later rose to lieutenant colonel and served as alcalde ordinario.

In association with at least two other officers, Miguel Antonio Anzuátegui and Jacinto Bejarano, the Arteta family engaged in shipbuilding enterprises and a cacao export business, which was of sufficient magnitude to justify various petitions to Spain for commercial favors. Anzuátegui, a captain of infantry, became alcalde ordinario in 1783. Bejarano, who served as alcalde in 1782, began his militia career as a mere lieutenant, but his stock rose suddenly following a contribution of 4,000 pesos to the aguardiente monopoly. In 1779 he became colonel of infantry, a position which he held until the end of the colonial period.[42] Thus, through the Arteta family the leadership of the business community, the municipal government, and the militia merged into a closely connected directorate.

Governor Ugarte attempted to obstruct Salcedo's emerging alliance with Guayaquil aristocracy by rejecting the commander's officer proposals, which he reviewed as inspector, but in the long run this tactic proved of little value. In Santa Fe, Viceroy Guirior overrode the governor's vetoes as a matter of course, explaining to the crown that Ugarte's objections stemmed from a personal vindictiveness intended to impede the progress of the reform.[43] Many of Ugarte's objections were valid, nevertheless, particularly the allegation that Salcedo was creating a militia with as many officers as troops.

Ugarte's chances of frustrating the designs of Salcedo suffered a fatal blow in 1774—actually before Salcedo's appointment—when a party or parties still unidentified submitted a fraudulent resignation for the governor. Guirior, who was disenchanted with Ugarte, hurried the renunciation to the crown, which accepted it and instructed the viceroy to select a temporary replacement. Ugarte knew nothing of the plot against him until he received the royal acceptance of his alleged resignation in October 1775. By this time Guirior had already appointed Lieutenant Colonel Domingo Guerrero y Marnara, who had just finished serving as interim governor of Portobelo, to act as provisional governor of Guayaquil. Seriously ill and friendless, Ugarte furiously pro-

42. Castillo, *Los gobernadores*, pp. 152, 155, 160, 188, 212, 239, 341; León Borja and Nagy, "El comercio," pp. 38–39; officer proposals, Guayaquil militia, 1775–79.

43. Expediente on the complaints of Ugarte, 1774–75; Ugarte to Guirior, Guayaquil, July 19, 1775, and reply, Santa Fe, December 17, 1775, ANC: MM, vol. 105, fols. 313–26; Guirior to Arriaga, Santa Fe, December 15, 1775.

tested the error to Guirior, and eventually to the crown, but the viceroy ordered the cabildo of Guayaquil to recognize Guerrero y Marnara as governor pending royal action. The cabildo, led by Alcalde Ordinario Pedro Arteta, who was also captain of militia, did just that, and Guerrero y Marnara assumed power upon his arrival in April 1776.[44]

Although the error was eventually rectified by the full reinstatement of Ugarte in early 1777, it was too late to halt Salcedo's appointments.[45] The various officer candidates had taken the precaution to woo Guerrero y Marnara by sponsoring a special celebration to honor his accession to the governorship, and Commander Salcedo opportunistically had exploited the period of good will that followed by rushing through most of his recommendations.[46] After his reinstatement, Governor Ugarte served until 1779 when he was finally relieved. Not surprisingly, the *residencia* (judicial review) of his term in office resulted in his conviction on numerous counts of misconduct in office. Not one resident spoke on his behalf.[47]

One consequence of the intimate social and political connection between the military and civilian leadership of Guayaquil was a relative absence of disruptive fuero cases. With both jurisdictions dominated by the same elite, there was little chance that the military fuero could become a dynamic vehicle for social mobility or, for that matter, that it might undercut existing local political institutions. If anything, the militia of Guayaquil reinforced the status quo. This experience sharply contrasted with that of Cartagena and Panama where the military corporate identity worked to blur class lines. An important difference was the leadership in those provinces of Spanish officers, who sympathized little with creole inhibitions and anxieties. Captain Salcedo's close collaboration with Guayaquil society precluded a similar occurrence. In any case, on at least one occasion Salcedo stated that he found creole-Spanish social differences insignificant for military purposes, a remark which also helps to explain his popularity in Guayaquil.[48]

One annoyance to Salcedo and the other militia officers was that Ugarte, as chief military officer in the province, acted as court of first instance in military cases. He exercised this power through his legal counsellor, *Auditor de Guerra* José Gabriel Icaza, a Panamanian lawyer who had found riches in Guayaquil by attaching himself to Ugarte. Icaza, who also acted as deputy governor, was

44. Practically anyone with influence could have perpetrated this fraud except Salcedo y Somodevilla, who arrived too late to have been the culprit. Castillo, in his study of Guayaquil, suspected that it was Lieutenant Ruiz Romero because of both his public animosity toward Ugarte and his association with anonymous satires and pamphlets. See *Los gobernadores*, pp. 156–70, 297; expediente on the resignation of Ugarte, 1775–77, AGI: Quito, legajo 237.

45. Castillo, *Los gobernadores*, pp. 171–72.

46. Ibid., p. 164; officer proposals, Guayaquil militia, September 19, October 16, and October 19, 1776, AGI: Quito, legajo 574.

47. Castillo, *Los gobernadores*, pp. 189–92.

48. Salcedo y Somodevilla to Guirior, Guayaquil, June 2, 1775.

Ugarte's principal henchman in the extraction of bribes and other favors, emerging as a petty tyrant in his own right. His judicial power was a sufficient nuisance to prompt the leadership of both the white and pardo militia to act with Salcedo in an attempt to unseat him. Although his friendship with Ugarte was destroyed by a violent altercation just before the governor's forced absence from office, the militia sought satisfaction anyway. The militia based its suit on the complaint that Icaza was not a military officer and therefore was not entitled to hear military causes. Flores rejected the petition, but José de Gálvez, new minister of the Indies, reversed this decision, stripping Icaza of his military powers. Meanwhile, the restored Ugarte launched his own vendetta against Icaza, who quickly departed the colony.[49]

The pardo militia, for its part, closely conformed to the general system fashioned by Salcedo y Somodevilla. As with the white units, pardo captainships were sold to those who would uniform their companies, with enough buyers appearing to justify the creation of one infantry battalion, two artillery companies, and one separate infantry company. Pardo possession of the financial means to meet this requirement strongly indicates that the prosperity of Guayaquil reached a considerable segment of the castas. Unfortunately, personal data for these officers are rare. It is worth noting, however, that at least one of the pardo captains, Joaquín Murillo, became an *hacendado*, thus imitating through his investment in land and his quest of public honors the behavioral pattern of the creole aristocracy.[50] Yet, despite their wealth, these men obviously were still too closely associated with the pardo reputation to advance into the higher social stratum.

One individual of "obscure birth," Juan Miguel de Vera, nearly did advance from his estate when he succeeded in purchasing from Salcedo the captainship of the tenth company of white dragoons. Governor Ugarte, however, seizing an opportunity to strike at Salcedo, foiled this appointment by exposing the candidate's lack of social quality and by questioning his ability to discharge his financial commitment because of large business debts. The cabildo had earlier derailed Vera's appointment as deputy alguacil mayor by the subdelegate of the Inquisition, and this lack of community acceptance further weakened his candidacy. Consequently, the viceroy sustained the objections of Ugarte, who thus scored one of his few victories over the militia commander.

Yet, in a sense, the Vera case is an exception that proves the rule. Had a spirit of harmony prevailed among the existing military authorities, in all likelihood nothing would have been said about Vera's undistinguished ancestry and he would have become a white officer. Furthermore, Juan Miguel

49. Expediente on the qualifications of Auditor de Guerra José Gabriel Icaza, 1776–77, ANC: MM, vol. 104, fols. 286–321, and vol. 106, fols. 225–27, 262–63; Castillo, *Los gobernadores*, pp. 142–43, 166–67, 178–80.

50. Officer proposals, Guayaquil, June 23, 1775, ANC: MM, vol. 108, fols. 645–52, 727–46; expediente on the qualifications of Auditor de Guerra José Gabriel Icaza, 1776–77.

Ponce, who similarly lacked social quality, did, according to the governor, become a captain of dragoons because there was no doubt about his capacity to fulfill his pledge to uniform his company. Ponce, unlike Vera, apparently enjoyed acceptance by the creole community, as no opposition arose to his candidacy. When all other conditions were favorable, it was therefore occasionally possible for mulattoes to assume the status of whites in the militia. Significantly, Ponce's social quality in the first set of service records compiled for Guayaquil's dragoons (1788) was buena or "good"; at that time this was also the description of two-thirds of the creole officers, most of whom must have been what in Cartagena were called "blancos de la tierra."[51]

Salcedo bestowed the commandership of the pardo battalion on Bernardo Roca, a wealthy mulatto merchant, and insured his preeminence by failing to create the white command and staff group demanded by militia regulations. Roca, a man always near the political pulse of the colony, was a close associate of Salcedo, obtaining, for example, nearly 100 per cent cooperation out of his unit in the attempt to unseat Icaza. He also acted as bondsman for Governor Guerrero, and in the following decade he closely attached his fortunes to Governor García Pizarro.[52] He was, in short, a man who could be trusted to handle the pardos, which helps to explain why Salcedo did not complicate matters by creating a separate white command structure. All in all, Salcedo involved the pardo in the militia far beneath his demographic potential, but, as demonstrated, the special commander was less interested in manpower than in financial influence.

The crown was cool toward the Guayaquil experiment from the beginning and never really accepted it. When presented with Guirior's claims of success in 1776, O'Reilly was incredulous, asserting that positive results were impossible given the size of the veteran cadre, and he insisted that in all cases a small but well-prepared militia was preferable to a large but poorly trained one. He did, however, recommend that the crown temporarily continue with Salcedo's creation pending the compilation of a census to determine a realistic size for the militia and then, presumably, the provision of proper support for it. In a later memo, the inspector general further suggested that Ugarte's replacement as governor be an officer with first-hand militia experience and that he be specifically instructed to consolidate the Guayaquil establishment. The crown found such a man in Ramón García de León y Pizarro, who had acted as sargento mayor of Mompós in the Cartagena reform. Given the continuing turbulence and political paralysis of Guayaquil, however, the authorities there

51. Officer proposals, Guayaquil, July 19, 1775, ANC: MM, vol. 105, fols. 313–26; service records, Squadron of Militia Dragoons, Guayaquil, 1788. By 1788, the Regiment of Militia Dragoons had been reduced to a squadron.

52. Castillo, *Los gobernadores*, pp. 178, 249, 294; anonymous letter to Spain, Guayaquil, December 4, 1787, AGI: Quito, legajo 271.

did not manage a militia census until 1782, by which time the empire was at war and it was too late to attempt immediate structural change.[53] Thus, although the militia of Guayaquil was destined for reorganization under Governor García Pizarro, Salcedo y Somodevilla's questionable work persisted into the 1780s.

Pleased with his accomplishment in Guayaquil, Viceroy Guirior recommended to his successor, Manuel de Flores, that the incoming viceroy continue the system he had devised.[54] Flores did so, extending the reform to Popayán in a manner similar to that employed in Guayaquil. However, Popayán, the first interior province of New Granada to raise a disciplined militia, reacted much differently to reform than did Guayaquil. Its powerful, entrenched creole aristocracy, which found itself threatened by the broader reforms of Charles III, soon came to view the military reorganization as a menace to its local preeminence. As a result, Popayán provides yet another dimension in the diverse history of the military reform in New Granada.

Popayán, a quiet isolated region of New Granada, did not generally share in the new prosperity of the Bourbon commercial revival. In the era of the *galeones*, merchants from Peru and Quito had passed through Popayán to deal in Cartagena, and Popayán had been sufficiently important as a commercial outpost to justify the maintenance of deputies there by the consulado of Lima. Following the liberalization of trade policy under the Bourbons, readjustments in the main commercial routes passed Popayán by, so that at the time of the military reform few merchants still remained in the region.[55] Hence, the circumstances of the creole merchants seeking officerships in Guayaquil, and to a lesser degree in Cartagena, would not be repeated in Popayán.

The absence of a strong commercial orientation in Popayán should not be construed to indicate a lack of productivity, however. Although overshadowed by the Chocó-Antioquia complex of the north, Popayán had traditionally been one of the leading gold producing areas of New Granada and the empire. During the late eighteenth century, the principal centers of mining activity were located near Cartago, bordering on the Chocó; Popayán, the provincial capital; and Barbacoas near the Pacific Ocean in the far southwest.[56] Much of the land in typical fashion had been given over to the raising of livestock, although not always for commercial purposes, as much beef had to be imported from the Province of Neiva to the east. In addition, Buga was known for its fine

53. O'Reilly thought that a militia with four infantry companies of pardos and four of whites at 100 men each, one moreno artillery company and one white, also at 100 men, and two cavalry companies of fifty men would be sufficient. Expediente on the formation of the disciplined militia of Guayaquil, 1774–83, AGI: Quito, legajo 574.

54. Manuel Guirior, in *Relaciones de mando*, pp. 186–87.

55. Flores to Spain, Cartagena, January 9, 1782, AGI: Quito, legajo 574; Juan and Ulloa, *A Voyage to South America*, pp. 152–53.

56. Robert C. West, *Colonial Placer Mining in Colombia*, pp. 4–18.

tobacco, Pasto for its flour, and Cali, as well as much of the rest of the province, for its sugarcane.[57]

Throughout much of Popayán, influential magnates held sway over the land and dominated the economy, with extensive portions of the population reduced to a marginal existence. Excluding Barbacoas, which failed to take a census, in 1779 there were 20,556 white, 27,764 Indian, and 32,765 "libre" subjects in the province, plus over 500 clerics.[58] Compared to the Caribbean provinces, the number of Indians was high and the number of libres relatively low. Yet, because much of the original sedentary and easily accessible Indian population had perished during the conquest and early exploitation, the colonists had imported Negro slaves to work the mines.[59] As a result, Popayán had a substantial slave population, the largest in New Granada, numbering nearly 19,000 exclusive of Barbacoas, which because of its extensive mines would doubtless have added considerably to that total.[60] A strict exploitation of slave labor probably contributed to the relatively small libre population. Moreover, the presence of a large slave population—over twice that of Cartagena, for example—had the effect of depressing wages. Combined with a growing monopolization of the land by the creole elite, the low wages contributed to the growth of a large, underemployed vagrant element, which caused political instability and became a serious concern to the viceregal authorities.[61]

Like the creation of the fixed company in 1771, the establishment of a disciplined militia in Popayán was, in part, one of the long-run consequences of the civil disorders of 1765. The aguardiente monopoly, which had been sold to enterprisers in the several districts, had, on the one hand, brought a reduction both in the price of cane and in the access to legitimate outlets and, on the other hand, had increased the cost of the liquor for the consumer. Particularly in the sugar producing zones of the Cauca Valley, this institution had exacerbated economic and social problems. Consequently, the rebellion in Quito against the aguardiente monopoly had struck a responsive chord in the inhabitants of Popayán. Ugly protests and occasional disorders occurred in Cartago, Cali, and Popayán, which forced an angry Viceroy Messía de la Cerda to curtail the monopoly for the immediate future.[62]

In the ensuing years, the authorities, including Captain Diego Antonio Nieto of the Fixed Company of Popayán and Viceroy Flores, continued to view the large vagrant population of Popayán as potentially dangerous. While on a temporary visit to Santa Fe, Captain Nieto proposed the organization of a

57. Ibid., pp. 112–19; Silvestre, *Descripción*, p. 21; Gustavo Arboleda, *Historia de Cali desde los orígenes de la ciudad hasta la expiración del período colonial*, 2: 325–26.
58. "Padrón general, 1778."
59. West, *Colonial Placer Mining*, pp. 78–90.
60. "Padrón general, 1778."
61. T. Lynn Smith, *Colombia: Social Structure and the Process of Development*, pp. 278–81; Arboleda, *Historia de Cali*, 2: 326.
62. Arboleda, *Historia de Cali*, 2:326–32.

disciplined militia, which he optimistically believed would serve the dual purpose of reorienting that idle population to a productive way of life and, simultaneously, of strengthening royal authority. Nieto argued that "ignorance and aversion to labor commonly dominate these people . . . vicious vagrants who contribute nothing to this place but disorder. But being trained as militiamen with their behavior guided by officers, they will in the future become most useful members of the community. And besides clearing the towns of the idle for a period that would not damage the population, a flowering will result in agriculture; crafts will advance; and good effects will ensue for commerce, society, and well-ordered discipline. . . ."[63]

Although less inclined than Nieto to predict an instant transformation of Popayán through the militia system, Viceroy Flores hoped to use it to strengthen the hand of royal authority in the province. He viewed a militia as a possible leverage to enlarge revenue collection, which he found unacceptably low, and, in particular, to underpin another attempt to strengthen the aguardiente monopoly (see chapter 4). Also, in the northern zone of the province, including the municipalities of Cartago, Cali, and Buga, he wanted a reserve military force to guard against the danger of a slave uprising in the gold fields of the neighboring Chocó Province or of an invasion by the unpacified Cuna Indians of that region. Once again, the military appeared—in the thinking of the royal administration—as an instrument to achieve unpopular political objectives.[64]

Another reason for an expansion of the militia system to Popayán was expediency. During the military reform in New Granada, a disciplined militia was formed only in those areas which already had a fixed contingent of regulars or had one nearby. Such an arrangement enabled the militia to draw upon the regular garrison for the formation and reinforcement of its veteran cadre. In Popayán, Nieto and Flores hoped to go one step further, reducing the fixed company to merely twenty-five men and using the resulting savings to support the militia. The existing fifty-man company was too small to support effectively royal authority throughout the province, but it was really larger than necessary to guard the mint and coffers of the provincial capital. A disciplined militia sustained in the several municipalities would permit greater geographic flexibility and provide a much larger force.[65]

Viceroy Flores issued the initiating order for the Popayán militia on February 17, 1777, and obtained royal approval on July 18.[66] By this time Alejandro O'Reilly, the father of Cuba's and New Granada's militia systems, had fallen

63. Expediente on the formation of the disciplined militia of Popayán, 1775–83 (hereafter cited as expediente, militia of Popayán), AGI: Quito, legajo 574.
64. Ibid.
65. Ibid.
66. Flores to the royal officials of Popayán, Santa Fe, April 26, 1777, and royal order, July 18, 1777, ACC: Colonia, MI–5P, sig. 7086; Nieto to the cabildo, 1778, ACC: Cabildo 29, fol. 7; Nieto to Flores, Mompós, April 6, 1780, ANC: MM, vol. 87, fols. 822–31.

from grace in Spain due to his disastrous failure as commander of an invasion of Algiers in 1775. Although he was later made captain general of Andalusia and nominally remained inspector general of the army of America until 1783, his role in shaping military policy faded quickly.[67] Meanwhile, José de Gálvez had become minister of the Indies. Until his death in 1787, the crown acted directly through him in guiding the military reform in New Granada.

During the early years of the military reform in Popayán, the captain of the local fixed company, in this instance Diego Antonio Nieto, acted (as in Guayaquil) as special commander of the militia. The governor functioned as inspector. Flores' reorganization plan envisioned the establishment of fourteen separate infantry companies modeled on the Puerto Rican modifications of the Cuban reglamento; most of the companies were to be located in the cities of the Cauca Valley in the north, but some were to range geographically as far southwest as Barbacoas.

It is instructive to note that in structuring the chain of command for the new militia, Flores, as had Guirior in the case of Guayaquil, bypassed the office of commandant general of Quito by working directly through the local governor. This arrangement may at first glance appear to have been a breach of protocol, but such was not the case. Both governors operated routinely on a largely independent basis in local military affairs. Moreover, when the reform was finally extended to Santa Marta, the commandant general of Cartagena was also excluded from direct participation. In all three cases the local governor possessed an independent veteran troop authorization, was a military officer himself, and, in consequence, had traditionally functioned with a large measure of local autonomy. This system reconfirmed the decentralized character of the military establishment of New Granada.

In contrast to the experience in Guayaquil, the relationship between Popayán's governor, Pedro de Beccaria y Espinosa, and the special commander, Diego Antonio Nieto, was relatively harmonious. Nieto, a native of Extremadura was a highly motivated, able officer, who eventually became president of Quito. He was a twenty-eight-year-old lieutenant in the garrison of Cartagena when selected in 1771 to serve as captain of the newly created fixed company of Popayán.[68] Finding routine service in Popayán an unsatisfactory challenge, however, he soon had applied for a transfer back to Cartagena. Guirior sympathetically had supported his request, recommending that,

67. During the late 1770s Gálvez consulted O'Reilly on the developments in the Guayaquil militia, which the latter had helped originate, but in the case of Popayán he merely informed him that a militia had been established. Expediente on the formation of the disciplined militia of Guayaquil, 1774–83; expediente, militia of Popayán. For the misfortunes of Alejandro O'Reilly, see Bibiano Torres Ramírez, *Alejandro O'Reilly en las Indias*, pp. 9–14; O'Reilly to Quiroga, Cádiz, October 17, 1783, AGI: Santa Fe, legajo 950.

68. Service records, Fixed Infantry Battalion of Cartagena, February 28, 1771, AGI: Santa Fe, legajo 944.

because of its slight responsibility, the post in Popayán be given to a man among the "weary" of Cartagena, definitely indicating that Popayán was a low-priority assignment. Although Spain acceded to Nieto's petition, Viceroy Flores suspended the transfer with Nieto's consent when the two men agreed to raise a disciplined militia in Popayán.[69]

The governor of Popayán at this time, Pedro Beccaria, was an elderly cavalry captain, who apparently had been assigned to Popayán as a form of semi-retirement. Once wounded in Italy, he could boast an honorable record of forty-two years of service when he became governor in 1777. At the time of his appointment he had been attached to the corps of retired and disabled veterans in Madrid.[70] His selection as governor was consistent with the traditional pattern of rewarding aging public servants with the quiet solitude of Popayán. Beccaria's predecessor, Juan Antonio Zelaya, who, it will be recalled, was the former governor of Guayaquil who had pacified Quito and acted as interim president, had passed his declining years in Popayán, dying in 1776.[71]

Beccaria possessed a comparatively gentle disposition, at least in comparison to his counterpart in Guayaquil, and he found working with the able Diego Antonio Nieto an easy affair. Because of the huge area encompassed by the enterprise, the two men divided responsibility for the formation of the new companies. The governor raised the militia of Pasto and Barbacoas, while Nieto directed action in the city of Popayán and the regions to the north.[72] Since Beccaria, while working in the southwest, was for all practical purposes beyond the range of immediate communication with the special commander, Nieto at times sent his officer proposals directly to the viceroy, although he also sent a duplicate list to the governor. This system preserved the technical chain of command, but it was sufficiently flexible to enable the viceroy, with advanced information, to reach his own decisions before receiving Beccaria's opinion.[73] Such cooperation would have been impossible in Guayaquil.

A new militia of fourteen companies had taken shape by 1779, with two each in the municipalities of Cartago, Buga, Cali, Pasto, and Barbacoas, and four in the provincial capital (see Table 4). To provide leadership and to supervise training, Flores' plan for Popayán envisioned a veteran cadre which, in addition to Nieto, would consist of two ayudantes mayores for the command and staff group and a veteran sergeant acting as ayudante in each municipality. Initially, however, Nieto enjoyed the assistance of only one lieutenant, Manuel de Mesa, and two sergeants, all three drawn from the fixed unit. In a

69. Expediente, militia of Popayán.
70. Expediente on the appointment of Beccaria, Madrid, 1776, AGI: Quito, legajo 238.
71. Petition of the royal officials of Popayán, Popayán, May 17, 1776, AGI: Quito, legajo 238.
72. Nieto to Flores, Cartago, February 2 and February 9, 1777, ANC: MM, vol. 52, fols. 332–48; idem, Mompós, April 6, 1780.
73. Nieto to Flores, Cartago, February 2 and February 9, 1777.

system similar to Guayaquil's, the veteran advisors journeyed periodically from one part of the establishment to another to impart the necessary technical advice, while local volunteer officers who were trained by the veterans handled the routine direction of their respective companies.[74] The veteran list was gradually filled by the mid-1780s, but this was too late to be of appreciable initial assistance. By the end of 1779, for example, at which time company formation was complete, only three sergeants and two ayudantes mayores were functioning. The second ayudante mayor, a cadet sent to Popayán from the viceroy's halberdiers, had just arrived.[75]

In staffing the volunteer officer position in the militia companies, Nieto and Beccaria, although generally seeking men of outstanding social reputation as directed by the reglamento, averted the kind of intimate alliance that had developed between the creole aristocracy and the militia leadership of Guayaquil, and they thus sustained the independence of the militia as an instrument of the central government. In instructing Nieto, Flores authorized him to award officerships in exchange for the uniforming of companies, but the special commander frequently managed to raise units without resorting to that contingency. In Cartago, Buga, and Cali, he recruited enough men who were willing to provide their own uniforms to fill the six companies, and in Popayán, although three of the four captains clothed from fourteen to twenty-five men, most of the soldiers also provided their own attire. Moreover, no one ever accused Nieto of accepting private favors in return for officerships, although Beccaria rather openly did so, citing local precedent in the urban militia and the need to defray his expenses as justification. The reformers offered many of the positions to men who had served in the preceding urban militia, and these individuals as well as the newcomers were usually from prominent local families, although in the city of Popayán itself the principal recipients were not closely tied to the inner elite.[76]

With his independence uncompromised, Captain Nieto and his staff were potentially in a position to assert considerable power in the Province of Popayán, especially in the capital. The fuero militar, for all intents and purposes, placed the enlisted man beyond the control of ordinary justice in the municipalities and worked to make the militia a vehicle for outside political penetration of the colony. The highest ranking officer in the city of Popayán was the

74. Ibid.; idem, Popayán, April 2, May 17, and May 24, 1779, ANC: MM, fols. 767–78; idem, Mompós, April 6, 1780.

75. Militia salary lists, November 1778, August 1779, and January 1785, ACC: Colonia, MI–5P, sig. 5562, sig. 6027, and sig. 5932; Flores to Beccaria, Santa Fe, June 23, 1778, ACC: Colonia, MI–5P, sig. 7086; Nieto to Flores, Mompós, April 6, 1780.

76. Nieto to Flores, Buga, September 13, 1778, ANC: MM, vol. 52, fols. 423–38; idem, Mompós, April 6, 1780; Beccaria to Flores, Popayán, January 2, 1778, ANC: MM, vol. 74, fols. 932–35; idem, Popayán, May 2, 1778, AGI: Quito, legajo 573; Regent-Visitor Juan Francisco Gutiérrez de Piñeres to Gálvez, Santa Fe, July 31, 1779, AGI: Quito, legajo 573; expediente on the causes of Governor Pedro Beccaria, 1776–88, AGI: Quito, legajo 238.

governor, who was assisted in dispensing military justice in the first instance by an auditor de guerra, José Ignacio Peredo, who also acted as deputy governor. In the outlying areas, the veteran ayudantes when available would normally exercise this responsibility on behalf of the auditor de guerra; as a practical matter, however, they were few in number, of less prestige, and probably had a limited impact. It was in the capital, where the authority of the governor stood directly behind military justice and where the militia was closely directed by the able Captain Nieto, that the reform most endangered existing political and social arrangements. Commander Nieto's men, shielded by the fuero militar, were potentially invulnerable to reprisals from the creole aristocracy through the cabildo, and the militia, therefore, could underpin a tightening of revenue collection, the establishment of royal monopolies, and the general assertion of viceregal political control. Not surprisingly, then, opposition to the military reform first crystalized in the capital and in ensuing years remained strongest there.

Almost from the beginning, the principal creole families of the city of Popayán viewed the reform with intense hostility and resisted the encroachment of the militia into their domain. On February 1, 1778, the cabildo of Popayán formally protested to Spain the establishment of a disciplined militia. The municipal government argued that the militia was completely useless because Popayán was far from any maritime port which might require a strong defense and because the city itself had throughout its history been governed "with the most exceptional bliss"; the latter portrayal showed a convenient lapse of memory which seemed to make an increase of governmental power superfluous. In reality, protested the cabildo, the militia was causing chaos. On the one hand, it failed to sustain satisfactorily existing social distinctions within the military corporation, shamelessly mixing those of nobility with those of lesser quality. On the other hand, the militia employed its fuero as an absolute license to disregard ordinary justice, promote lawlessness, and disrupt communal tranquility, which only an adherence to the traditional sense of hierarchy could preserve.[77]

For its part, the militia leadership complained of continued harassment and intimidation by the cabildo of Popayán. Nieto charged that while he and the governor were absent organizing the militia, the ordinary justices of Popayán vengefully exacted penalties on those who dared profess the fuero, thereby forcing many to conceal or deny their claim to it. Moreover, lampoons appeared daily protesting the establishment of taxes, and matters so deteriorated that Nieto was forced to abbreviate his expedition and hurry back to the provincial capital. Despite his return, Nieto found himself seriously handicapped

77. Expediente, militia of Popayán. Among others, this cabildo contained Joaquín Valencia, the son of Pedro Valencia, Francisco del Campo y Larraondo, and Francisco Basilio Angulo, all of whom became personally involved in the struggle against the military reform.

in asserting military rights because the deputy governor and auditor de guerra was a civilian, who in the absence of the governor proved more responsive to pressure from the cabildo than from the militia commander.[78] Describing his tenure in Popayán as the unhappiest period in his forty-eight years of royal service, Governor Beccaria likewise bitterly complained of extensive local obstructionism that frustrated his endeavors to sustain a disciplined militia.[79] He was particularly angered by a cabildo allegation that the militia was not suited, because of its lack of honor and character, even to be permitted to provide detachments to guard the jail during a temporary absence of the regular garrison.[80] In effect, two competing forces for control of the colony had joined battle in a struggle that was by no means uneven.

The most serious single incident arising from local resistance to the military reform in Popayán occurred when four young vassals refused to accept appointments as officers in the new militia. These men were Francisco García and José Lorenzo Largacha, lieutenants, and Joaquín Menoyo and Manuel Larraondo, second lieutenants. The least significant of the four was García, whose motives are not entirely clear, although he was obviously influenced by the general climate of discontent in the creole community and by an expressed reluctance to serve under the captain of his company, Alberto Pastoriza, a merchant who had offered to uniform twenty-five men. Unfortunately, the military never compiled service records for the officers of the Popayán militia, so social data are at best fragmentary. It is possible, however, to make a number of important observations based upon the evidence available. Pastoriza had served as lieutenant in the Third Company of Mestizos in the old urban militia, which indicates that his social standing may not have been the highest. On the other hand, the three other captains were all Spanish, which also may account for some of the friction.[81] In all cases, it appears that the militia reformers had carefully selected captains who were not intimately connected to the inner elite of Popayán.[82]

The motives of the other three men who declined subordinate offices de-

78. Nieto to Flores, Mompós, April 6, 1780. Although Gálvez had ruled against the auditor de guerra of Guayaquil, Icaza, by this time, no clear prohibition against civilian occupancy of this office had yet developed.

79. Beccaria to Flores, Popayán, January 2, 1778.

80. Cabildo of Popayán to Flores, 1778, ANC: Cabildos, vol. 2, fols. 73–105.

81. Officer proposals, Popayán, July 2, 1777, AGI: Quito, legajo 574; urban militia report, Popayán, November 18, 1776, AGI: Quito, legajo 574. Captain Gerónimo de Torres had served in the urban militia as the second lieutenant of the Company of *Forasteros* and was Spanish; Captain Juan Saavedra and his brother Pedro, who served as *sargento mayor* without salary, were born in Lugo. Juan Antonio Pombo, the other captain, was also Spanish. Flores to Gálvez, Santa Fe, August 11, 1778, AGI: Quito, legajo 574; statement of merits, Pedro Saavedra, Popayán, July 28, 1786, AGI: Quito, legajo 574; Luis Martínez Delgado, *Popayán, ciudad prócera*, p. 178.

82. A number of creoles from important families did accept positions as junior officers, including Mariano Quijano, José Joaquín Mosquera, and Manuel Hurtado, the latter as a replacement in one of the rejected second lieutenantships. These acceptances may have resulted from fear

rived directly from a basic hostility toward the reform, as well as from probable resentment that they had been passed over for captainships. Manuel Larraondo was the eldest son of Francisco del Campo y Larraondo, hidalgo, wealthy mine operator and landowner, and regidor. José Lorenzo Largacha and Joaquín de Menoyo were nephews and wards of Francisco Basilio de Angulo y Gorvea, one of Popayán's few wholesale merchants, *juez de comercio* (commercial magistrate), regidor perpetuo, and among the most powerful men of Popayán. Actually, both Angulo and Campo y Larraonda were Spaniards by birth, but they had been incorporated into the local patriciate through marriage, and the colonial authorities identified Angulo as the instigator and leader of the resistance to the military intrusion. In all probability, the selection of Angulo's two nephews as junior officers was a token gesture from Nieto and Beccaria intended to win his neutrality or perhaps to disarm him. The gesture, however, obviously not only failed but led to further humiliation for the militia. Nieto apparently had not offered to sell captainships to these men, because they surely could have topped the number of uniforms promised by the successful candidates.[83]

Much of Angulo's power derived from his personal connections with a leading family of Popayán, the Valencias. Angulo had married a niece of Pedro Agustín de Valencia, who was not only a dominant creole power in Popayán but one of the most prominent men in New Granada.[84] Among the beneméritos of the viceroyalty, Valencia claimed hidalguía and his son eventually acquired the title of count.[85] With his wealth being in gold mining and land, Pedro Valencia's greatest triumph was his founding of a royal mint in Popayán, one of two in New Granada.[86] This service ingratiated him with the monarch, who made him permanent treasurer, dispensed his "protection" to the family, and accepted Valencia's oldest surviving son and one daughter at Court under his personal care. That son, Francisco, was assigned to the secretariat of the Ministry of the Indies and managed to contract marriage with the daughter of Felipe Codallos, a minister on the Council of Castille.[87]

---

of royal recrimination or perhaps simply stemmed from a different reaction to the militia system. None of the three remaining replacements, Félix Pérez, Miguel Yangues, and Manuel Saavedra, seems to have come from well-established families. Gustavo Arboleda, *Diccionario biográfico y genealógico del antiguo departamento del Cauca*, pp. 214, 282, 365.

83. Nieto may have offered the companies to the men in question and been refused, but this possibility seems unlikely because he made no mention of ever having made such a gesture. Expediente on the refusal of militia officerships, Popayán, 1778–80, AGI: Quito, legajo 573; expediente, militia of Popayán; Martínez Delgado, *Popayán, cuidad prócera*, pp. 178, 210.

84. Martínez Delgado, *Popayán, cuidad prócera*, pp. 235–36; Flores to Gálvez, Cartagena, January 9, 1782, AGI: Quito, legajo 574.

85. Informe on the distinguished circumstances of Antonio Valencia, Popayán, 1794, AGI: Quito, legajo 226.

86. Vicente Restrepo, *Estudio sobre las minas de oro y plata de Colombia*, p. 84.

87. Expediente on the merits of Pedro Valencia, Popayán, April 19, 1776, AGI: Santa Fe, legajo 555.

In all, Valencia had thirteen surviving children as well as six nephews and nieces under his guardianship, many of whom found public positions through his influence.[88] On one occasion, for example, he succeeded in placing his nephew, Rafael Fernández de Córdova y Valencia, in the Fixed Regiment of Cartagena as a second lieutenant, in spite of a complete lack of previous experience, normal tenure as a cadet, or any new financial contributions.[89] In other instances, his family managed through marriage to absorb powerful outsiders, such as Angulo. Significantly, Francisco del Campo y Larraondo had married Valencia's daughter, Ignacia, as prerequisite to his entrance into Popayán's elite. Manuel Larraondo, who refused to collaborate with the militia, was, then, the grandson of Pedro Valencia.[90]

Despite the esteemed recognition that the crown accorded to the Valencias, this powerful family did not readily accept royal initiatives in Popayán. A coincident tragedy seems to have destroyed irrevocably any real Valencia identity with the regime of Charles III. Pedro Valencia's eldest son, Pedro Vicente, had been a member of the Society of Jesus serving in Popayán when Charles expelled the order. Like other members of the society, young Pedro had been taken into custody and forced to depart America; unhappily, however, he perished in Panama on the journey to Spain.[91] Thus, in addition to those political, social, and economic reasons that might have led a man such as Valencia to resent the Bourbon reforms, he harbored deep personal motives as well.

As a recipient of royal favors, Pedro Valencia remained in the background while his nephew through marriage, Francisco Angulo, overtly worked to frustrate the military reform, although Beccaria, Nieto, and Flores fully appreciated the connection between the two men. Even before the military reform, the patriciate of Popayán had forcefully demonstrated its ability to derail unwelcome government initiatives. During the regime of Guirior, an outsider named Babilonia had won authorization to establish a government tobacco monopoly in Popayán. Prior to this time the concession had belonged to Joaquín Fernández de Córdova, the brother-in-law of Pedro Valencia, who appears to have acquired it as a preemptive move, because he never seriously attempted to do anything with it. The arrival of an outsider threatened this arrangement, and Francisco Angulo quickly had himself elected procurador general (city attorney). From this base, and aided by Governor Zelaya, who had discovered that it was more comfortable and profitable to deal with the Valencias than to oppose them, Angulo harassed Babilonia with an endless series of claims. Against hopeless odds, the tobacco monopolist soon fled to

88. Ibid.; expediente on the petition of Pedro Valencia, 1777, AGI: Quito, legajo 556.

89. Expediente on the petition of Francisco Valencia, Madrid, 1773, AGI: Quito, legajo 1001.

90. Arboleda, *Diccionario biográfico*, pp. 89, 448–49.

91. Juan Manuel Pacheco, "La Universidad de San José de Popayán," pp. 456–58.

avoid further abuse and certain imprisonment, leaving the tobacco monopoly once again inactive.[92] The military reformers now faced this same formidable opposition.

When Viceroy Flores learned of Nieto's difficulties in Popayán, he moved directly to meet the crisis. Unfortunately, Manuel Antonio Flores has been remembered more for his frustration at the hands of Regent-Visitor Gutiérrez de Piñeres and his ultimate physical and emotional collapse following the Comunero Rebellion than for the strength and vision he demonstrated while an unencumbered viceroy. Rational but sharp-tongued, he was a hard-hitting, tough administrator, who ranks as one of the two or three ablest men to serve as viceroy in New Granada. Although perhaps a bit too quick to condemn, he had little tolerance for the ubiquitous bureaucratic haggling of his time, vain pretenses, or insubordination.[93] As will be recalled, it was Flores who sought to rectify and rationalize the pretentious but chaotic militia establishment that Guirior had left in Cartagena. And it was Flores' desire to assert effective authority in Popayán that led him to return Nieto to that province with orders to organize a militia which could back the royal administration.

Already annoyed by the difficulties that the reform was experiencing in Popayán, Flores moved forcefully against the four men who had refused militia offices. He declared Campo, Lorenzo Largacha, and Menoyo ineligible for further appointments of public distinction and ordered the cabildo of Popayán to deposit a copy of this decree in the municipal archives as well as in all others in the province. In addition, although Beccaria wanted to "score a blow for justice" by sending García off to royal labors at Cartagena, Flores, recognizing the secondary role that García had played, merely retired him, but without the uniform or fuero he deserved from previous service.

Banishment from public distinctions was a harsh blow to the creole accustomed to seeking titles, honors, and public positions; consequently, both Angulo and Campo y Larraondo appealed to the crown. In their petitions they asserted that their dependents had extensive responsibilities that conflicted with militia service. These involved the administration of landed estates and gold mines as well as educational and family demands. They also asserted that, by reason of their "nobility," they could not be forced to assume such responsibilities against their will. The latter contention is revealingly indicative of the extent to which the eighteenth-century patriciate had become removed from the martial function which formed the original basis for its social status.

In defending his action in August 1778, Viceroy Flores depicted the confrontation as a test of the determination of royal government to assert itself

92. Expediente, militia of Popayán; Flores to Gálvez, Cartagena, January 9, 1782.
93. Flores repeatedly demonstrated these qualities. They can be seen in previously cited correspondence concerning Guayaquil's Governor Ugarte. An amusing example can be found in his action over a dispute in Panama between Commandant General Pedro Carbonell and Governor Félix Bejarano of Veragua, AGI: Panama, legajo 256.

in Popayán. Beginning with the disorders of 1765, he described the inability of the viceregal government to advance revenue collection as due to persistent obstructionism by the local aristocracy. Asserting that the common people would not act without encouragement from those above, he blamed the creole magnates for secretly fomenting popular disorders when it suited their purposes and he underscored the necessity of standing firm in the present instance. Concerning the fate of the three men, Flores argued that those who refused to discharge the noble military responsibility hardly deserved consideration for other positions.[94]

In a later commentary on the crisis, Flores specifically attacked Angulo and Valencia for their roles in disrupting the militia system, and in the process he delivered a particularly revealing and biting commentary on the patriciate of Popayán. "Serving in the militia does not infringe upon the privileges of the nobility, for bearing arms has always been the glory most dear to it, from which its origin and distinction principally derive. But in that [nobility] of Popayán, it appears enthusiasm still pursues that which has made the misguided chivalry of Don Quixote so celebrated in the world, which consists of viewing disdainfully all those men it considers inferior, without appreciating the interdependence that God has placed among all classes of the state for the preservation of society and that only those that excell in moral and civil virtues are worthy as superiors . . . because birth is luck, not choice."[95]

At this critical juncture, the struggle over the military reform in Popayán merged with other, broader issues and lost its separate identity. In January 1778, Regent-Visitor Juan Francisco Gutiérrez de Piñeres arrived in Santa Fe with broad powers including extraordinary authority to revitalize the royal treasury (see chapter 4). Confronted with the appeals of the dishonored young creoles of Popayán, the crown solicited an opinion from the regent-visitor. Gutiérrez de Piñeres should, presumably, have warmly applauded Flores' tough policies in Popayán, directed as they were toward tightening government control and enhancing revenue collection, but the regent-visitor, who consistently sought to embarrass and undercut Flores as a rival power, instead supported the entrenched aristocracy. He warmly applauded the principal families of Popayán for their faithful and cooperative behavior, and he assured the crown that the only real menace to law and order in Popayán was the militia itself, although he did not go so far as to recommend its abolition. Moreover, he seized upon rumors coming out of Popayán to charge Governor Beccaria with gross misconduct and malfeasance in office. By the time the regent-visitor's communication reached Spain, however, war with England had broken out, largely precluding any basic changes in Popayán's militia.

94. Expediente on the refusal of militia officerships, Popayán, 1778–80.
95. Flores to Gálvez, Cartagena, January 9, 1782. Although the creoles involved in this controversy classified themselves as "nobles," none of them possessed an actual title of Castile.

The crown did, nevertheless, by an order of January 20, 1780, lift the restrictions Flores had placed on the three men who had refused officerships.[96] This action amounted to a personal defeat for the viceroy, although it actually mattered little. Flores had already gone to Cartagena to assume direct military command, abandoning domestic affairs to Gutiérrez de Piñeres.

While the controversies generated by the military reform moved through the viceregal and royal bureaucracies, the predicament of the military in Popayán continued to worsen. Much to his regret, Beccaria soon found himself alone and isolated, and the simple old gentleman was no match for the magnates of Popayán. When Flores discovered that the governor had exacted fees for the officerships of Pasto, he withdrew his support for him, sternly admonishing him and suspending his salary to cover the amount of his illicit increment. Moreover, Nieto had transferred to the comparatively peaceful but more important garrison of Mompós, Province of Cartagena, when the war broke out, replacing as sargento mayor of militia Ramón García Pizarro, who became governor of Guayaquil.[97] Thus, of the three men originally associated most closely with the reform in Popayán, Beccaria alone remained.

Governor Beccaria's personal difficulties had begun when he toured southern Popayán to organize militia in Pasto and Barbacoas. In addition to selling offices, which cost him the support of Flores, he permitted his wife, who was alone and new in a strange land, to accompany him, which was an illegal but common practice in that vast province. Matters were complicated when a priest he brought along for spiritual comfort made improper advances to Mrs. Beccaria and the governor felt compelled to denounce him to the vicar in Pasto. This action, although open and honorable, bared his own breach of regulations and exposed his spouse to public scandal, delighting the hostile creoles of Popayán. To aggravate his situation, it was soon discovered that Beccaria was operating a gambling establishment in his home. Again, the simple old gentleman made no attempt to conceal his action because he believed it a perquisite of his office.

Beccaria's misconduct was, in reality, less serious than his political mistakes. His close association with the military reform aroused the wrath of Popayán's patriciate, but while he had too much integrity to seek an accommodation with the local aristocracy, he still naïvely sought the same unspoken privileges and perquisites that his predecessors had enjoyed. His deputy governor, José Ignacio Peredo, made a number of attempts to explain the political facts of life to him, but succeeded only in insulting his sense of honor.[98]

Inexperienced as he was, the old governor was stunned by the difficulties

96. Expediente on the refusal of militia officerships, Popayán, 1778–80.
97. Expediente, militia of Popayán; expediente on the causes of Beccaria, 1776–88.
98. Expediente on the causes of Beccaria, 1776–88.

that befell him. Lampoons threatened his life; he found himself without salary and the means to survive; and his actions were consistently overruled from above. Gutiérrez de Piñeres rudely pushed him aside and vested Deputy Governor Peredo with the authority to reform and to supervise royal monopolies. And, finally, the crown itself sternly admonished him with a clear warning that further incidents would bring harsh punishment.[99] Politically helpless, his lines of authority dissolved, Beccaria's life became a nightmare. Once again the power of the great magnates of Popayán had prevailed. The military reform was in disarray and would remain so until the great Comunero Rebellion of 1781 altered the political realities of upland New Granada.

In the remainder of the province, opposition to the reform was much less apparent than in the capital. This tranquility can be at least partly explained by the success of the reformers in wooing leading families into the militia system. In Pasto, for example, Beccaria recruited three members of the Burbano de Lara family for captain, lieutenant, and second lieutenant of the first company and a son of the Pérez de Zúñigas as captain of the second company. Both were patrician families.[100] In Cali, Nieto awarded the captainship of the first company to Manuel Caicedo Tenorio, benemérito, titled nobility, and head of one of the most powerful and distinguished families of the province. Antonio Cuero, captain of the second company, was distinguished in his own right, and, like many of the officers, he was related to the Caicedos and was a frequent public servant.[101] Data are less conclusive for the other municipalities, but the available evidence indicates conformity to the pattern in Cali and Pasto. Captains Casimiro Cortés and Manuel Díaz del Castillo of Barbacoas, for example, both derived from extremely wealthy and well-established creole families.[102] In Buga, Nieto named Santiago de Soto y Zorrilla captain of the first company. The Soto y Zorrilla family traced its lineage back to the first conquerors and colonists of the Cauca Valley.[103] Finally, in Cartago, the captainship of the first company went to Pedro Cerezo y Figueroa, a Spaniard, but one who had integrated into the community through numerous public services

99. Ibid.

100. Compare Beccaria's list of officers in his report to Flores, May 17, 1780, in the expediente, militia of Popayán, with the list of noble families of Pasto in Sergio Elías Ortiz, Crónicas de la ciudad de Sant Joan de Pasto, p. 13.

101. Caicedo's son, Manuel Joaquín Caicedo y Cuero, was second lieutenant in his company. His name indicates marriage connections with the Cueros. He was related by marriage to the other second lieutenant, Ignacio Lourido, who in turn was connected by marriage to Lieutenant José Ramos. Including the remaining lieutenant, Luis Vergara, lawyer of the Audiencia of Quito, these men owned cattle herds, some of them sugar mills, and all served frequently in varying capacities on the cabildo. See Arboleda, Historia de Cali, 2: 272–78, 322–32, 341–49, 355–78, 385, 399–405; 3: 15–17, 30–33, 49–53, 67–89, 104–6, 113–15, 121–29, 137, 148–51, 169–70, 186–87, 200–203, 211.

102. Arboleda, Diccionario biográfico, pp. 130, 145–46.

103. Arboleda, Historia de Cali, 2: 152–53.

and marriage to Micaela Gómez de la Asprilla y Valencia, who had all the proper family connections.[104]

With more problems than they could handle in the capital, the reformers were not immediately inclined to undercut the local aristocracy in the communities of the outer province; and the aristocracy in turn, finding itself at a safe distance from the central authorities, feared less for its vested interests. These factors largely account for recruitment successes. Moreover, it should also be recalled that Beccaria sold offices in the south, presumably to the highest bidder. North of Popayán, the primary motive for organizing the militia was the danger of slave uprisings in the gold fields. Hence, it was possible for Nieto to cooperate with Manuel Caicedo and Antonio Cuero, both large slave owners, even though Caicedo was deeply implicated in the popular disorders of 1765 as the owner of a sugar mill and as an alcalde on the cabildo which, claiming popular duress, had conveniently suspended the aguardiente monopoly.[105] In effect, a policy of accommodation prevailed in the outlying towns, while the reformers directed their energy toward asserting viceregal authority in the provincial capital.

When taken as a whole, the early militia reform could hardly be classified as an unqualified success in either Guayaquil or Popayán. The reform in Guayaquil produced only a paper militia, which was more significant as a vehicle to promote social pretenses than as an instrument of defense. The close relationship that developed between the reorganized military and the creole aristocracy, however, was destined to endure throughout the colonial period with important long-run implications. In Popayán, by contrast, where a hostile, arrogant aristocracy managed to keep the reform off balance, no such marriage emerged, and the militia, suffering extreme harassment, encountered great difficulty in asserting its corporate identity. Yet not all was lost, for Governor Beccaria and a few faithful officers stubbornly continued the struggle to promote at least some semblance of military capability. Future events would demonstrate that this effort was not in vain.

Adjustments in the regular army of the Commandancy General of Quito were much more limited in scope than those of Cartagena and Panama, but considering the small size of the original garrisons the modifications were, nevertheless, relatively substantial (see Table 4). The first major change came in Popayán when Viceroy Flores reduced the fixed company to a detachment of twenty-five men to compensate for the cost of raising the new militia.[106] Then, in March 1779, in response to recommendations by Flores, the monarchy increased the size of the three companies of Quito from fifty to seventy-

104. Miguel W. Quintero Guzmán, "Valencia: Una ilustre familia Cartagueña." This family is distinct from the Valencias of Popayán. For officer lists see reports in the expediente, militia of Popayán, and officer proposals, 1777–83, in AGI: Quito, legajo 574.

105. Arboleda, *Historia de Cali*, 2: 328–32, 405.

106. Royal order, July 18, 1777.

five men and doubled the size of the company of Guayaquil to one hundred. This expansion of the army of the Commandancy General of Quito in 1779 was another expression of the monarchy's increasing dependence upon the military to support its policies, particularly as it moved to expand revenue collection. Moreover, Portuguese incursions against settlements in the Amazon Governorship of Mainas and painful, inept efforts to muster an expedition to the area from Quito in 1776–77 added yet another reason for a stronger garrison in the south of the viceroyalty. Although the boundary dispute was settled by the Treaty of San Ildefonso in October 1777, uncertainty about the future of the area was a strong consideration in Flores' request for a strengthened force.[107] Finally, the continued growth and importance of Guayaquil as a maritime stronghold made its original fifty-man garrison appear ridiculously small.[108] When taken as a whole, these readjustments in the regular army of the southwest under Flores netted a substantial forty per cent increase in manpower and, at the very least, represented a further expansion and revitalization of the military establishment of New Granada.

As the 1770s drew to a close, plans were already under way to extend the reform to much of the remaining interior of the viceroyalty. In May 1777, acting on a royal request, Flores ordered the governor of Antioquia to explore the possibility of forming a disciplined militia in his province. And in August of the same year he sent a plan to Spain for the expansion of the reform to the provinces of Pamplona, Tunja, and Mariquita. The crown approved Flores' proposal, but it ordered him to delay further action until Regent-Visitor Juan Francisco Gutiérrez de Piñeres had completed his work. Evidently, the court was skeptical of the low-cost results in Guayaquil and Popayán and wished to delay further reforms until sufficient funds were available. Fearing that disorders would result from the regent-visitor's mission, Viceroy Flores for his part contended that, before daring to introduce tax innovations, the government should organize additional disciplined militia to sustain royal authority, an argument consistent with his own record in Popayán. In view of the viceroyalty's past experiences, Flores' arguments deserved careful consideration, but he spoke in vain.[109]

107. An Indian uprising in the town of Guano, Corregimiento of Riobamba, against the visit of Fiscal Juan José Villalengua of the Quito audiencia in 1778 had intensified the ever present fear of public disorders. Expediente on the expansion of the Quito garrison, 1779, AGI: Quito, legajo 573; expediente on the destiny of the Fixed Company of Popayán, 1777, ANC: MM, vol. 52, fols. 520–29; Diguja to the royal officials of Popayán, Quito, July 29, 1777, ANC: MM, vol. 52, fols. 508–11; Diguja to Flores, Quito, September 3, 1777, ANC: MM, vol. 110, fols. 82–85; Flores to Diguja, Santa Fe, February 2, 1778, ANE: Pres., vol. 117, fol. 5.

108. Flores to Gálvez, Santa Fe, November 15, 1778; royal order, March 14, 1779.

109. Antonio Caballero y Góngora, in *Relaciones de mando*, pp. 199–202; Flores to Governor Cayetano Buelta Lorenian, Santa Fe, May 31, 1777, ANC: MM, vol. 3, fols. 81–87; royal order, February 13, 1778, ANC: MM, vol. 30. fols. 937–39.

4. The Impact of the Comunero Rebellion

As THE MILITARY REFORM entered the decade of the 1780s, former experience and emerging projects promised a slow but steady expansion of the disciplined militia system to all the remaining provinces of New Granada. But on March 16, 1781, in the town of Socorro, Province of Tunja, the great Comunero Rebellion began and soon engulfed much of the interior of the viceroyalty. Before the authorities could restore order, the insurrection, because of its unprecedented severity, had humiliated the regime in Santa Fe and had clearly demonstrated an alarming weakness in the fabric of royal control in New Granada. As a result, the royal administration, consistent with its previous behavior, sought to reassert its authority by increasing the political role of the army; in the process, it irrevocably altered the course of the military reform. Because of the rebellion's importance to the subsequent history of the military in New Granada, pause must be given to briefly sketch its course.

Historians have been nearly unanimous in attributing the immediate cause of the Comunero Rebellion to the ambitious attempt of Juan Francisco Gutiérrez de Piñeres to reform revenue collection in New Granada.[1] Gutiérrez de Piñeres, commissioned as both regent of the royal audiencia and visitor general, possessed extraordinary powers over the royal exchequer, superseding

1. Another source of great bitterness during this same period was the reorganization of Indian administration in the altiplano of Cundinamarca, which resulted in the resettlement of Indians and the sale of vacant lands.

those of the viceroy. His immediate task was to convert an annual deficit of some 170,000 pesos into a surplus in the royal coffers. Revenue collection in New Granada had languished under Guirior and, although Flores laid the foundation for a stricter policy, full implementation had awaited the arrival of the regent-visitor.

Arriving in Santa Fe in early 1778, Gutiérrez de Piñeres initially addressed himself to the strict enforcement of tax and monopoly laws, the reduction of inefficiency and waste, and the elimination of fraud and other forms of corruption. Further, to strengthen his hand in effecting these policies, he cleared the fiscal administration in Santa Fe of a clique of deeply entrenched creole bureaucrats. Viceroy Flores, a properly cautious administrator in the area of taxation, soon feared that the regent-visitor was overzealous in effecting his commission. Flores argued that substantial revenue increases could only safely follow additional economic growth and a strengthened governmental authority; he anticipated that Gutiérrez de Piñeres' attempt to squeeze firmly more funds out of the viceroyalty's inhabitants would be likely to produce an unfavorable political reaction. His expression of concern went unheeded by the crown, however, which sharply rebuked Flores and advised him to support Gutiérrez' measures. When word reached Santa Fe in the summer of 1779 that Spain had entered the American War of Independence, Flores turned over his remaining civil powers to the regent-visitor, abandoning the capital for Cartagena, where he assumed personal military command.[2]

Although Gutiérrez de Piñeres appreciated the value of military support to the government, he strongly opposed the disciplined militia system of the empire. For example, he actively supported the expansion of the regular army of Quito in 1779, but consistently argued that the viceroyalty's militia was more trouble than it was worth. In a March 1780 report on the continuing controversy in Popayán, he warned that the militia system posed a serious danger to social and political stability. He feared, most perceptively, that the fuero militar, with its broad definition as both active and passive, would shortly transform the governmental institutions in America into purely military affairs, making civil authority (ordinary justice) meaningless. In this regard, the regent-visitor quite accurately prophesied the emergence of a praetorian tradition from the exercise of military privilege. To arrest the anticipated danger and to promote political stability, he urged the monarchy at least to restrict the militia fuero to a passive definition, with that of enlisted men limited to solely criminal causes.

On the other hand, Gutiérrez de Piñeres' social views had obviously benefited little from the egalitarian spirit of the Enlightenment. Arguing that the stability of the hierarchical social structure in New Granada depended upon a

2. David Phelps Leonard, "The Comunero Rebellion of New Granada in 1781 . . . " (Ph.D. diss.), pp. 72–76; Phelan, "El auge y la caída de los criollos," pp. 607–13.

white monopoly of the instruments of force, he strongly objected to the general practice of arming the castas. Educating the lower classes in the art of combat, he stressed in his report, provided them with the means to escape their proper, subordinate position.

> I have said and repeat that the humility in which the people of color have remained until now and the ascendancy that the few whites and Spaniards have possessed over them, has been the principal or perhaps the only cause to which the subordination of the commoners [*plebe*] should be attributed; and the preservation of good order wholly worked to make these people comprehend the obscurity of their birth and respect the nobles, the distinguished, and even any ordinary Spaniard, in such form that they dared not to oppose them; and with one voice they instilled a kind of reverent fear in them, that easily restrained any prejudicial or sinister movement. What most intimidated the commoners was firearms, as the use of them was absolutely prohibited, and they viewed the power to use them as a special and laudable privilege of the whites.
> With the establishment of the militia those ideas are destroyed. The most vile Negro, mulatto, or quadroon [tercerón] now considers himself equal to any white man, instead of respecting nobility as before; rather, he places himself at its level; [or] at least the subordination that served so much to conserve the harmony that results from hierarchy has disappeared, and the ascendancy that sustained it has dissipated.
> From the time that the man of color enlists in the militia, martial feelings that he did not know or dare to express inspire him; he is reminded each moment of the privileges and exemptions that he enjoys. Almost absolute independence from ordinary justice is manifested to him. He is instructed in the use of arms that was prohibited to him. In a word, he is made to know all that he can, and to develop his natural faculties, that fortunately he did not know or only possessed remotely because of the impossibility of exercising them.[3]

The regent-visitor, writing during wartime, recognized the need to arm limited numbers of pardos in the strategic maritime provinces but only with the strictest controls. In no sense could he find justification for maintaining a privileged militia in Popayán or any other interior province. He therefore opposed Flores' plan to prevent possible opposition to revenue reforms by expansion of the militia system and, indeed, urged the crown to replace the Popayán militia with a resurrected full company of regulars.[4] Gutiérrez de Piñeres' arguments closely resembled those then circulating in Popayán, and in one shape or another they frequently reappeared during the remaining history of

3. Gutiérrez de Piñeres to Gálvez, Santa Fe, March 31, 1780, AGI: Quito, legajo 574.
4. Expediente, militia of Popayán, AGI: Quito, legajo 574.

the military reform in New Granada. With war confronting the empire, however, the crown had more immediate concerns and essentially settled for the status quo, electing not to expand further the militia into the interior but permitting those establishments already in existence to continue.

The outbreak of international hostilities and the problem of war finance immensely complicated the endeavors of Gutiérrez de Piñeres. In Cartagena, Flores vigorously executed emergency defense preparations for those coastal strongholds which might be subject to British attack: he ordered the governors of the maritime provinces to place their garrisons on alert; he mobilized much of the coastal militia; and he ordered the construction of additional fortifications.[5] He also reclassified as "disciplined" the urban militia of Quito, which by this time was well developed.[6] Finally, a naval expedition was raised and outfitted in Cartagena for the Captaincy General of Guatemala to help resist British adventurism on the Mosquito Coast. These measures drastically increased military expenditures—Cartagena alone consumed over 50,000 pesos a month—and consequently the demand for additional revenues was immediately intensified.[7] The crisis was momentarily alleviated by the procurement of a loan of 200,000 pesos from the merchants of Cartagena and by the withdrawal of a comparable sum from the royal mints of Santa Fe and Popayán, but these were only stop-gap measures.[8]

In late 1779, the crown authorized Gutiérrez de Piñeres to raise additional revenue by increasing both royal monopoly prices and taxes. The visitor general acted in the following year by issuing a series of controversial edicts. The alcabala list was extended to include almost all goods except bread; the *Armada de Barlovento*, an excise tax long combined with the alcabala for payment but by this date largely forgotten and uncollected, was revived on a separate basis; and finally, the prices of tobacco and aguardiente, both royal monopolies, were doubled. Increases in tax rates were always unpopular, but feelings ran especially high against such a drastic expansion of the alcabala list and, particularly, against the resurrection of the Armada de Barlovento, logically believed to be a new tax. To make matters worse, the regent-visitor entrusted the enforcement of his edicts to an extensive array of thoroughly hated royal agents, mostly Spanish-born, who were reportedly arrogant, abusive, and unsympathetic toward the people.[9] A similar judgment would probably have befallen any revenue agent, no matter how urbane, who efficiently attempted to enforce the new measures.

The Socorro sector of Tunja Province, in which the upheaval began, was

5. Caballero y Góngora, in *Relaciones de mando*, p. 200.
6. Flores to J. García Pizarro, Cartagena, January 5, 1780, ANE: Pres., vol. 134, fol. 11.
7. Caballero y Góngora, in *Relaciones de mando*, pp. 200–203; see also Troy S. Floyd, *The Anglo-Spanish Struggle for Mosquitia*, pp. 152–62.
8. Leonard, "The Comunero Rebellion," pp. 75.
9. Ibid., p. 7.

one of the areas most adversely affected by the Gutiérrez edicts. Cotton, the basis for an extensive textile industry of the poor, was placed on the tax list, and the cultivation of tobacco, traditionally the region's main cash crop, had been restricted to a zone near the city of Girón shortly after Gutiérrez' arrival, thereby depriving many poor of their livelihoods. Moreover, a powerful landed aristocracy, similar to that of Popayán, also recoiled from this blatant assertion of royal authority.[10] Although a loud chorus of complaints followed the promulgation of the revenue measures, the regent-visitor refused to be dissuaded from making every possible effort to replenish the exhausted royal coffers.[11] Whether more sympathy and understanding might have averted the uprising or, perhaps, mitigated its intensity is uncertain; once under way, however, its full wrath fell upon the agents and devices employed in implementing the fiscal reform.

Proclaiming allegiance to the crown but demanding an end to unjust taxes, the insurgents of Socorro destroyed or pilfered the property of the government monopolies, chased revenue agents through the streets, and, in general, defied the local authorities.[12] Sometimes prompted by outside agitators, similar upheavals soon followed in neighboring settlements. Enjoying deep-rooted support among the inhabitants, the movement contained members from all the native-born classes; rather than subside, it continued to gain momentum, and within a short time the rebellion enveloped much of the Province of Tunja. Faced with this turmoil, local authorities stood helplessly by, either unable or unwilling to act, and frequently they were swept into the insurgency themselves. The movement eventually began to institutionalize, and on April 18, 1781, over 4,000 insurgents gathered in Socorro to select a council of leaders to direct their struggle. They bestowed command upon four creoles, with Juan Francisco Berbeo of Socorro soon emerging as commander. Although the various municipalities participating in the rebellion each selected its own leaders to manage local government, the men chosen at Socorro, apparently because the rebellion began there, acted as the supreme directorate.[13]

Finally comprehending the seriousness of the unrest, Gutiérrez met with the royal audiencia of Santa Fe in early April, at which time it was resolved to crush the sedition by force. They selected Oidor José Osorio to supervise the action, but military command was entrusted to Captain Joaquín de la Barrera of Santa Fe's company of halberdiers.[14] Short of outright capitulation, there

10. For a general description of the landed aristocracy of upland Colombia during the colonial period, see Smith, *Colombia: Social Structure*, pp. 62–69.
11. Leonard, "The Comunero Rebellion," pp. 78–84.
12. Indalecio Liévano Aguirre, *Los grandes conflictos sociales y económicos de nuestra historia*, 2:20–22.
13. Leonard, "The Comunero Rebellion," chap. 5; Pablo E. Cárdenas Acosta, *El movimiento comunal de 1781 en el Nuevo Reino de Granada*, 1: chap. 3.
14. Leonard, "The Comunero Rebellion," p. 122.

was no other course of action open to the authorities, although the troops available for the venture were hopelessly inadequate. The garrison of Santa Fe, created in 1750, possessed only two companies, one cavalry, the other halberdiers.[15] Originally consisting of fifty men each, Viceroy Messía de la Cerda had increased them to seventy-five. Even so, this force was much smaller than the garrison of less significant Quito, and it had been further weakened in 1781 because Viceroy Flores had taken the company of viceregal cavalry with him to Cartagena to insure his personal safety.[16]

Not daring to leave Santa Fe totally undefended, the authorities divided the remaining company; fifty of its men formed the core of the expedition, while twenty-five stayed to protect the capital. In addition to the regulars, twenty-two revenue guards and a small number of volunteers were incorporated into the operation. The authorities also sent an additional 100 firearms with ample ammunition, hoping that many additional loyal vassals could be recruited on the march to the confrontation. Efforts at further enlistment, however, encountered little enthusiasm and did not appreciably strengthen the force.[17] On April 22, the first elements of the tiny army arrived at Puente Real, an important transportation crossroad, where Osorio and Barrera decided to entrench and make a stand. The rebels on May 7 established positions on the heights surrounding the town with a force believed by the defenders to number at least four thousand men. Although the Comuneros possessed only rudimentary weapons, resistance proved to be hopeless. In the initial confrontation on the following day, the new recruits broke ranks at the first serious threat of combat and deserted to the insurgents, while the revenue guards took refuge in a nearby church. The remaining forces then surrendered without a fight, and Oidor Osorio, Captain Barrera, and all the weapons and supplies fell captive to the Comuneros. The insurgents later permitted the captured men to return to Santa Fe.[18]

It is unlikely that the presence of the cavalry company would have altered the outcome at Puente Real. Although subsequent testimony revealed that the defenders greatly overestimated the strength of the Comunero army—which actually numbered no more than 500 men—the Comuneros held the high ground and a favorable strategic position. Moreover, they were supported by a massive political movement, which could hardly have been contained militarily at this point, even had the army performed respectably.

In any event, the stunning Comunero victory at Puente Real soon inspired

15. Actually, although the royal authorization for these companies provided for 100 cavalrymen and 60 halberdiers, Viceroy José Alonso Pizarro chose to limit them to 50 men each. Royal order, July 17, 1751, ANC: RO, vol. 53, fol. 188.

16. *Tribunal de Cuentas* to Viceroy Messía de la Cerda, Santa Fe, August 9, 1768, ANC: MM, vol. 51, fols. 601–2; Cárdenas Acosta, *El movimiento comunal*, 1: 116.

17. Cárdenas Acosta, 1:151.

18. Leonard, "The Comunero Rebellion," pp. 126–31.

further insurgency. During the next several weeks, the authorities of the provincial capital of Tunja capitulated to Comunero pressure; Pamplona in the far northeast incorporated itself into the movement; and the insurrection spread into the far eastern Province of Los Llanos. On May 29, the Comuneros occupied the loyalist city of Girón, favored by the crown in the cultivation of tobacco and a possible base for counterinsurgency forces from the coast. The ranks of the rebel army, now firmly resolved to drive on Santa Fe, soon swelled to more than 15,000 men.[19]

The authorities in Santa Fe attempted to mobilize the existing urban militia and enlist new, trustworthy personnel in order to organize a defense for the city. On paper the various units totaled 678 men, but in typical prereform tradition, they quickly melted away when faced with a crisis. Consequently, Santa Fe's commander in chief of arms, Oidor Pedro Catani, realistically concluded that an effective defense of Santa Fe was impossible.[20] The only remaining hope of preventing the Comuneros from entering the city was negotiation or, possibly, capitulation. At this point the archbishop of Santa Fe, Antonio Caballero y Góngora, offered to mediate with the rebels. He addressed his offer to the *Junta General de Tribunales*, an emergency body composed of the royal audiencia acting in *real acuerdo* (executive session) and other leading officials in the city. The junta accepted his offer, and commissioned Oidor Joaquín Vasco y Vargas and Alcalde Ordinario Eustaquio Galavis with full powers to assist in the bold venture. This trio set out for the nearby town of Zipaquirá on May 13 in an attempt to meet with the insurgents. Gutiérrez de Piñeres left Santa Fe the same day fleeing toward Honda to depart for Cartagena via the Magdalena River.[21] On May 25 Berbeo dispatched José Antonio Galán, a deserter from Cartagena's fixed regiment, to intercept the regent-visitor and to capture arms being sent to Santa Fe from Cartagena. Galán failed to apprehend Gutiérrez but he carried the standard of rebellion into the Province of Mariquita, which had already experienced major upheavals, including one in the important city of Ibagué.[22]

On May 14 the archbishop's commission directed a communication to the insurgent forces advancing on Santa Fe, inviting its leaders to concur in discussions at Zipaquirá. Following an exchange of communications with the Comunero chief, Berbeo, the two sides agreed to meet in Nemocón, a small settlement several leagues from Zipaquirá. The first session occurred on May 26, and a lengthy series of further meetings, consultations, and diplomatic maneuverings followed. Events climaxed on June 5 when Berbeo, in the name

19. Cárdenas Acosta, *El movimiento comunal*, 1:221–24, 240–48, 250–55, 288–92, and 2: 340.
20. Ibid., 1:211–13.
21. Ibid., pp. 203–8. Gutiérrez returned to Santa Fe after the rebellion ended, but this time was subordinated to the viceroy. His stay was shortlived for on February 25, 1783, he was appointed to the Council of the Indies. Ibid., 2: 192, 221, 362.
22. Ibid., 1:266–68, and 2:75–89, 176.

of the Comuneros, presented a list of thirty-five articles. Known as the Capitulations, these articles demanded the repeal of the new revenue measures as well as remedies for many long-standing grievances. The commission immediately relayed the document to Santa Fe where the authorities, labelling it preposterous and outrageous, returned it without approval. Rumblings in the ranks of the Comuneros prompted the commission, after obtaining some minor concessions, to return the list to Santa Fe with the recommendation that it be immediately approved, lest the Comuneros enter the city. This was no time to raise objections! The Junta General de Tribunales ratified the Capitulations that evening, June 7. The following day in Zipaquirá, the agreement was promulgated after the archbishop celebrated a solemn Mass; the commission swore to comply with the terms of the Capitulations; and a Te Deum was sung. The Comuneros then disbanded and returned to their homes. Meanwhile, in Santa Fe the Junta General secretly declared the Capitulations null and void by reason of duress.[23]

Even following the Zipaquirá accord, shock waves continued to roll outward from the area of initial insurgency. In the south of the viceroyalty, the capital city of the Governorship of Neiva rose on June 19 in violent rebellion. Governor Policarpo Fernández was assassinated, but because of the forceful resistance of local government functionaries, two rebel leaders were killed and the government won the day. In the far northeast, insurgents from Pamplona carried the rebellion into the backlands of the Province of Maracaibo, now of the Captaincy General of Caracas, in the months of June, July, and early August. Finally, in September upheavals over the introduction of the tobacco monopoly erupted in the Province of Antioquia. The governor averted serious violence by making rapid concessions to the insurgents, including the free cultivation of tobacco and a general pardon. Viceroy Flores, who granted a pardon to the Comuneros on October 20, also confirmed the action of the Antioquian governor.[24]

In Cartagena, Viceroy Flores learned of the trouble in the backlands shortly after it started, but like the authorities in Santa Fe he initially underestimated its magnitude and expressed confidence that the company of halberdiers could cope with the problem.[25] The disaster at Puente Real made clear the need for a major relief expedition, but Flores could not respond immediately because British naval forces had been sighted off Maracaibo and Santa Marta, which led him to believe that Cartagena was in grave danger of attack. Moreover, he was fearful that the Fijo, comprised mainly of recruits from the troubled areas, might be unreliable if sent to confront the Comuneros, and for a time he con-

23. Ibid., 1: 255–58; 265, 269–302, and 2:8–49.

24. Ibid., pp. 95–96, 129–35, 163, 166–71; Roberto María Tisnes, *Movimientos pre-independientes grancolombianos*, pp. 61–69.

25. Cárdenas Acosta, *El movimiento comunal*, 1:154–55.

templated dispatching an all-militia force.[26] Ultimately, he elected to employ a force of 250 militiamen, half from the battalion of whites and half from the battalion of pardos, and 250 regulars, all of whom he placed under the command of Colonel José Bernet of the Fijo.[27] The employment of so many militiamen on this delicate mission was partly motivated by Flores' reluctance to weaken Cartagena by withdrawing too many regulars and by his fear that natives of the rebellious provinces might prove untrustworthy; but his decision also reflects, at least in part, a measure of confidence in the ability of the militia to perform. The expedition did not leave Cartagena, however, until July 1, reaching Santa Fe on August 6, by which time the main crisis had already passed. Although the Capitulations were not officially nullified until March 18, 1782, the government in Santa Fe began violating the accord as soon as sufficient military forces were available to sustain its authority.[28]

When the behavior of the authorities in the late summer indicated that they did not intend to honor the terms of the Capitulations, José Antonio Galán, the man Berbeo had dispatched to capture the fleeing regent-visitor, attempted to regenerate the movement in hopes of marshalling another drive on Santa Fe. Although operating in the heart of former rebel territory, his endeavors met little enthusiasm. Viceroy Flores, when informed of the new insurgency, ordered Colonel Bernet to employ the forces under his command to apprehend the new leader, but this did not prove necessary. Salvador Plata, a patrician from Socorro and one of the men selected along with Berbeo to lead the original movement, who was always a personality with nebulous designs and who now was seemingly committed to royal service, succeeded in capturing Galán with his personal forces on October 13. The prisoner was taken to Santa Fe where the royal audiencia tried him, found him guilty of sedition, and sentenced him to die by hanging. Death was administered on February 1, 1782. The body was then partitioned and its various members were distributed for public display in former insurgent cities and villages.[29] With that, the Comunero Rebellion was dead. For the next decade, the voices of open dissent would

26. Narváez to Flores, Santa Marta, October 19, 1779, ANC: MM, vol. 99, fols. 790–97; Caballero y Góngora, in *Relaciones de mando*, pp. 204, 206–7.

27. Most historians have incorrectly stated the composition of this expedition, probably because Caballero y Góngora himself was very nebulous on the subject in his relación de mando. José Manuel Groot, in his 1889 *Historia eclesiástica y civil de Nueva Granada*, 2:240, stated the force consisted of 500 militiamen; more recently Indalecio Liévano Aguirre, in *Los grandes conflictos sociales y económicos de nuestra historia*, 3:65, quoted Caballero's statement that Flores intended to send 500 militiamen, thereby creating the impression he actually did so; and Roberto María Tisnes, in *Movimientos preindependientes grancolombianos*, p. 59, indicated the component consisted of 500 regulars. Pablo E. Cárdenas Acosta, in *El movimiento comunal de 1781 en el Nuevo Reino de Granada*, 1:293, set the record straight. Corroboration can be found in Bernet to Flores, Santa Fe, August 31, 1781, ANC: MM, vol. 10, fols. 246–80.

28. Cárdenas Acosta, *El movimiento comunal*, 2:110–12, 162, 193–94.

29. Ibid., pp. 149–66, 175–92.

be silent in New Granada, although they were never far beneath the surface of events.

The results of the Comunero Rebellion brought to a climax the increasing militarization of political life in New Granada. The royal government had coped with the insurgents through a combination of finesse, malleability, and deception, not through preparedness or an ability to call upon the fidelity of its vassals. Viceroy Flores, whose petitions for a stronger internal defense system and greater moderation in advancing revenue reforms had gone unheeded, was, at least momentarily, vindicated. Although desperately ill and pleading for a replacement, the viceroy, in January 1782, reminded the crown that the one interior province in which he had installed the militia system, Popayán, had remained peaceful. He attributed this to the deterrent value of the militia along with the principles of order and obedience that it taught.[30] The badly shaken monarchy more than readily accepted this viewpoint.

Curiously, there did indeed seem to be a connection between the availability of military force and the preservation of domestic peace. An examination of the overall dimensions of the Comunero Rebellion reveals that it failed to take firm hold in any province that possessed a strong military establishment, although it spread everywhere else except in the Chocó. A thorough analysis of the geographic dimensions of the Comunero Rebellion, something still not attempted by historians, would require the study of many diverse, non-military factors. These factors would include the separate geographical, cultural, and ethnic character of the coast; the reform of revenue collection in the Presidency of Quito by a separate regent-visitor; the relationship between an unsuccessful rebellion in 1765 and peace in 1781; and the implicit assumption in most writings on the subject that the rebellion's core movement was halted before it had an opportunity to advance any farther.

There is, nevertheless, good reason to believe that the correlation between domestic peace and the presence of military establishments was more than a mere coincidence. An available military force not only discouraged any possible defiance of royal authority, but also, in the key cities, many of the active members of the community, men who might otherwise have provided leadership in seditious movements, were enlisted in the militia and subject to military discipline. Moreover, there were several instances where the military did act directly as a deterrent or did actually halt insurgency before it could spread. The best example of this phenomenon occurred in the Governorship of Maracaibo, Captaincy General of Caracas. Upon receiving word that the rebellion had overflowed into his jurisdiction, Governor Manuel de Ayala dispatched an expedition of 125 regulars reinforced by additional troops from Caracas. In the face of this opposition, the Comuneros dispersed.[31] At the same time, Viceroy

30. Flores to Gálvez, Cartagena, January 9, 1782, AGI: Quito, legajo 574.
31. Cárdenas Acosta, El movimiento comunal, 2: 132.

Flores in Cartagena, fearful that the insurgency would spread into the coastal provinces of Riohacha and Santa Marta, ordered an expedition of 200 regulars and militiamen to take position in Chiriguaná, a strategically located town in Santa Marta's backlands.[32] Notified of the possible trouble, Governor Antonio de Narváez of Riohacha and Santa Marta also sent 150 of Riohacha's militia cavalrymen to Chiriguaná, and he then went to Santa Marta to ready additional forces.[33] Perhaps because of these precautions, the rebellion failed to reach the coast.

In Popayán, Pedro Beccaria, with moral authority now clearly shifted to his side, reasserted his power as governor and mobilized part of the capital city's militia to deter and, if necessary, to arrest possible sedition.[34] When on November 7, 1781, the inhabitants of Tumaco, a small settlement on the Pacific coast, rose somewhat belatedly in rebellion, seizing the royal revenue building, freeing prisoners, and incarcerating the deputy governor, Beccaria dispatched his forces, and their arrival in late November quickly dispersed the rebels.[35] To officials examining the wreckage of 1781, the success of Popayán in maintaining order, despite its upland location contiguous to the zones of insurgency, was most significant.

An exception to the generalization under consideration occurred, however, in the city of Pasto, which possessed two of the Province of Popayán's fourteen militia companies. On June 22, Indians from surrounding villages joined Pasto's inhabitants in a violent protest against Deputy Governor José Ignacio Peredo's attempt to introduce a number of revenue measures, including the aguardiente monopoly. Peredo, who had earlier lectured Governor Beccaria on the wisdom of cultivating harmony with the creoles of the capital, had become Gutiérrez de Piñeres' agent for Popayán, and he now found himself in a difficult position. Under very suspicious circumstances, the Pasto cabildo, claiming popular duress, had petitioned (or warned) him to suspend the aguardiente monopoly; but, in an uncharacteristic display of determination, Peredo had refused to be dissuaded and rioting ensued. Despite the assistance of a small military escort, which killed or wounded several insurgents, Peredo was eventually forced to take refuge in a public building. The following day, however, his enemies succeeded in capturing him, and a mob of Indians beat him and four of his escort to death. Gabriel Valdés, the veteran sergeant of Pasto's militia and commander of the escort, managed to escape only by taking refuge in a monastery. The army later tried him for cowardice in the face of the enemy, but he claimed that his troops had found themselves without car-

32. Ibid.
33. Narváez to Flores, Santa Marta, August 26, 1781, ANC: MM, vol. 124, fols. 638–42. By this time Riohacha had created two mounted companies of disciplined militia (see chapter 6).
34. This force at one time comprised as many as 93 men. Beccaria to Flores, Popayán, July 2, 6, 1781, ANC: MM, vol. 19, fols. 908–15.
35. Cárdenas Acosta, *El movimiento comunal*, 2: 171–72.

tridges for their weapons and in consequence could do nothing. Valdés was later reinstated to duty but this time with the militia of Buga.

Action in Santa Fe rescinding the revenue measures ultimately quieted the tumult in Pasto, and, perhaps significantly, the insurrection did not spread.[36] Pasto's importance as an exception to the general peacekeeping role of the military is somewhat mitigated by the fact that its militia, along with that of Barbacoas, was the most neglected in the Province of Popayán. It had never really been established as an independent entity because of the absence of strong leadership from outside the community. It should also be remembered that Pasto, located midway between Quito and Popayán, was remote from any strong military base. In short, Pasto's military capability was not substantially superior to that of the other regions overrun by the Comuneros.

The fact that Quito remained at peace is of special interest because the presidency was flanked by revolutionary activity, not only on the one side by the Comuneros, but on the other by the famous Peruvian insurgent, Túpac Amaru. It is perhaps significant that Regent-Visitor José García de León y Pizarro, who also became president of the royal audiencia and commandant general, shared Flores' belief that military reform was a necessary adjunct to fiscal reform.[37] Apparently aware of Flores' desire to see the military reform extended and of the crown's reluctance to do so until the royal exchequer had been replenished, and also fully realizing that Quito was impoverished, he approached the problem of strengthening his military forces by indirect, but effective means. His requests for military concessions were always moderate and invariably cloaked with proper and extensively professed desires to avoid expenditures, but his deeds were highly ambitious. He first petitioned for merely three urban companies, two of these infantry and the other cavalry, for which authorization from Santa Fe was sufficient. He submitted this request on May 18, 1779, expressing concern for the potential problem of sedition. In his proposal, he specified that the members would, for the most part, be obliged to provide their own equipment and would deserve at least the criminal fuero.[38] A sympathetic Flores granted his approval on July 16, for which he received a warm letter of gratitude.[39] García Pizarro then proceeded to establish a militia similar in character to those of Guayaquil and Popayán. Instead of the three companies proposed, however, he raised two regiments, one of infantry and the other of dragoons, as well as a company of artillery.

---

36. The relationship of Peredo to the cabildo of Pasto, and its relationship with the June mob, are subjects which require further study. Governor Beccaria believed that the cabildo and the creole aristocracy were deeply involved in Peredo's death. Ibid., pp. 97–98; Sergio Elías Ortiz, *Agustín Agualongo y su tiempo*, pp. 37–43; militia salary list, January 1, 1785, ACC: Colonia, MI-5P, sig. 5932.

37. Royal order, September 16, 1779, ANC: MM, vol. 110, fol. 830.

38. J. García Pizarro to Flores, Quito, May 18, 1779, ANE: Pres., vol. 134, fols. 1–3.

39. Flores to J. García Pizarro, Cartagena, July 16, 1779, and reply, Quito, August 18, 1779, both in ANE: Pres., vol. 134, fols. 4–5.

The volunteer positions of captain were usually given to those who would uniform their own companies, with the president assuming the role of inspector. To supervise the formation of the new units and later to train the volunteer officers, he selected two officers from the city's regular companies.[40]

The outbreak of war with Great Britain provided President García Pizarro with the opportunity to press for additional concessions. In a communication of November 3, 1779, he expressed concern over the weakness of the armed forces of Guayaquil, and he emphasized the advantage of having a strong military force in the backlands to reinforce Guayaquil should it come under attack.[41] Although García Pizarro did not specifically request a reclassification of his units to disciplined, he sought authorization from the viceroy to select from the regular companies one veteran sergeant for each company and as many corporals as possible to staff the militia. In addition, he hoped for firearms and sabers to equip them.[42] Flores replied on January 5, 1780, that, although he did not have the authority to raise disciplined militia without the consent of Spain, he would, in view of the outbreak of war and emergency considerations, consent to García Pizarro's proposal and grant a disciplined classification for the new units on a provisional basis. He added, however, that for the time being he could not provide additional weapons.[43] Without further ado, the president then expanded the militia to the outlying provinces of Cuenca, Riobamba, Ibarra, Ambato, Guaranda, and Loja (see Table 5).[44]

As a consequence of García Pizarro's actions, Quito and its dependencies possessed a militia of at least partial combat capacity by the time the Comunero Rebellion swept through the undefended provinces of New Granada's interior. Ironically, José Ignacio Peredo had petitioned the president of Quito just nine days before his death for a detachment of troops to sustain an extension of his tax reforms southward into Barbacoas. García Pizarro responded affirmatively only to learn a few days later that Pasto itself was in a state of rebellion.[45] To contain the new sedition he quickly dispatched 150 militiamen from Quito to the Corregimiento of Ibarra, adjoining Pasto, and he also placed the newly organized militia of that jurisdiction on a program of intensive training and

40. J. García Pizarro to Flores, Quito, November 3, 1779, ANE: Pres., vol. 134, fols. 9–10; troop inspection report, Quito, August 17, 1783, ANE: Pres., vol. 194, fols. 55–58.
41. This argument seems sincere because at a later date he did dispatch detachments from Quito's militia to Guayaquil. J. García Pizarro to Flores, Quito, March 18, 1780, ANE: Pres., vol. 134, fols. 12–13.
42. Ibid., fols. 9–10.
43. Ibid, fol. 11.
44. Troop inspection report, Quito, August 17, 1783; J. García Pizarro to Flores, Quito, March 18, 1780; Colonel Manuel Guerrero to J. García Pizarro, Quito, June 27, 1783, ANE: Pres., vol. 203, fol. 126; Villalengua to Caballero y Góngora (copy), Quito, November 18, 1786, ANE: Pres., vol. 234, fol. 89.
45. Expediente on the request of Peredo for troops and ammunition, Quito and Pasto, June 1781, ANE: Pres., vol. 179, fols. 251–60.

preparation.[46] However, the trouble did not spread beyond Pasto as feared; nor did other areas within the presidency experience serious disorders. The question of whether the reformed military of Quito and the other regions of New Granada was really a decisive factor in containing the geographic scope of the great insurgency of 1781 can probably never be conclusively answered; but the correlation between military preparedness and domestic peace is impressive.

The government based its response to the Comunero Rebellion upon the conviction that the surest way to prevent future popular uprisings was greater military preparedness in potential trouble zones. This view, justified by the 1781 pattern of peace and rebellion, had been the argument developed by Flores early in his administration. The principal government reaction was not structured by Flores, however, but by Antonio Caballero y Góngora, the archbishop of Santa Fe. Flores, whose health had so deteriorated in Cartagena that he could not sign his own correspondence, had repeatedly begged for a replacement.[47] By 1782 he had served six years, but apparently because of the war, the crown had made no provision to relieve him. When finally convinced of the gravity of Flores' condition, the monarchy was forced to look inside New Granada for a replacement, selecting Field Marshal Juan Pimienta, governor of Cartagena, as interim viceroy.[48] Pimienta, however, became ill on the ascent to the capital and died there three days after his arrival. Pimienta's death left the viceregency in the hands of Caballero y Góngora, who by authority of a royal cédula of November 1777 was second to him in line for emergency succession.[49] No doubt in part because of his skillful performance during the Comunero Rebellion, the archbishop obtained full appointment as viceroy the following year.[50]

Caballero y Góngora was a tough, enlightened viceroy, who was eager to foster reform from above. Although perhaps too ambitious given the available resources, he was a most aggressive and imaginative administrator and represented the most advanced manifestation of the Enlightenment and the Bourbon reforms in New Granada. Included in his activities were a renewed effort to expand and enforce government monopolies, the drafting of a general plan for an intendant system of provincial administration, the organization of a mining reform commission, and a further liberalization of trade policy through

46. Expediente on the dispatch of troops to Ibarra, Quito and Ibarra, 1781, ANE: Pres., fols. 197–250; expediente on the death of Peredo, 1781, AGS: GM, legajo 7070.

47. Flores to Gálvez, Cartagena, October 5, 1779, October 22, 1781, and February 27, 1782, AGI: Santa Fe, legajo 578.

48. Royal cédula, November 26, 1781, AGI: Santa Fe, legajo 578. Flores recovered his health and later became viceroy of New Spain.

49. Caballero y Góngora to Gálvez, Santa Fe, June 19, 1782, and royal cédula of November 16, 1777, AGI: Santa Fe, legajo 1011.

50. Antonio Caballero y Góngora was the only civilian to serve as viceroy in New Granada. See Ernesto Restrepo Tirado, *Gobernantes del Nuevo Reyno de Granada durante el siglo XVIII*.

various commercial concessions to foreigners.[51] Despite his civilian background, he also became New Granada's most avid viceregal proponent of the military reform.

The archbishop-viceroy's administration (1782–89) also featured undertakings which, if not precisely part of the reform movement, were connected to the broader spirit of enlightened innovation. Under his auspices the famous botanical expedition of José Celestino Mutis first received official sanction.[52] An independently organized economic society for the advancement of applied learning was founded in Mompós in 1784 and obtained viceregal approval the same year, and plans for another were initiated in Quito.[53] The government conducted large-scale colonization enterprises on the coastal frontiers. And, in connection with the latter ventures, the viceroyalty greatly expanded its coast guard.[54]

There was nearly complete continuity between the regimes of Flores and Caballero y Góngora with respect to their views on the need for, and the function of, the militia and their outlook on the military in general. Both men were keenly aware of a weakening in the fabric of royal control, and they saw the emerging military as a solution to the problem of state power. Since Flores left no relación de mando, Caballero y Góngora summarized his predecessor's activities during the Comunero Rebellion and did so with deep sympathy and understanding. It is evident that he believed Flores was correct in his wish to establish a military force in the interior prior to tax reform and that, in a large measure, the failure to do so was responsible for the government's inability to control the events of 1781.[55] Caballero y Góngora, after all, had gone naked of power to Zipaquirá to capitulate to the Comuneros; he had seen the regime in Santa Fe forced to abandon honor for trickery and treachery; and, on several occasions, he had suffered personal insults at the hands of the Comuneros.[56] Once vested with the powers of viceroy, he moved decisively to strengthen the military establishment and to employ it to sustain the political prerogatives of royal administration.

On June 15, 1783, Caballero y Góngora submitted a proposal for royal consideration which envisioned an extensive shift of military resources from Cartagena to Santa Fe. He proposed a strengthening of the regular army of the viceregal capital through the creation of an auxiliary regiment, with a core of nine hundred men in nine companies, plus an additional six companies of fifty

---

51. Arthur P. Whitaker, "The Elhuyar Mining Missions and the Enlightenment," pp. 573–85; Caballero y Góngora, in *Relaciones de mando*, pp. 253–54, 257–59, 267–68.
52. Caballero y Góngora, p. 253; R. Frías, "La expedición botánica al Nuevo Reino de Granada," pp. 137–38.
53. R. J. Shafer, *The Economic Societies in the Spanish World (1763–1821)*, pp. 154–56, 168–77.
54. Caballero y Góngora, in *Relaciones de mando*, pp. 272–73.
55. Ibid., pp. 197–208.
56. Cárdenas Acosta, *El movimiento comunal*, 1:277, and 2:8, 41–42, 60–61.

men each, attached to the regiment but deployed in the important regional capitals and former rebel centers of Pamplona, Girón, Tunja, San Gil, Los Llanos, and Neiva. The archbishop also urged a reduction of the viceregal guard to a mere half company of cavalry, because it had proven largely useless for anything beyond ceremony. The disciplined militia would include a regiment of cavalry, with twelve fifty-man companies, and an infantry regiment of nine companies. Meanwhile, the veteran regiment of Cartagena, though retaining a full plana mayor, would be reduced to nine companies, and the sprawling militia would be condensed into two infantry regiments and one infantry battalion, two artillery companies, and two dragoon companies.[57] The crown quickly approved Caballero y Góngora's proposal.[58] In separate but related actions, it also resolved to preserve the controversial militia of Popayán and extended a general approval for the recently contrived militia of inland Quito.[59]

These measures dramatically refocused New Granada's military power toward the challenge of preserving domestic peace. The transfer of troops into the interior, especially the redeployment of a regular infantry battalion from strategic Cartagena, betrayed a deep erosion in the confidence of the crown in the fidelity of its vassals. The traditional bonds of loyalty and obedience that for so long had linked New Granada to the crown of Spain had beome dangerously strained. To fill this vacuum the army had been converted into an internal striking force, oriented toward achieving for the reforming Bourbon monarchy what its moral prestige and simple persuasion could not.

The experience of Peru during this same period provides an interesting contrast to that of New Granada. Peru had developed an extensive disciplined militia in its upland provinces before the Túpac Amaru Rebellion, but the authorities largely dismantled it once peace had been restored and thereafter depended mainly upon the regular army as an instrument for internal security. This course of action, taken in consultation with José de Gálvez, appears superficially to contrast sharply with the strategy employed in New Granada; however, there were sound underlying reasons for the differences. The militia of Peru, unlike that of New Granada, proved nearly worthless in combating insurgency. Further, the crown believed that the upland creole population, which dominated the militia, was deeply involved in the disorders.[60] In New Granada, as will be seen in the following chapter, the creole elite was also

57. The three militia infantry regiments envisioned in this plan differed from battalions only in their command and staff groups, which were larger, usually including both a colonel and lieutenant colonel, but they consisted of merely nine companies. Caballero y Góngora's proposal (hereafter cited as troop plan, Caballero y Góngora) can be found in AGS: GM, legajo 7089.

58. Royal order, March 6, 1784, ANC: MM, vol. 12, fols. 103–14; troop plan, Caballero y Góngora.

59. Royal order, April 6, 1783, AGI: Quito, legajo 574; royal order, November 15, 1783, ANC: MM, vol. 52, fols. 81–85.

60. Leon Campbell, "The Army of Peru and the Túpac Amaru Revolt, 1780–1783."

strongly implicated in the Comunero disorders. Unlike Peru, however, New Granada's capital was located in the uplands; consequently, there were enough Spanish-born subjects (bureaucrats, tax collectors, and the like) to staff a "safe" militia to complement the regular army in sustaining internal control, and there was an urgent need to do so.

The authorities, nevertheless, dared not develop a militia system in upland provinces which had been directly involved in the Comunero movement. The previously charted expansion of the military reform into the interior provinces of Antioquia, Pamplona, Tunja, and Mariquita was dropped because the inhabitants of those regions were too closely identified with the great rebellion. The new cavalry regiment did, however, contain components from Tunja and Sogamoso as well as from Boza, Cáqueza, Chocontá, and Zipaquirá.[61] At first appearance, this would seem to be a contradictory and dangerous move because of the course of the Comunero Rebellion, but actually the viceregal authorities did not appear particularly worried about possible sedition in the cavalry.

This lack of concern about further sedition can be traced to events which occurred during the tense and delicate negotiations at Zipaquirá. When the peace talks had threatened to collapse because radicals from the Comunero center of Socorro voiced a strong desire to seize Santa Fe, the Comuneros from Tunja and Sogamoso, together representing about one-third of the rebel army, had physically maneuvered themselves between the mass of the troops and the capital to block any advance.[62] The motive for this action is not entirely clear, but the Tunjans had always claimed to be acting in the interest of the crown. Indeed, when Tunja was first swept into the insurgency, the cabildo members, speaking for their city's inhabitants with whom they had met in open session, emphasized in a proclamation for royal authorities that they had submitted only because of coercion and that they hoped that in so doing they could function in the royal interest.[63] Tunja's council of Comunero leaders had also issued a similar proclamation.[64] Such professions of loyalty were commonplace throughout the course of the upheaval; the distinction of Tunja and Sogamoso was that they acted accordingly—or seemingly so—during the negotiations at Zipaquirá.

Elements of pure regional self-interest were also present in this chain of events. The Tunjans and Sogamosans were apprehensive that provincial political control might shift from their cities in favor of Socorro if Socorran

61. Zejudo to Caballero y Góngora, Santa Fe, September 1, 1783, ANC: MM, vol. 12, fols. 103–14.

62. Cárdenas Acosta, *El movimiento comunal*, 2: 8–12.

63. "Acta del cabildo abierto," Tunja, May 23, 1781, in Cárdenas Acosta, *El movimiento comunal*, 1: 245–48.

64. "Instrumento de exclamación," Tunja, May 17, 1781, in Cárdenas Acosta, *El movimiento comunal*, 1: 242–44.

forces seized the capital.[65] Archbishop Caballero y Góngora perceived this jealousy between the provincial capitals and Socorro, and he exploited it during the course of the Zipaquirá negotiations. When the Tunjans and Sogamosans moved to protect the capital, they were acting at his request, and he gave them much credit for their deed.[66] In the words of the archbishop: "Those of the districts of Tunja, Sogamoso, and San Gil, which comprised the considerable number of from five to six thousand men, adhered to my stipulation with Berbeo, and they performed this task against the sentiment of the opposition; for although the latter group outnumbered them, they possessed other advantages in as much as their troops were the finest of that army, the most formidable, and the most subordinate to their leaders. These assisted me vastly in my enterprise, either because the village of Socorro intended to promote itself at their expense in government, or because the most of them, especially those of Tunja and Sogamoso, came [to Zipaquirá] under coercion."[67] Significantly, Caballero y Góngora was the viceroy who raised the cavalry regiment.

As a clergyman, Antonio Caballero y Góngora lacked expertise in military affairs, but he found counsel in a trusted military officer, Lieutenant Colonel Anastasio Zejudo. Zejudo, whose career spanned the period of the military reform, was the most impressive officer of his time in New Granada. He arrived in Cartagena as sargento mayor of the newly created Fixed Infantry Regiment in 1773, and he served in the viceroyalty until his death in 1808. Born in Carmona near Seville in 1741, he was the son of Antonio Zejudo, who had served fifty-eight years in the Spanish army prior to his death in action in Portugal in 1762. Anastasio Zejudo had performed with distinction in the Regiment of León for seventeen years before his incorporation into the Fijo. He was promoted to lieutenant colonel in 1776 and served as interim governor of Riohacha in 1777.[68]

Anastasio Zejudo was a shrewd, highly motivated officer whose ambition could verge at times on ruthlessness. Although he managed to accumulate a fair number of personal enemies during his years of service, he was universally admired by those who were not in his way, and he unfailingly managed to obtain the friendship and respect of those in positions of influence. When he

65. Liévano Aguirre, Los grandes conflictos, 3: 48.

66. Cárdenas Acosta, El movimiento comunal, 2: 8.

67. Account of the happenings at Zipaquirá by Caballero y Góngora, June 1781, in Cárdenas Acosta, El movimiento comunal, 2: 9. Liévano Aguirre goes beyond regional differences and argues that class tensions also help to explain the Tunjan and Sogamosan behavior in that the powerful creole leadership of those jurisdictions sought only limited concessions from the royal administration, while fearing the possible social consequences of a popular invasion of Santa Fe led by radical Socorrans. Liévano Aguirre, Los grandes conflictos, 3: 44–52.

68. Service records, Auxiliary Infantry Regiment, December 1787, AGS: GM, legajo 7280; expediente on the conduct of Colonel Anastasio Zejudo, 1784–85, AGI: Santa Fe, legajo 950.

later acquired extensive personal military authority, Zejudo demonstrated a definite willingness to use it, leading him not infrequently into direct and sometimes shattering confrontations. The Emerging in the wake of the Comunero Rebellion, Zejudo was a dominant figure during the remainder of the military reform in New Granada, and, in the long run, he did much to bring some semblance of reason and order to the reform despite its chaotic early beginnings.

Zejudo's rise to prominence at the viceregal level resulted directly from his success in winning command of the army of the interior. When Flores ordered the 500-man expedition to Santa Fe in 1781, he placed Colonel José Bernet in command; Zejudo remained with the Fijo in Cartagena. Zejudo, however, enjoyed the confidence of Viceroy Flores, who had earlier seen him both handle a difficult assignment in Riohacha and conduct a revealing inspection of the militia of Cartagena. He also enjoyed the respect of both Governor Juan Pimienta and Lieutenant Governor Roque de Quiroga, and he had cultivated the friendship of Regent-Visitor Gutiérrez de Piñeres, who had taken refuge on the coast.[69] Colonel Bernet, who, it will be recalled, had been selected by Alejandro O'Reilly to command the Fijo on the basis of his record in Cuba, jealously mistrusted his subordinate, but he was personally vulnerable and easily outmaneuvered. Although a courageous combat officer, Bernet was a most inadequate peacetime leader. He despotically and corruptly exploited his troops; he failed to sustain proper levels of discipline; and he was himself chronically insubordinate to his superiors. Upon Bernet's expeditionary force's arrival in Santa Fe, its discipline collapsed, and much to the consternation of the archbishop, a number of embarrassing altercations with the local population followed.[70]

In early 1782, just before he was relieved, Flores ordered 200 troops withdrawn from Santa Fe, and, with the support of Gutiérrez de Piñeres, who returned to the capital at this time, he ordered Zejudo to replace Bernet. Flores acted on the pretext that the diminished Santa Fe mission did not require a full colonel. Once in Santa Fe, however, Zejudo quickly became the personal military advisor of Viceroy Caballero y Góngora, as well as commander of all the forces of the capital. Moreover, he applied for promotion to colonel, which he obtained in late 1783, and Caballero y Góngora selected him to command the newly formed Auxiliary Regiment.[71]

69. Ibid. Gutiérrez de Piñeres corresponded extensively with Zejudo on a personal basis, normally using the salutation "Amigo."
70. Expediente on the conduct of Colonel José Bernet, 1783–85, AGI: Santa Fe, legajo 951. Among his many offenses, Bernet extorted fees from his men in return for their rations and uniforms and for favors in his official reports and recommendations. Further, his personal abuse of individual enlisted men occasioned a jump in the desertion rate.
71. Expediente on the conduct of Colonel Anastasio Zejudo, 1784–85; service records, Auxiliary Infantry Regiment, December 1787; troop plan, Caballero y Góngora.

Bernet's protests over this turn of events and, specifically, over Zejudo's promotion drive ended his career in New Granada. Zejudo retaliated against the colonel by producing massive documentation which convincingly exposed Bernet's years of misconduct as commander of the Fijo. Roque de Quiroga, who had again become interim governor of Cartagena, joined in the attack on Bernet, accusing him of insubordination and dereliction of duty, and recommended that he be separated from his command. After earlier vetoing an application by Bernet for a governorship, Caballero y Góngora strongly supported Quiroga's recommendation in a December 1784 message to Spain, claiming that all prudent means of controlling Bernet had failed.[72] The crown consequently summoned Bernet to court with the intention of retiring him.[73] The colonel made the journey in mid-1786, but he died a short time after reaching Spain.[74] The case against Bernet was overwhelming; yet it is unlikely that anything would have been done about his misconduct had he not attempted to block the rise of Anastasio Zejudo.

Zejudo had been the immediate architect of the military reorganization proposed by the archbishop-viceroy in June 1783, and he was the officer who implemented it.[75] In organizing the new defenses of Santa Fe, Caballero y Góngora and Zejudo were able to build upon foundations already laid by Flores. When the latter dispatched the relief expedition to Santa Fe, he also began successful efforts to secure outside reinforcements; a battalion from the Regiment of the Crown, garrisoned in Havana, reached Cartagena in mid-1782. Caballero y Góngora summoned the battalion to Santa Fe in late 1783, and through the direction of Zejudo, he converted it into the core of the Auxiliary Regiment, although incorporating additional personnel from the Fijo.[76] Earlier Flores, while still viceroy, had also ordered Bernet as commander of the relief expedition of 1781 to organize an urban militia which might become the basis for a permanent disciplined militia.[77] By the time Caballero y Góngora became viceroy, Bernet had formed an infantry battalion which with little effort could be converted into a disciplined unit. Zejudo, functioning much the same as had the special commanders during earlier phases of the reform, formally placed the infantry on a disciplined footing in 1783, and he then

72. Expediente on the conduct of Colonel José Bernet, 1783–85.

73. Royal order, December 3, 1785, AGI: Santa Fe, legajo 951; royal order, August 18, 1786, AGS: GM, legajo 7089.

74. Caballero y Góngora to Gálvez, Cartagena, April 29, 1786, AGS: GM, legajo 7089; Deputy Governor Pablo de Arroyo to Gálvez, Cádiz, May 22, 1787, AGS: GM, legajo 7089.

75. Troop plan, Caballero y Góngora.

76. Ibid.; Colonel Basilio Gascón to Caballero y Góngora, Cartagena, September 26, 1783, ANC: MM, vol. 86, fols. 959–82; Quiroga to Caballero y Góngora, Cartagena, November 24, 1783, ANC: MM, vol. 30, fols. 387–422.

77. Bernet to Flores, Santa Fe, September 15, December 31, 1781, ANC: MM, vol. 12, fols. 1042–45, vol. 31, fol. 699.

proceeded to raise the proposed cavalry regiment.[78] Under these conditions, the organization of a permanent military establishment for the viceregal capital went smoothly and quickly.

In the following year, 1784, Caballero y Góngora ordered Zejudo to the coast to restructure the forces of Cartagena.[79] Despite the end of the war in 1783, the reduction of the Fijo to nine companies was a painful step because the reasons for its original expansion still remained valid. To be sure, the descent down the Magdalena from Santa Fe de Bogotá was quite rapid, and the Auxiliary Regiment could therefore assist in the event of a lengthy siege, but as a practical matter, one battalion was insufficient to garrison Cartagena, and Spain soon found itself again dispatching rotating units to the coastal stronghold (see chapter 6). Upon completing his commission on the coast, Zejudo escorted the excess veteran personnel to Santa Fe to complete the organization of the Auxiliary Regiment.[80]

A consolidation of the Cartagena militia had been long overdue. As will be recalled, various military authorities, including Viceroy Flores, had strongly advocated a more productive and efficient arrangement. On the eve of the war with Britain, the crown had commissioned Brigadier of Engineers Agustín Crame from Spain to conduct a general review of New Granada's Caribbean defenses and to prepare a strategy to be implemented in the event of hostilities. Crame's plan for Cartagena envisioned the employment of only the military units of the city of Cartagena itself, plus some 1,000 militiamen from the interior of the province—principally from the Mompós and Lorica districts—to work in reserve and to protect Cartagena's lines of communication with the interior.[81] The effect of this strategy was to render the maintenance of the other numerous, outlying units in the province unnecessary.

Zejudo reorganized both the white and pardo battalions of the provincial capital to encompass additional surrounding towns, including some in the district of Barranquilla on the Magdalena River to the east. This step reduced enlistment pressures by increasing the population base for the units, and, in effect, it amounted to a practical response to the discrepancies between their authorized and actual strength that had appeared during the war. In the south of the province, Colonel Zejudo organized a line of infantry companies from Mompós, the strategic river port, across the back country to Lorica in the

78. Caballero y Góngora to Zejudo, Santa Fe, May 8, 1783, ANC: MM, vol. 10, fols. 274–80; Zejudo to Caballero y Góngora, Santa Fe, July 14, September 1, 1783, ANC: MM, vol. 18, vols. 51–57, vol. 12, fols. 103–14. These units were formally approved by royal order of March 6, 1784, ANC: MM, vol. 10, fols. 743–44.

79. Service records, Auxiliary Infantry Regiment, December 1787.

80. Troop plan, Caballero y Góngora; Zejudo to Caballero y Góngora, Cartagena, June 26, 1784, ANC: MM, vol. 11, fols. 379–87.

81. Defense plan of Crame, Cartagena, December 29, 1778, ANC: MM, vol. 41, fols. 405–54.

west, into a regiment of all colors to protect Cartagena's lines of communication as prescribed by engineer Agustín Crame. As part of the same strategy, Zejudo also positioned two companies of dragoons in Lorica, where they could also assist in defending the western flank of the province from Indian invasions out of the Chocó and Darién regions.[82] The remaining units were demoted to an urban status, and were expected to provide replacements for the disciplined units.[83]

The net effect of Zejudo's measures was to reduce the authorized strength of the Cartagena militia from 7,230 men to merely 3,098, which included the nearly complete elimination of the militia of Barranquilla. (It will be recalled, nevertheless, that both battalions of the city of Cartagena maintained companies in Barranquilla.) Events to the east of Cartagena in the provinces of Santa Marta and Riohacha, however, facilitated this latter development. During the Indian wars of the late 1770s and the conflict with Great Britain, a disciplined militia of two regiments and two companies had sprung up there, considerably strengthening the approaches to the Magdalena Valley (see chapter 6). These units won royal approval in 1783, which further diminished the necessity of sustaining the numerous separate companies originally created by Pérez Dávila in eastern Cartagena. When reducing peripheral units to an urban status, Zejudo reassigned the numerous veteran advisors to the new militia establishments of New Granada, including those of Santa Marta, Santa Fe, and Quito.[84] Although newly created disciplined units in the viceroyalty totaled far more than those eliminated in Cartagena, no serious strain on regular troop resources developed, because Zejudo discontinued the position of veteran lieutenant and in the Presidency of Quito the various militia establishments continued to operate with a very low ratio of veteran advisors.[85]

When viewed as a whole, the significance of the reorganization of 1783–84 was profound. Insurgency from within had stimulated the fastest and the most comprehensive military reorientation in the history of the viceroyalty. Whereas the character of the military establishment had traditionally been coastal, it was now almost evenly balanced, and whereas royal authority had traditionally rested upon the fidelity of its vassals, it now rested squarely upon military force.

Archbishop Caballero y Góngora succinctly summarized this transition in

82. Quiroga to Gálvez, Cartagena, September 14, 1784, with copy of Caballero y Góngora to Quiroga, Santa Fe, March 25, 1784, AGI: Santa Fe, legajo 949; troop inspection report, Cartagena, July 1, 1784, AGI: Santa Fe, legajo 1156.

83. Urban militia inspection report, Cartagena, May 1787, ANC: MM, vol. 14, fols. 417–20, and vol. 15, fols. 107–32.

84. Quiroga to Gálvez, Cartagena, September 14, 1784.

85. It will be remembered that Guirior anticipated the official elimination of the veteran lieutenants by his actions in Guayaquil. Troop inspection report, Cartagena, July 1, 1784.

his relación de mando. "In the past, when the policing of the interior provinces, the administration of justice, and the authority of the King's Ministers, lay in the fidelity of the people, the military forces were concentrated in the maritime provinces. But, once the inestimable original innocence was lost, the government needed and the loyal vassals—which eventually came to include all of them—desired the establishment of military bodies in order to perpetuate order and tranquility."[86]

86. Caballero y Góngora, in *Relaciones de mando*, pp. 268–69.

5. The Army under Caballero y Góngora

BECAUSE THE CREOLE constituted the vital cultural center of New Granada, it is evident in retrospect that his participation in, and his identification with, the emerging military was indispensable, if, in the long run, a tradition of military elitism—inherent in the military constitution advanced by the reforms of Charles III and encouraged by the extensive political role assigned to the colonial army—were to take strong root in the colony.[1] On the other hand, the contrary could be postulated for those situations where the creole was excluded and alienated from the military system, which was in effect what happened nearly everywhere in New Granada except the Presidency of Quito. In the aftermath of the Comunero Rebellion, the government of Charles III, its confidence in the fidelity of its American vassals shaken, sought through policies developed by Viceroys Flores and Caballero y Góngora to exclude whenever possible the creole from military positions of primary responsibility in favor of the Spanish-born. As a consequence, not only the regular army but the disciplined militia as well came to appear to the creole as a foreign army of occupation and they invoked a fiercely hostile native resistance which blended dramatically into the earlier history of the military reform in the Governorship of Popayán. Although some creoles found meaningful identification within the military corporation, the army never came to enjoy the broad

1. McAlister, in The "Fuero Militar," has argued convincingly that a widespread dissemination of military privilege in New Spain led to the praetorian tradition of the Mexican military.

support which would have permitted militarism to become an enduring feature in the life of New Granada.

The decision to raise a large disciplined militia in the interior of New Granada involved the obvious risk of arming vassals of questionable loyalty. A militarily capable citizenry was a double-edged sword; in time of domestic crisis it might turn either way. Creoles had provided much of the Comunero leadership both in Socorro and in the other regions swept into the movement, and although the disciplined militia of Santa Fe was not positioned in an area directly associated with open insurgency, the authorities had suspected widespread sympathy and some collaboration in the viceregal capital.[2] Moreover, Flores was mindful of the recent events in North America which led to the independence of the thirteen English colonies. He correctly suspected the existence of a similar sentiment in New Granada, although he realistically believed that it lacked sufficient support to pose an immediate danger to the existence of the empire.[3] Thus, when Flores and Caballero y Góngora moved to establish military forces in the interior of New Granada, they found themselves compelled to proceed with extreme caution.

When Flores, in September 1781, ordered Bernet to raise the urban infantry battalion which preceded the disciplined regiment, he instructed him to select for enlisted men only those whose loyalty was clearly above suspicion. More important, in filling officerships Flores ordered Bernet to favor Spaniards on the assumption that their loyalty to the Spanish crown would surpass that of the American-born.[4] Flores' concern is illustrated in the following passage from his instruction to the colonel: "it is indispensable that you (as ordered in the original instructions and as repeated in those of August and here again) have exact information about the character of the men that are enlisted and of the confidence that can be had in them before proceeding with their training, in order to avoid the peril of augmenting the number of the enemy who will with instruction become skillful in the handling of arms; because, as I have been reminded by the cabildo of this city, the conspiracy that was discovered here and past events necessitate examining this matter with intense scrupulosity and circumspection; and with this knowledge, I once again reiterate that you must know who the people of distinction and the city's loyal vassals are, and what type of people should be rejected with the end of preventing those grave inconveniences that could result from enlisting some who will be difficult to dispense with later."[5]

2. Partial exceptions to this rule were cavalry companies in Tunja and Sogamoso. For an excellent treatment of the interplay between the Comuneros and their sympathizers in Santa Fe, see John L. Phelan, "La trayectoria enigmática de Manuel García Olano durante la revolución comunera."

3. Flores to Gálvez, Cartagena, July 11, 1781, AGI: Santa Fe, legajo 578.

4. Flores to Bernet, Cartagena, September 27, 1781, ANC: MM, vol. 49, fol. 103.

5. Ibid., fol. 71.

Caballero y Góngora refined the policy of favoring Spaniards over creoles by introducing a calculated tokenism. Although ordering a superiority of Spaniards in both number and rank, he envisioned sufficient creole participation to allay suspicions by the native-born of their exclusion from real influence and responsibility.[6] Thus, when Zejudo organized the officer corps of the two Santa Fe regiments, he contrived to place creoles at all officer levels while still preserving Spanish dominance. In both units the colonel was Spanish; the lieutenant colonel of infantry was a creole, that of cavalry a Spaniard. In the latter it is significant, however, that the two men who acted as squadron commanders along with the colonel and lieutenant colonel were creoles. In both units the highest placed captain was Spanish; the second was a creole. Overall, Spaniards dominated captainships six to three in infantry and six to two in cavalry. Because creoles prevailed in the lower offices, they slightly outnumbered Spaniards, thirty-six to thirty-four, in volunteer positions.[7] Thus, although creoles were highly visible in the new establishment, with some appearing in high offices, Spaniards controlled most key positions.

An interesting example of the execution of the archbishop-viceroy's policy was the case of Jorge Miguel Lozano de Peralta Maldonado de Mendoza, the first Marqués de San Jorge de Bogotá, who was probably the most distinguished creole in Santa Fe. Jorge Miguel Lozano possessed an immense fortune, much of it in land. He was the grandson of Oidor Jorge Miguel Lozano, who had established an entailed estate for his descendants and who had named him, his surviving male heir, first holder. The mother of the Marqués de San Jorge was Josefa de Caicedo y Villacís, through whom he had inherited the Dehesa de Bogotá, an entailed estate which dated from the sixteenth century and which covered roughly one-fourth of the savanna of Bogotá.[8] In accordance with his social status, Lozano had sought military titles, having served as sargento mayor in the urban militia; he also had exercised various civic responsibilities in the municipal government of Santa Fe. When Charles III authorized the creation of two titles of Castile in New Granada in 1771 to honor the birth of Prince Carlos Clemente, son of the princess of Asturias, Lozano had acquired one of them, becoming the Marqués de San Jorge de Bogotá. And, when the Comunero Rebellion threatened the viceregal capital, he had raised a special mounted company of noblemen at considerable per-

6. Troop plan, Caballero y Góngora, AGS: GM, legajo 7089.
7. The twelve companies of the cavalry regiment were divided into four squadrons of three companies each. In addition to the colonels and commanders on the command and staff group of the cavalry regiment, there were two creole and one Spanish flag bearers. There were seven creole and five Spanish lieutenants, and eight creole and four Spanish second lieutenants. In infantry there were one creole and one Spanish standard-bearers, five creole and four Spanish lieutenants, and five creole and four Spanish second lieutenants. Officer lists, Regiments of Militia Infantry and Cavalry of Santa Fe, 1783, AGS: GM, legajo 7089.
8. Camilo Pardo Umaña, *Haciendas de la sabana: Su historia, sus leyendas y tradiciones*, pp. 24, 217–21.

sonal expense, ostensibly to protect the viceregal palace and to patrol the streets of the city.[9]

The Marqués de San Jorge was not, however, an ideal royal subject. He exhibited a strong sense of personal independence, as well as an apparent dislike for the exalted status of the European-born. His arrogant failure to deliver a number of required fees connected to his title led the audiencia to suspend his claim to it in 1777, although he continued to use it.[10] More important, while he was making a conspicuous display of his loyalty to the crown at the head of his cavalry company during the desperate days of May 1781, the insurgents camped at Zipaquirá mysteriously named him one of four Comunero captains for Santa Fe. The authorities soon came to suspect that he was a hidden instigator of the rebellion and one of its silent leaders, although in view of the general pardon and perhaps for a lack of evidence they did not attempt legal action at that time.[11]

Lozano constituted a troublesome obstacle to the structuring of a secure militia. Although believed untrustworthy, he was too important to bypass, especially given his conspicuous record of military service. When Zejudo assumed command of the forces of Santa Fe, he found him still in command of the cavalry company, which Colonel Bernet had formally incorporated into the new emerging militia structure.[12] Zejudo's challenge was to move the marqués out of the militia without overtly betraying the government's fear of the creole elite.

Lozano soon provided Zejudo with the pretext he needed. A crisp, efficient, and an exacting officer, Zejudo was the kind of Spaniard that most antagonized the marqués. When, in May 1783, Zejudo ordered him to mobilize his company for immediate service, he balked three days before acting, claiming a lack of proper notification. Pronouncing Lozano quarrelsome, unstable, and unsuitable for military service, Zejudo, supported by Caballero y Góngora, omitted his name from the list of officers for the disciplined militia. He did, however, employ many men from Lozano's company as officers, and he attempted to disarm the Lozano family by appointing Jorge Miguel's son, José María, the future Marqués de San Jorge and a more pliable individual than his father, as cavalry squadron commander with the rank of lieutenant colonel. The marqués belligerently but unsuccessfully protested his exclusion from the militia, and his alienation from the colonial system was undoubtedly thereby reinforced.[13] The military authorities had managed, nevertheless,

9. Raimundo Rivas, "El Marqués de San Jorge," pp. 721–29.
10. Ibid., pp. 725–29.
11. Cárdenas Acosta, *El movimiento comunal*, 1: 28–29, 33, 59–60, 119–35.
12. Troop inspection report, October 1, 1781, ANC: MM, vol. 10, fols. 253–57.
13. Expediente on the plea of Jorge Lozano de Peralta, Marqués de San Jorge, 1784–85, AGI: Santa Fe, legajo 950. With the approval of Gálvez, Caballero y Góngora exiled Lozano to Cartagena in 1786, using his disputes with the audiencia as justification. He died there in 1793. Phelan, "La trayectoria enigmática," pp. 181–82.

to remove a troublesome individual who under normal circumstances should have been named colonel, and they had outwardly accomplished this objective on personal rather than social or political grounds.

Beyond placing Spaniards in key positions, government success in shaping a politically satisfactory militia officer corps seems doubtful. Of the creoles who served, the overwhelming majority claimed noble status, which at least indicates success in recruiting from the better creole families. In some instances these men, including Eustaquio Galavís, lieutenant colonel of infantry, had demonstrated solid political loyalty. As alcalde ordinario of Santa Fe and one of those commissioned along with Caballero y Góngora by the Junta General de Tribunales in Santa Fe to negotiate with the Comuneros, Galavís had achieved an unassailable record of faithful and able service to the monarchy. Moreover, he was also the son-in-law of Jorge Miguel Lozano de Peralta, which further aided in disguising the reasons for the exclusion of the marqués from officership.[14] On the other hand, it would have been most difficult for alienated or reluctant creoles to refuse officership at this time without raising suspicions concerning their fidelity, and there is some reason to believe that efforts to screen out the unfaithful failed. At the rank of cavalry lieutenant, for example, served the nephew of Pedro Valencia, Gaspar, who held a position in the Santa Fe mint.[15] More significant, among the junior officers there were at least eleven creoles, who later emerged as active figures in the struggle for independence. In addition, both Jorge Tadeo Lozano, son of the marqués and later the first president of Cundinamarca, and Joaquín Ricaurte, famed general of the revolutionary armies, were subsequently recruited as second lieutenants.[16] While these facts prove nothing directly concerning political attitudes in 1783, they at least raise the suspicion that not all the creole officers enthusiastically embraced the purpose of the disciplined militia, and they do demonstrate the prudence of the archbishop-viceroy's Spanish-oriented approach toward fashioning the system.

The Spanish portion of the officer corps was derived largely from bureaucrats, revenue officers, and merchants. Caballero y Góngora's official secretary, Juan Casamayor, acted as colonel of cavalry, while Manuel López de Castilla, an Andalusian noble with extensive previous militia service in Peru,

14. Cárdenas Acosta, *El movimiento comunal*, 1: 205 ff.; Rivas, "El Marqués de San Jorge," p. 747.

15. Expediente on the petition of Pedro Agustín de Valencia, 1777, AGI: Santa Fe, legajo 556.

16. The eleven officers were Primo and Pedro Groot, Pantaleón Gutiérrez, Pedro Lastra, Pantaleón Santa María, Antonio Baraya, José Ortega y Mesa, José Arce, José María Ricaurte, Justo Castro, and José Ayala. It is also noteworthy that both brothers of the famed revolutionary Antonio Nariño, José and Juan, were second lieutenants in the infantry regiment. Officer lists, 1783; militia officer appointments, Santa Fe, June 5, 6, 1787, AGS: GM, legajo 7075; Rivas, "El Marqués de San Jorge," p. 730; M. Leonidas Scarpetta and Saturnino Vergara, *Diccionario biográfico de los campeones de la libertad de Nueva Granada, Venezuela, Ecuador i Perú, que comprende sus servicios, hazañas i virtudes*.

acted as colonel of infantry. At the company level, eight captains, seven lieutenants, and seven second lieutenants were government employees by 1789, nearly all of them from the royal treasury.[17] Because their occupations frequently were transient in nature, the Spanish officers experienced a relatively high turnover rate, which prompted a need to promote Spaniards from the lower ranks and to recruit others in order to preserve and improve upon the desired social balance. This situation necessarily led to the frequent bypassing of able creoles, which must have further exacerbated social tensions.[18] On another level, the veteran cadres, which supervised the development of the militia, were overwhelmingly Spanish. The viceroy's own nephews, Gerónimo Segovia and Juan José Caballero, served as sargentos mayores of infantry and cavalry respectively, which, although indicating a high degree of nepotism, also reflects the close personal connection that Caballero y Góngora cultivated with the militia.[19]

Despite the danger of arousing further creole antagonism through discriminatory policies, the government could not relax its security precautions. In 1784 it received word that an Italian ship captain, Luis Vidalle, and two unknown companions, who claimed to speak for the Comuneros, had gone to England to seek military and political assistance. This incident was in fact a minor occurrence if measured by any real danger to the empire; but, given the frightening dimensions of the events of 1781 and the example of the English colonies, the authorities could ill afford to take chances. As a result, during 1784–85 the government maintained an intense vigil in the ports of Cartagena, Santa Marta, Panama, and Guayaquil to arrest any possible infiltration of men and supplies, and Colonel Anastasio Zejudo was commissioned to lead a special expedition of 300 men into dangerous Indian territory on the Riohacha Peninsula for the same reason.[20] Under these circumstances it was hardly feasible to hand over the militia to creoles.

17. Ezpeleta to Valdés, Santa Fe, September 15, 1789, AGS: GM, legajo 7089.

18. Unfortunately, the authorities did not prepare service records for these units and consequently it is not possible to ascertain fully the composition of the officer corps during the late 1780s. However, later proposals to fill officer vacancies reflected the same kind of concern over social status as the original recommendations. Thus, while it is impossible to construct a complete picture, enough evidence is available to demonstrate a clear trend. Compare the officer lists, 1783, of Santa Fe, with officer listings in the troop review reports for the same units, June 6, 1787, and see officer appointments, 1787–88, AGS: GM, legajo 7075. The meager level of creole captainships remained stable, but significant erosion occurred at the level of lieutenant as the decade progressed.

19. It was not unusual for viceroys to place relatives in military offices, although Caballero y Góngora was particularly ambitious in that his nephews reached sargento mayor while still very young. Caballero y Góngora to Gálvez, Cartagena, November 28, 1786, and royal orders of May 23, 1786, and March 21, 1787, AGS: GM, legajo 7089.

20. Cárdenas Acosta, *El movimiento comunal*, 2: 224–67. A number of historians believe that Vidalle was an emissary of Juan Francisco Berbeo and Jorge Lozano de Peralta. Ibid., p. 256; see also Manuel Briceño, *Los Comuneros: Historia de la insurrección de 1781;* expediente on secret security measures, 1783–84, AGI: Santa Fe, legajo 578.

The disciplined militia of Santa Fe quickly became the center of a heated controversy. From its inception with an urban status under Colonel Bernet, it suffered harsh criticism from the municipal government. The position of the Santa Fe cabildo toward the militia was essentially the same as that assumed by the magistrates of Popayán during the previous decade. The cabildo argued that an armed citizenry threatened community stability and simply could not be trusted politically. It reminded the viceregal authorities that when the city was under siege from the Comuneros hardly a soul could be found who would raise a hand to defend it; yet now, large numbers of inhabitants eagerly sought membership in the militia, many of whom were related to people believed to have been conspirators. The magistrates also complained about disorderly conduct by volunteers following their drills and dutifully reported one clearly seditious shout of "Long live the King, down with his bad government." The cabildo argued that the employment of more regular troops instead of a militia would both provide better security and prove less disruptive of community life.[21] There may have been some substance to these complaints and fears, but a more fundamental issue was the intrusion of the military fuero into the Santa Fe community, which removed a sizeable portion of the population from the jealous authority of the cabildo and the native aristocracy, placing it under Spanish officers who were closely associated with the central government.

Probably because of its role as a political instrument of the reforming Bourbon monarchy, the military also aroused widespread popular hostility, which frequently was manifested through public ridicule. Colonel Juan Casamayor of the cavalry regiment was so stung by jest and satire directed at his command that he ordered an investigation. The probe focused on events in Zipaquirá, where there was one cavalry company and where rumors of disrespectful behavior abounded. The investigation, as anticipated, uncovered widespread popular disdain for the militia, which found expression through indirect but perceptible means. A current vogue in the community, for example, was to give black servants or dogs names such as "colonel" or "soldier." People sang anti-military satires. And in one instance, an ass adorned with militia-like epaulets had been led into the delighted town. Although no judicial processes resulted from the improprieties uncovered by Casamayor's inquiry, it did confirm the unpopularity of the militia experiment.[22]

Confronted with such deep-seated hostility, military reformers were particularly hard pressed to educate their new recruits and the citizenry to the honor, glory, and advantages of military life. This challenge often moved the

21. Expediente on the formation of the urban militia of Santa Fe, 1781–82, ANC: MM, vol. 31, fols. 694–725.
22. Expediente on the investigation into indecorous behavior in Zipaquirá, 1784, ANC: MM, vol. 4, fols. 38–51.

militia leadership to an aggressive, sometimes distorted, assertion of military privileges, which further exacerbated anti-military sentiments. In Santa Fe, for example, a clash erupted between Lieutenant Justo Castro of the infantry regiment and Alcalde Miguel Galindo, who apparently was antagonized by Castro's participation in the militia. When approached by the sister of the lieutenant concerning an investigation into the theft of a piece of diamond jewelry, the alcalde rudely stunned the lady by ordering her not to pester him further and by insulting the honor of her brothers, including Lieutenant Castro, whom he termed a "concubine-ridden bum." This insult prompted Castro to seek redress through the military jurisdiction under his active fuero. Eager to assert military prestige, both Colonel Manuel López de Castilla and the auditor de guerra supported his suit, although there was in fact no provision in military law which authorized the military prosecution of civil magistrates. Probably aware of their feeble legal position, however, the militia authorities took the precaution of consulting the viceroy as captain general before actually attempting to arrest the alcalde.

Despite his close association with the military reform, Caballero y Góngora, who after all was not a military man, was sensitive to the difficulties caused by the creation of a privileged militia in the interior of New Granada, and during his administration he arbitrated between the rival jurisdictions with equanimity. In this instance, he instructed the militia that it had no authority whatever to prosecute Galindo, although complaints could be registered during the magistrate's residencia, and the matter ended there. Nevertheless Galindo's original behavior and the audacious attempt of the militia to prosecute him illustrate the ill will between the rival jurisdictions and their propensity to clash frivolously.[23]

An incident in Cogua, an outlying village which maintained one company, further illustrates the dispute among military and civil authorities. A distinguished soldier, José Antonio Forero, disappointed over the handling of the sale of some wheat and brandishing his fuero, profanely abused by word Alcalde Francisco Javier Forero, a distant cousin. In the ensuing judicial processes, Corregidor Carlos Burgos of Zipaquirá, obviously ruffled by the arrogance of those immune from the reach of ordinary justice, came to the defense of the offended magistrate and angrily demanded satisfaction for ordinary justice. "Some of the individuals enlisted in the newly created militia companies of this district . . . made insolent by a defective knowledge of their privileges and considering themselves shielded with militia arms—not in order to assist the justices and sustain their authority, the end for which they have been established in this kingdom—belittle and affront authority with them, refusing directives and responding in an insolent manner that they do not

23. Expediente on the petition of Lieutenant Justo Castro, 1785, ANC: MM, vol. 6, fols. 750–63.

have to obey, because they [the ordinary justices] are not their judges. . . ."
Because the incident occurred in the presence of much of the community, the
distinguished soldier could hardly deny the nature of his conduct toward the
alcalde, but he did emphasize his conviction that the alcalde had no authority
whatever over him in the matter. In fact, the militiaman was in error, because
abuse of royal justice constituted a case of desafuero. In any event, the appeal
reached Caballero y Góngora who once again had little choice but to act against
the militia, assessing Forero a penalty of fifteen days in jail.[24]

By far the most dramatic clash between military and civil authority occurred
in Zipaquirá in 1785. This incident vividly illustrates the natural propensity
of the rival jurisdictions to come into conflict, their deep-seated rivalry, and
their mutual vindictiveness, and it reinforces the supposition that harmony
was the exception, not the rule. Finally, it demonstrates that the vengeful attitude of ordinary justice extended even to the royal audiencia.

The immediate conflict derived from acts perpetrated against Alcalde Juan
de Dios Ramírez, who was also a corporal of the Zipaquirá militia company.
As a soldier, Ramírez performed most unsatisfactorily. He was a chronic
complainer and a frequent absentee from both Sunday drills and the special
training sessions held on market days for sergeants and corporals. Such behavior not only precluded proper military discipline for himself, but set a bad
example for the ranks as well. As a consequence of reports concerning Ramírez'
misconduct, José María Lozano, who at that time was acting regimental commander, issued a written order on January 9, 1785, for his disciplinary con-
finement in military prison. Residing in Santa Fe, Lozano acted without the
knowledge that Ramírez had recently acquired the position of alcalde ordinario of Zipaquirá. The officer charged with conducting the arrest was Second
Lieutenant Francisco de Moros, a personal enemy of Ramírez and the chief
source of complaints about his military behavior.

Moros proceeded against Ramírez on January 12, a market day when the
corporal was again absent from training. By what appears to have been a total
coincidence, both the corregidor of Zipaquirá, Carlos Burgos, and his assistant
had gone to the nearby settlement of Nemocón. Consequently, the dispensation of justice during the day's business transactions reverted to the new
alcalde. It was during Ramírez' execution of the duties of this office in the
central plaza that two cavalrymen acting under orders from Second Lieutenant
Moros apprehended him. Pointing to the insignia that he bore—cape, hat,
and staff—as proof that at the moment he personified royal justice, Alcalde
Ramírez vigorously protested, but to no avail. With typical disregard for the
dignity of ordinary justice, the militiamen roughly escorted him to Moros who
awaited in a nearby store. A violent shouting match ensued, including lan-

24. Expediente on the cause of Alcalde Ordinario Francisco Javier Forero, 1784–85, ANC:
MM, vol. 53, fols. 575–97.

guage so vile from Moros that in the subsequent examination one witness to the occasion declined to repeat it out of deference for modesty. The scandalous spectacle soon attracted a large crowd of onlookers, which much to its astonishment witnessed Second Lieutenant Moros strip Alcalde-Corporal Ramírez of his insignia and hurl it to the ground. Indeed, for a moment it appeared that the military delegation might go so far as to bind the beleaguered alcalde with ropes, but the timely intervention of Moros' own mother prevented that excess. An even greater humiliation followed, nevertheless, for the militiamen disdainfully dragged Ramírez off to the military jail and placed him in stocks where he remained in public shame.

The arrest of Juan Ramírez was a serious offense against ordinary justice regardless of the validity of the military charges against him. Not only had an alcalde been abused by word and deed during the execution of his duties, but royal insignia had been desecrated. These acts were direct violations of the Cuban reglamento which, in addition to provisions regarding interference with ordinary justice, stipulated that alcaldes, if members of the militia, were not subject to military jursidiction.[25] Moreover, the fact that the incident occurred in public compounded the gravity of the abuses. Upon his return to Zipaquirá, Corregidor Burgos, who had earlier resolutely defended ordinary justice in Cogua, immediately filed a protest with the royal audiencia. Commander Lozano, for his part, when receiving word of the affair, ordered Ramírez' release and thereby seemingly extricated himself from what was certain to be a dangerous entanglement.

The audiencia initiated correctional procedures by instructing Burgos to gather evidence to substantiate his complaint. It then directed him to obtain a statement from Moros explaining his actions. Contrary to expectations, the second lieutenant lengthened the list of complaints against himself by refusing to testify on the grounds that the audiencia had no jursidiction in matters pertaining to military personnel. No friend of military privilege, the audiencia was duly incensed at the arrogance and disobedience of the second lieutenant. In a communication to the viceroy on April 30, 1785, it demanded punitive measures, warning that if capricious insubordination of this kind were not vigorously stifled there would be no end to jurisdictional conflicts, which would undermine the administration of justice.

Viceroy Caballero y Góngora was on the coast directing a campaign against the Indians of Darién (see chapter 6) and consequently could not respond until June. When he did act, he ordered Moros to comply with the audiencia's directive and asked for clarifying material from Lozano as well. Moros complied but noted he was submitting to the audiencia only upon orders of the viceroy as captain general. In any case, he was unable to justify satisfactorily his excesses, offering only the feeble explanation that the arrest had been ordered by

25. *Reglamento . . . de Cuba*, chap. 2, art. 26.

his superior officer and that extreme measures had been necessitated because of Alcalde Ramírez' resistance. Commander Lozano contributed nothing more than proving that Ramírez was in fact a discipline case for the militia, thereby justifying his action in ordering the arrest. In August, by which time all evidence was before him, and agreeing with the audiencia that the new evidence in no way altered the nature of Moros' offenses, Caballero y Góngora sentenced the second lieutenant to four months in prison. Upon completion of his sentence Moros was to appear before the audiencia to give evidence that he had repented for his defiance of royal justice.

Meanwhile, the *fiscal* (prosecuting attorney) of the audiencia pressed for further satisfaction. Claiming that Commander Lozano's role in the humiliation of royal justice was far from clear, he asked that the officer be ordered to exonerate himself. Here the fiscal appears to have acted out of spite. The relationship between the audiencia and the Lozano family had been strained; it will be recalled that the high tribunal had stripped the senior Lozano of his title of marqués just a few years earlier. Responding in September, Lozano conclusively explained his actions but failed to produce a specifically requested letter from Moros, although this was irrelevant to his case. Vengefully seizing upon this omission, the fiscal sought to reopen the entire incident by strongly recommending that the cavalry commander be severely punished for his failure to comply with superior orders. In so doing he also warned that unless superior authorities pursued a strict policy, the creation of the new militia would bring about the downfall of the viceroyalty. Caballero y Góngora realistically declined to pursue the matter, although he did issue a mild rebuke to Lozano for failing to maintain proper records.

The Zipaquirá episode was still not finished, however, for a sequel developed in the meantime. Although in the Ramírez-Moros case justice appears to have been dispensed fairly, the decision could not, and indeed did not, instantly soothe all ruffled sentiments. Local friction continued, and to aggravate matters Alcalde Ramírez, apparently hoping to regain face, reportedly persisted in treating the militia in a most high-handed fashion. Events climaxed in early August 1785, when Sergeant Ignacio Nieto threatened to break the alcalde's staff over his head. Legal action similar to that of the previous case ensued and persisted into the following year before a conclusion was reached. On June 26, 1786, Viceroy Caballero y Góngora sentenced Sergeant Nieto, like Second Lieutenant Moros before him, to imprisonment for disrespect to ordinary justice, although for the lesser term of three months.[26]

The jurisdictional clashes which reached the viceroy were only the most sensational expressions of the struggle between the military and ordinary jursidictions. On a lower level, daily friction, bickering, and ill will were the

26. Expediente on the judicial dispute in Zipaquirá, 1785–86, ANC: MM, vol. 26, fols. 35–70, and vol. 34, fols. 48–130.

rule rather than the exception. Although in some instances ambiguities in military law, or an ignorance of it, may have contributed to these conflicts, a spirit of good will and cooperation would certainly have prevented most difficulties. Quite predictably, however, such virtues were conspicuously absent. Chafing under the weight of popular scorn and anxious to expand its corporate prestige, the militia belligerently asserted its fuero, while municipal authorities defended their prerogatives with equal jealousy. As a consequence, the military reform, rather than strengthening respect for law as anticipated, worked to foment disorder and to undermine the power and prestige of municipal magistrates, who were the most visible symbol of royal authority.

No overt relationship appeared between social origins and an advocacy of either the military or ordinary jurisdictions in these disputes. Indeed, in the incidents described, most of the participants on both sides were creoles, the most notable example being the Forero family of Cogua. An underlying social factor did nevertheless exist, closely connected to the native hostility toward the reforms of Charles III. Much of the creole community regarded the militia as a threat to their traditional independence and widespread de facto immunity from effective royal administration. Indeed, those creoles who willingly served in the militia must have appeared as collaborators, a consideration which may well explain why the harshest jurisdictional conflicts in Santa Fe pitted creole against creole. Under these circumstances, significant creole identification with the emerging military was limited, and an acceptance of military elitism failed to take strong root in the hostile cultural heartland of New Granada.

In the Province of Popayán the struggle between the militia leadership on the one hand and the creole aristocracy and the cabildo on the other continued into the 1780s, although at a more subdued level. It will be remembered that during the war with Britain the special militia commander, Captain Diego Antonio Nieto, had transferred to Cartagena, leaving the aging governor, Pedro Beccaria, to manage alone while besieged by charges of misconduct and malfeasance in office. The fortunes of Governor Beccaria improved markedly, however, as a result of the Comunero Rebellion. Not only did his stature increase because of his decisive action in halting disorders during the crisis but his judgment as a resolute defender of the militia system seemed vindicated. In expression of its gratitude, the crown promoted Beccaria to lieutenant colonel and as a special concession excused him from payment of the *media anata* tax.[27] In addition, it ordered Viceroy Caballero y Góngora to console the governor concerning his earlier predicaments. The local creole aristocracy of the provincial capital found itself at a momentary psychological

---

27. The *media anata* was the payment to the royal treasury of one-half of an officeholder's first year's salary.

disadvantage and was forced prudently to subdue its overt opposition to the military reform. Neither Beccaria nor the militia ever won acceptance, however. The governor found himself so completely ostracized socially that he bitterly characterized the province as a "purgatory" and a "vale of tears." He begged repeatedly for a transfer, but Spain, which could ill afford to lose the services of a faithful vassal in that hostile land, kept him there until his death in 1788.[28]

Despite the tensions that simmered between the army of the interior and the creole aristocracy, New Granada remained outwardly peaceful for the duration of Caballero y Góngora's regime. The archbishop-viceroy and the royal treasury vigorously advanced revenue reform in the troubled upland provinces, as elsewhere, with highly visible results. Annual income in the viceroyalty, which had languished around the 1 million peso mark during the 1770s, rose to approximately 3,354,000 pesos by the late 1780s. Prominent contributors to this increment were the expanding tobacco and aguardiente monopolies and customs receipts, while the numerous other sources of royal income generally benefited from more zealous collection.[29] Although the reformed army occasionally provided direct support for revenue officials as in the ill-fated mission of José Ignacio Peredo in Pasto, its normal role was simply to deter violent resistance by its continuing presence in the uplands, where troops stood ready to crush any dangerous protest.

On the coast, the disciplined militia of Cartagena, as restructured by Colonel Anastasio Zejudo in 1784, closely resembled that of Santa Fe in the social composition of its officer corps. Men of European birth occupied all volunteer positions of command, including the offices of colonel and lieutenant colonel of the two regiments of whites and all colors and the two captainships of the dragoon companies of Corozal. Moreover, as in Santa Fe, Spanish captains outnumbered creoles three to one in the two infantry regiments, while creoles dominated the lower officerships.[30] The new policy of conscious discrimination, however, actually seems to have produced little visible change over the previous decade with its de facto favoritism of Spaniards. In the Regiment of White Militia, for example, which was the only unit to maintain service records during both periods, social composition remained nearly constant.[31]

28. Expediente on the causes of Governor Pedro Beccaria, 1776–88, AGI: Quito, legajo 238.

29. Caballero y Góngora, in *Relaciones de mando*, pp. 256–61.

30. The company officers of the two infantry regiments and two dragoon companies totaled fourteen Spanish captains, three creoles; four Spanish lieutenants, six creoles; and seven Spanish second lieutenants, eight creoles. At the time the service records were formulated there were a number of vacancies and the regiment of whites still had not replaced its veteran lieutenants with volunteers, which accounts for the uneven figures. Adding the volunteers of the *plana mayor*, Spanish officers outnumbered creoles twenty-eight to seventeen. Service records, Cartagena, June 1785, AGI: Santa Fe, legajo 1156.

31. In 1776, the Militia Battalion of White Infantry contained six Spanish captains, one creole; four Spanish second lieutenants, four creoles. In 1785, as the Militia Regiment of White Infantry,

More subtle discrimination appeared in the frequent inability of creole officers to advance despite a relatively high turnover of Spaniards and in the incredible failure of any of seven creole cadets who were engaged in training during 1776 to secure positions in the units organized by Zejudo. As in the interior, the veteran officers assigned to the planas mayores, including those attached to the pardo battalion, were nearly solidly Spanish by birth.[32]

The type of resistance to the fuero that flared in the interior of New Granada did not, however, develop on the coast during the 1780s. This calm can be explained at least partly by the traditional presence and acceptance of a European-dominated army in Cartagena with an overt responsibility to repel foreign invasion rather than merely to sustain royal authority. Moreover, the crisis over pardo privilege abated considerably. The passage of time after the initial shock undoubtedly contributed to this quiet, but there were other important considerations as well. The reorganization of 1784 reduced the number of pardo units by twelve companies and, hence, substantially curtailed the extent of the disruptive impact of pardo privileges (compare Table 4 to Table 6). Also, during the middle and late 1780s the pardo militiaman was bearing a disproportionate share of combat duty in the Indian wars in Darién, a consideration which undoubtedly made his privileges appear less offensive to creoles who managed to remain in Cartagena because of the pardo's sacrifices (see chapter 6).

The controversy over the status of transient merchants that had developed in the previous decade continued during the eighties. It will be recalled that militia colonel Juan Fernández de Moure, supported by Flores, had strongly objected to Viceroy Guirior's original dispensation for merchants from militia duty, but that in 1778 the crown had sustained the exemption for those who were transients. Despite this clear royal decision, however, Colonel Moure refused to permit the matter to rest.

Moure was an immensely wealthy merchant, who had acquired a certificate of hidalguía and who had demonstrated a strong sense of public responsibility through the building of roads and bridges and by occasionally serving in municipal offices.[33] As colonel of the white militia, Moure emerged quickly as a dogged defender of military prerogatives and privileges; he belligerently opposed not only the merchant exemption but the broad recruitment prerogatives of the matrícula de mar as well. Moure's one weakness as a spokesman for the militia was his quarrelsome nature, which was too frequently

it contained six Spanish captains, one creole; four Spanish second lieutenants, two creoles. It will be recalled that the 1776 records included only the six companies based in the city of Cartagena itself. Ibid.; service records, Cartagena, December 1776, AGI: Santa Fe, legajo 946.

32. Service records, Cartagena, December 1776; service records, Militia Regiment of White Infantry of Cartagena, December 31, 1790, AGS: GM, legajo 7280.

33. Flores to Gálvez, Cartagena, March 31, 1780, AGI: Santa Fe, legajo 948.

manifested by an unfortunate lack of diplomatic skill and an obtuse ability to alienate those of superior authority.[34]

The arrival of the war in 1779 presented a psychologically favorable moment to assert the cause of the armed forces, so Colonel Moure reopened his campaign against the merchant exemption. This time he shifted ground to the question of the fuero militar, which he sought to enhance at the expense of ordinary justice and particularly the business community. In an appeal to Viceroy Flores, Moure argued that the fuero as currently defined was insufficient and appealed for a reinterpretation to the effect that crimes, commercial contracts, and other obligations consummated prior to enlistment would be included under military competency. Such latitude would have dramatically enhanced the judicial advantage that merchants serving in the militia would enjoy over outsiders and thereby indirectly coerce the latter into entering the militia for their own self-protection, especially since militiamen often received preferential treatment in their own tribunals. Colonel Moure's arguments notwithstanding, however, no legal basis existed for such claims. Obligations contracted prior to enlistment were plainly cases of desafuero, and the viceroy had no choice but to refuse his petition.

Flores did, however, sympathetically suggest that the colonel might wish to take the matter to Spain.[35] Moure did so in June 1780, arguing that a narrow interpretation of the fuero had hurt morale and had contributed to the present wartime shortage of personnel. In the same petition, he asked for a curtailment of coast guard recruitment prerogatives as well. In a second communication in March 1781, he renewed his plea, this time harshly criticizing all of his military superiors, including Lieutenant Governor Roque de Quiroga, Governor Juan Pimienta, and Viceroy Manuel Flores, for failing to sustain his interpretation of the fuero.[36]

In the matter of recruitment, the crown aided the militia by declaring that militiamen could not be deprived of their fishing rights or of the use of boats and canoes to transport produce to Cartagena simply because they were not registered in the matrícula de mar.[37] This decision eliminated a major obstacle to militia recruiting and the maintenance of authorized troop levels. The crown, confronted by the exigencies of war, however, elected to skirt the fuero issue that Moure presented. It ruled that military justice should be governed by a newly promulgated reglamento for the militia of Campeche; this action only increased confusion, because the new code added nothing of substance regarding Moure's issue but at the same time left the colonial authorities un-

34. By 1781 he had clashed with Roque de Quiroga, Juan Pimienta, and Manuel Flores. Fernández de Moure to Gálvez, Cartagena, March 30, 1781, AGI: Santa Fe, legajo 948.

35. Expediente on the militia fuero, Cartagena, 1780, ANC: MM, vol. 17, fols. 781–85.

36. Fernández de Moure to Gálvez, Cartagena, June 4, 1780, and March 30, 1781, AGI: Santa Fe, legajo 948.

37. Royal order, September 22, 1781, AGI: Santa Fe, legajo 948.

certain as to the actual royal intention. The new legislation did employ the term "all" in reference to the cases which pertained to military jurisdiction, and Colonel Moure shrewdly demanded a literal interpretation of that clause. Caballero y Góngora, lacking clear guidance in the matter, granted this concession by a decision of June 12, 1784.[38] Colonel Moure and the militia of Cartagena momentarily had scored a major victory over their rival jurisdictions.

Moure's triumph proved only temporary, however. Three years later, Miguel Antonio Anzuategui, the mercantile magistrate of Guayaquil, challenged the right of military tribunals to hear commercial causes of any sort, contending that all such actions pertained to mercantile tribunals. To support his case, he cited a royal cédula of September 28, 1779, stemming from a dispute in Santiago de Chile, which denied the military any jurisdiction whatever in mercantile causes. The crown had not circulated this decision throughout the empire and, for that matter, had even contradicted it in the ruling made shortly thereafter for Cartagena. Yet it now seemed to represent a strong precedent for merchant privileges and forced the viceregency once again to review its policy toward the commercial community.

By this time, 1787, the exaltation of the military, which had characterized the period immediately following the war and the Comunero Rebellion, had begun to fade, and the trouble-making capacity of the military fuero had become even more evident. Furthermore, Moure's intemperate behavior had eroded whatever personal sympathy his long list of public services might have generated. In his decision, Caballero y Góngora reversed his previous policy and stunned militia leadership by declaring that causes pertaining to commercial affairs were outside the military jurisdiction and subject only to mercantile tribunals. Colonel Moure quickly appealed the viceroy's decision to Spain but the action stood.[39] The ruling by Caballero y Góngora had the effect of reestablishing the independence of the wholesale merchant class of Cartagena from military authority, thus frustrating the attempt of Colonel Moure to coerce its members into the militia system. While individual merchants chose to serve in the disciplined militia of Cartagena in the following years, they were few in number, a situation that perpetuated the chronic problem of attracting enough acceptable officers. Thus, as Cartagena moved calmly through the decade of the 1780s, Europeans continued to dominate the militia officer corps, but that advantage rested upon extremely weak foundations.

An important exception to the general pattern of anti-creole discrimination in the disciplined militia of New Granada and the alienation of creoles from the military reform developed in the Presidency of Quito. Although flanked

38. Expediente on the militia fuero, Cartagena, 1781–84, ANC: MM, vol. 13, fols. 814–23; *Reglamento para las milicias de infantería de la provincia de Yucatán, y Campeche . . .* , título 11.

39. Fernández de Moure to Valdés, with documents, Cartagena, March 6, 1788, AGI: Santa Fe, legajo 951; *Reglamento . . . del Nuevo Reyno de Granada*. chap. 2, art. 24.

by insurrection on all sides, Quito had enjoyed domestic peace throughout the war with England. Consequently, the crown exhibited less distrust bf its American-born vassals there than in those regions directly involved in the Comunero Rebellion, and it did not attempt to limit creole participation in the Quito defense system. The very fact that the presidency had remained quiet in 1781, however, somewhat irrationally tended to diminish the strategic importance of its disciplined militia—or at least it received less credit—despite the general recognition that it had contributed directly to that tranquility. As a result, the militia of the southwest, especially that of inland Quito, escaped the close scrutiny accorded the establishments in other areas; it followed its own line of development and in the long run created a distinct colonial tradition.

The upland provinces of Quito presented a picture of general stagnation at this time. A large Indian population, which outnumbered whites by over three to one, had survived the conquest and had endured with relatively little miscegenation into the eighteenth century. This population provided manpower for an extensive textile industry, which in earlier times had found profitable markets in Peru and New Granada.[40] With the liberalization of trade regulations under the Bourbons, however, European products arrived in large quantities via Cape Horn, underselling the Quito industry and bringing about a severe economic decline. As a result, a large vagrant population drifted through the uplands. Others lived by subsistence agriculture or as debt peons on the large haciendas which dominated the mountain valleys.[41] In the white estate a fair number of creoles held titles of nobility, often acquired either by their families during the more prosperous seventeenth and early eighteenth centuries or by being descendants of recent presidents of the royal audiencia. By the period of the military reform, however, a significant number of them had become badly debt-ridden.[42] This class generally lacked the vigorous commercial orientation that characterized the creole community of Guayaquil, and its isolation seemed firmly to wed it to the conservative traditions of earlier times.

During the eighties, Colonel José García de León y Pizarro and his family dominated the Presidency of Quito politically and shaped the defense system

40. John L. Phelan, *The Kingdom of Quito in the Seventeenth Century: Bureaucratic Politics in the Spanish Empire*, chaps. 3, 4; Magnus Morner, "Aspectos sociorraciales del proceso de poblamiento en la Audiencia de Quito durante los siglos XVI y XVII," pp. 265–87. The general census for Quito, taken in 1779, registered 211,745 Indians, 68,257 whites, and 11,553 libres for the corregimientos of Quito. Cuenca was credited with 54,364 Indians, 25,377 whites, and 994 libres. "Padrón general, 1778," AGI: Estado, legajo 54.

41. Juan and Ulloa, *A Voyage to South America*, pp. 143–45, 154–72; Manuel Guirior, in *Relaciones de mando*, pp. 133 ff.

42. José Alejandro Guzmán, *Títulos nobiliarios en el Ecuador*, chaps. 1, 2; Regent Estanislao de Andino to Ezpeleta, Quito, November 5, 1794, and Ezpeleta to Eugenio de Llaguno, Santa Fe, March 19, 1795, AGI: Quito, legajo 234.

to meet their personal needs. An ambitious, enterprising individual, García Pizarro in late 1778 became both president and regent-visitor of Quito, promoted from the Royal Chancery in Seville, his birthplace, where he had served as fiscal. Pizarro's primary responsibility, like that of other regent-visitors of this period, was to reform royal revenue collection, an assignment which he performed with unmerciful efficiency. In only four years he raised over 1 million pesos just to support the defenses of Cartagena, which was more than the entire sum sent there during the eleven-year administration of José Diguja, who had only collected some 700,000 pesos.[43] Pizarro's success in increasing royal revenues further depressed the economy of Quito, but it earned him considerable latitude in the conduct of his office, a liberty which he shrewdly turned to considerable personal advantage. Through sheer ruthlessness he intimidated the local aristocracy; he ruled willfully, arrogantly, and despotically; and through extortion and graft he boldly converted his office into a vehicle for self-enrichment.[44]

President García Pizarro's political strength solidified when his daughter married the fiscal of the local audiencia, José de Villalengua y Marfil, and when his younger brother, Ramón, acquired by royal order of March 19, 1779, the governorship of Guayaquil, a subordinate but potentially dangerous rival jurisdiction. Ramón had earned a solid reputation in his own right as a militia reformer in Mompós, where he had served as sargento mayor during the early years of the military reorganization.[45] He had also acted as interim governor of Riohacha and in 1777 won full appointment as governor of Mainas in the Amazon basin.[46] Shortly after he assumed that office, however, an unusual turn of events brought him the appointment in Guayaquil. Colonel Ramón Carvajal originally had been selected to succeed Governor Ugarte; but when the crown relieved Governor Pedro Carbonell of his duties in Panama as a result of his clash with Regent-Visitor Gutiérrez de Piñeres, it ordered Carvajal to Panama, which was a more important assignment than Guayaquil, especially with war at hand. This action left Guayaquil without a governor and opened the way for Ramón García Pizarro, who, being in the Presidency of Quito at the time, was readily available.[47] During his administration, President García Pizarro found his younger brother a faithful and

---

43. This was for the *situado*, the special fund earmarked for the maintenance of Cartagena's fortifications and miscellaneous defense expenses. González Suárez, *Historia general*, 5: 295, 307.

44. Ibid., pp. 299–309.

45. Ramón García Pizarro's zeal in structuring the Mompós militia sharply contrasted with the generally dismal record of the military reformers in the backlands of Cartagena. Report of Zejudo, Cartagena, September 15, 1779, AGI: Santa Fe, legajo 948.

46. Statement of merits of R. García Pizarro, Madrid, March 14, 1786, AGI: Quito, legajo 237.

47. Royal order, March 19, 1779, AGI: Panama, legajo 257. Presumably the president of Quito influenced this decision, although no direct evidence has been uncovered to support that suspicion. See Castillo, *Los gobernadores*, pp. 194–99.

valuable political ally on the coast. Moreover, the marriage of García Pizarro's daughter to Villalengua proved especially significant when García Pizarro managed to arrange for his son-in-law's succession to the presidency upon his own transfer to the Council of the Indies in 1784.[48]

When President García Pizarro received provisional authorization from Viceroy Flores in 1779–80 to raise a disciplined militia in the upland provinces of Quito, he solicited the cooperation of the principal noble families of the region. Probably fearful of social chaos, the *quiteño* creole aristocracy had remained slavishly obedient during the Aguardiente and Aduana Rebellion of 1765, outdoing itself with professions of fidelity. A leading noble of the city, for example, Manuel Ponce de León Guerrero, who was the Conde de Selva Florida, had not only demonstrated his loyalty by publicly refusing offers to lead the movement, but had proceeded to take personal custody of the royal coffers to protect them from the rioters.[49] The aristocracy had given no indication that it would ever behave disloyally when García Pizarro organized the militia of Quito, which was, significantly, before the Comunero Rebellion had raised serious doubts about creole loyalty elsewhere in the viceroyalty. Once that insurrection had passed without incident in Quito, there was no compelling reason to alter his orientation. Thus, the military reformers of Quito unhesitatingly recruited leadership from the very group denied unrestrained access to officerships in other provinces.

For their part, the leading creoles of Quito generally appeared willing to collaborate with the system. Under the García Pizarro regime, those who cooperated prospered while those who did not suffered. Militia service at least humored the president, and through the system of command it provided an additional device to fasten a grip upon potential labor supplies.[50]

The aristocracy, moreover, sought a stronger domestic security force for reasons of its own. Quito, probably more than any other province in New Granada, faced the danger of social revolution along lines that emerged at this time in Peru under Túpac Amaru, with the massive impoverished Indian population striking out at the great landed estates and the men that owned them. The period of the military reform was dotted by a rash of local Indian uprisings, including one in 1777 in Otavalo where Indian rebels destroyed property worth over 100,000 pesos on the haciendas of the Marqués de Villa Orellana.[51] A militia promised at least some security against this danger.

48. González Suárez, *Historia general*, 5: 299, 309.
49. Ibid., pp. 216–25; Oscar Efrén Reyes, *Breve historia general del Ecuador*, 1: 299.
50. As in the case of the backlands of Cartagena, the viceregal authorities never systematically investigated the possibility that militia officers abused their authority to exploit the enlisted men of their units. However, such practices were suspected in Quito and, as demonstrated later, there is some direct evidence to support that supposition.
51. Expediente on the travel petition of Jacinto Sánchez de Orellana, Quito, 1781, AGI: Quito, legajo 314; Regent Andino, as part of a special investigation for Ezpeleta, reported in 1794 that the nobility lived in constant fear of the masses; ibid., legajo 234.

Finally, the militia offered the quiteño aristocracy, which was typically engaged in an eternal search for honors and titles, an excellent opportunity to win public prestige of a coveted military nature, which must often have been sufficient incentive in itself to induce participation. García Pizarro shrewdly exploited the creole mentality and fears to strengthen his position as president and to win support for his revenue reforms. Indeed, his ability to manipulate the quiteño aristocracy may well have been a key factor in the preservation of domestic peace during the disorders of 1780–81.

President and Commandant General García Pizarro, it will be remembered, raised one infantry regiment and one cavalry regiment in the city of Quito, one infantry battalion each in Riobamba and Cuenca, and nine separate companies in Quito, Guaranda, Ibarra, Loja, and Ambato. Some of the members of the creole aristocracy recruited to command these units were Manuel Ponce de León Guerrero, who was the Conde de Selva Florida, for colonel of Quito's infantry regiment, and Joaquín Sánchez de Orellana, who was the son of the Marqués de Villa Orellana, for lieutenant colonel. Mariano Flores de Vergara y Jiménez de Cárdenas, who was the Marqués de Miraflores, became colonel of dragoons. Significantly, he was the brother of Ignacio Flores, who was to become instrumental in the pacification of the Túpac Amaru Rebellion in Peru and in lifting the siege of La Paz, and who would become the president of Charcas. The lieutenant colonel was Diego Sánchez, who became the Marqués de Solanda. When in 1784 the two companies of Ibarra were expanded into a nine-company battalion, two additional noble families joined the militia establishment. Manuel de Villavicencio, son of the Conde del Real Agrado, became colonel and Juan Pío de Montúfar, the Marqués de Selva Alegre, became lieutenant colonel.[52] With the recruitment of this kind of leadership the militia system had embraced the cultural heart of the Quito colony.

A second category of officer commanded most of the remaining units: tax collectors and bureaucratic allies of the García Pizarro family. President

---

52. Lists of the commanding officers of the Quito militia can be found in J. García Pizarro to Caballero y Góngora, Quito, January 18, 1783, AGS: GM, legajo 7051, and in Ezpeleta to Alange, Santa Fe, November 19, 1791, AGS: GM, legajo 7060. Verification for the social status of these men can be found in Flores to Gálvez, Cartagena, January 21, 1780, AGS: GM, legajo 7051; petition of Juan Pío de Montúfar, 1787, AGS: GM, legajo 7051; expediente on the cause of the Marqués de Selva Alegre v. Simón Sáenz de Vergara, 1795–97, AGI: Quito, legajo 362; petition of Manuel Villavicencio in Caballero y Góngora to Valdés, Cartagena, November 25, 1787, AGI: Santa Fe, legajo 951; petition of the Marqués de Miraflores for the grade of colonel of the army, Quito, 1791, AGI: Quito, legajo 337; expediente on the travel petition of Jacinto Sánchez de Orellana. See also Guzmán, *Títulos nobiliarios*, chaps. 1, 2. Guzmán states that upon the death in 1784 of the third Marqués de Solanda, Fernando Félix Sánchez, his sister succeeded him. However, the officer list for 1788 contained in the above cited communication from Ezpeleta to Alange, November 19, 1791, lists the lieutenant colonel as the Marqués de Solanda, who in all likelihood was the same Diego Sánchez who was the original lieutenant colonel. Data on the brother of the Marqués de Miraflores, Ignacio Flores, can be found in Lillian Estelle Fisher, *The Last Inca Revolt, 1780–1783.*

García Pizarro placed his personal secretary from Spain, Agustín Martín de Blas, in command of the Volunteer Infantry Battalion of Riobamba. Martín de Blas also served as director of revenue collections for that same province and was the man who exposed a plot by one Miguel Tovar y Ugarte of Quito to enter into communication with Túpac Amaru during 1781.[53] Corregidor José Corral y Narro, another close associate and former secretary of President García Pizarro, successfully petitioned in 1784 for authorization to consolidate the separate companies of Guaranda and Ambato and to add five more to them in order to create a battalion under his command. His lieutenant colonel, José Renxijo, was the computer of Indian tribute for the Province of Quito and a close personal friend of García Pizarro's son-in-law and successor, Juan José Villalengua. Officers of this sort solidified García Pizarro's personal grip on the militia. However, Cuenca, which had its own governor, blended less smoothly into the president's system. José Antonio Vallejo, who was stubbornly independent as that jurisdiction's first governor, assumed the colonelship, with Felipe Nieto Polo, the son of one of Cuenca's most distinguished families, becoming lieutenant colonel.[54]

The amount that the colonels invested in uniforms to acquire their positions varied considerably. Men such as the Marqués de Villa Orellana, who had lost his fortune in the Otavalo Indian uprising of 1777, and the chronically debt-ridden Marqués de Selva Alegre left most of that expense to the men they accepted as captains, while the wealthy tax collector José Corral y Narro, in a bid for respectability through conspicuous public generosity, bore the cost of uniforming over half of his battalion.[55] In any event, most of these units were far understrength, possessed few weapons, and rarely, if ever, drilled. The colonels nearly all lived in Quito, a great distance from their units, and largely relied upon Indians—probably peons from their own estates—to fill company quotas.[56]

The militia of Quito fell far short of the standards required of disciplined units in other ways as well. Only a handful of veterans were ever assigned to these units, which can be explained in part by the general lack of available

53. Audiencia of Quito to Gil y Lemos, Quito, June 18, 1789, AGI: Quito, legajo 271. Tovar was convicted of sedition and died in prison in the Castle of Chagres. Boleslao Lewin, *La insurrección de Túpac Amaru*, pp. 88–89.

54. Expediente on a petition by Corral y Narro for appointment as colonel of the militia of Guaranda and Ambato, 1784, ANE: Pres., vol. 205, fols. 132–73; expediente by Felipe Nieto Polo on the disposition of a sum of pesos, Madrid, 1794, AGI: Quito, legajo 354; Renxijo to Valdés, Quito, August 18, 1788, AGS: GM, legajo 7089.

55. Expediente on the establishment of the militia of Guayaquil and Quito, 1775–87, AGS: GM, legajo 7051; expediente on a petition by Corral y Narro . . . , 1784.

56. Fernando Antonio de Echeandia, former corregidor of Chimbo and Guaranda, provided an illuminating insight into the hollow nature of Quito's militia in a memorial to the crown, Madrid, April 20, 1789, AGS: GM, legajo 7089; Corral y Narro to Valdés, Guaranda, July 26, 1788, AGS: GM, legajo 7054; Andino to Ezpeleta, Quito, November 5, 1794; expediente on the petition of Villavicencio, 1785–87, AGI: Quito, legajo 574.

regular troops in the region.[57] More important, however, was the absence of any real desire on the part of the president and commandant general to share his authority with high-ranking military officials. As matters stood, García Pizarro's colonels were uninhibited by the normal checks on volunteer authority which had been built into the disciplined militia system and were therefore free to abuse it for their own purposes. During the war with England, for example, when detachments from most of the upland units were deployed in Guayaquil as a reserve force, Quito's troops were exploited as forced laborers for private purposes by Ramón García Pizarro, an undertaking which no doubt profited the commanding officers and the commandant general as well as the governor.[58]

In short, the militia of upland Quito deserved nothing even approaching a disciplined classification. Rather than serving as an instrument of royal policy, either domestic or foreign, it functioned as the personal tool of President García Pizarro, his successor Villalengua, and their cronies. In 1783 the crown ordered Caballero y Góngora to complete and formalize action taken during the war to establish these units, steps which presumably could have led to improvements.[59] No such undertaking materialized, however, because the perfection of the Quito militia was a matter which commanded little immediate urgency. During this period, the viceroy was occupied by the more critical reorganizations in Santa Fe and Cartagena as well as the Darién Indian war, and for the time being he simply permitted the reform in Quito to drift.

Meanwhile, the militia of Guayaquil did register some improvement over the system devised during the seventies by Special Commander Víctor Salcedo y Somodevilla. Governor Ramón García Pizarro was a capable militia officer, and under the stress of war he managed to convert the nearly worthless self-serving organization of Salcedo into a disciplined militia worthy of the name. He reduced the number of units to a more realistic size of two battalions of infantry, four companies of dragoons, and two of artillery. To train these units he requested a substantial increase for the cadre of veteran advisors, and following the war he received some increment from those freed by the consolidation of the Cartagena militia.[60] His brother, the president of Quito, assisted him by successfully engineering the transfer to Quito of Salcedo, the man most responsible for the underdeveloped condition of the Guayaquil militia and a potentially dangerous rival.[61]

---

57. Expediente on the establishment of the militia of Guayaquil and Quito, 1775–87.
58. Expediente on the conduct of R. García Pizarro, 1787–89, AGI: Quito, legajo 271.
59. Expediente on the establishment of the militia of Guayaquil and Quito, 1775–87.
60. R. García Pizarro to Gálvez, Guayaquil, June 7, 1782, AGI: Quito, legajo 262; Caballero y Góngora to Gálvez, Santa Fe, October 5, 1782, AGI: Quito, legajo 574; idem, Santa Fe, March 23, 1784, AGS: GM, legajo 7089.
61. J. García Pizarro to Gálvez, Quito, May 18, 1783, and royal order, November 29, 1783, AGI: Quito, legajo 225.

Despite the improvements made by Ramón García Pizarro, the crown withheld final approval for his work, urging him after the war to effect additional consolidations to bring that establishment more closely into line with the province's resources and peacetime needs.[62] The governor, however, never bothered to attempt further action, and as a consequence the final status of the militia of Guayaquil, like that of the upland units, remained unresolved. When Colonel Anastasio Zejudo reviewed the military units of the Presidency of Quito on behalf of Viceroy Caballero y Góngora at the end of the decade, he nevertheless found the Guayaquil militia to be the only force in good condition in that entire jurisdiction.[63]

Governor Ramón García Pizarro quickly proved as enterprising as his brother in exploiting public office and the military for personal purposes. Shortly after his arrival, he moved to assert his uncontested command of the city. First, he barred the cabildo from conducting sessions without his assistance. This act posed an open challenge to custom in the municipality, but it predictably found support from the president of Quito. Thereafter, the governor boldly intimidated the cabildo, even daring on occasion to employ troops to dictate its proceedings and to influence the outcome of its elections.[64] A key element in García Pizarro's despotic assertion of authority was his success in winning the personal loyalty of the local military leadership once Salcedo had departed, something his unhappy predecessor, Francisco Ugarte, had never managed to do.

With the local military leadership loyal to the governor, with the cabildo reduced to impotence, and with most able-bodied creoles enlisted in the militia, the militia system of command, as reinforced juridically by the fuero militar, served to reinforce García Pizarro's sway over the city. Under this arrangement the military dominated the colony, scoffed at civilian authority, and penalized those who did not cooperate. Indeed, the military soon exhibited in its own right an open disdain for the cabildo. On one occasion, Jacinto Bejarano, colonel of whites, dared to shock the city during an official Mass by arrogantly refusing to rise in deference to the arrival in the church of the city magistrates, an indiscretion which predictably went unpunished.[65]

García Pizarro used his despotic command of Guayaquil to extend his personal control over the vast, expanding cacao and lumber export industries, including both legal trade and contraband. In so doing, he collaborated with the principal local military authorities, whom he accepted as partners in his business ventures and who in turn supported his authority. These men included Manuel de Guevara, the officer who replaced Salcedo; Colonel Jacinto

---

62. Royal order, April 27, 1783, AGI: Quito, legajo 574.

63. Expediente on the subinspectorship of Zejudo, 1787–89, AGS: GM, legajo 7053.

64. Castillo, *Los gobernadores*, pp. 202–4; expediente on the conduct of R. García Pizarro, 1787–89.

65. Castillo, *Los gobernadores*, pp. 205–10.

Bejarano of the white battalion, who as previously stated was among Guayaquil's wealthiest creole merchants and a close friend of the Arteta family; militia captain Juan Antonio Rocafuerte; and Bernardo Roca, the mulatto commander of the pardo battalion.[66] As discussed earlier, Miguel Antonio Anzuátegui, the local mercantile magistrate and, incidentally, a captain of militia, successfully challenged the jurisdiction of the military fuero in commercial suits in 1787. That ruling, however, had less impact in Guayaquil than in Cartagena, where military and political structures were more complex. In Guayaquil, with its one-man rule, the judgment merely permitted merchants dealing with militiamen to avoid the first instance jurisdiction of an unpopular auditor de guerra, Lieutenant Governor José Mejía del Valle; but Governor García Pizarro, backed by the military and his brother in Quito, still ruled the province.[67]

The domination of the Presidency of Quito by the García Pizarro family dissolved by the end of the decade. President José García Pizarro, the one regent-visitor who completed his work without provoking an uprising, returned to Spain with honor in 1784 to assume a position on the Council of the Indies. It will be remembered, however, that he arranged the succession of his son-in-law, Juan José Villalengua, who ruled until 1790. In 1789 the crown transferred Ramón García Pizarro to the Intendancy of Salta in the Viceroyalty of Río de la Plata. His exit led to a stormy investigation of his tenure in office, but Villalengua and those who were his allies on the audiencia managed to block it, with the outcome proving inconclusive.[68] The García Pizarro family had ruled despotically and corruptly during its dominion in Quito, but had incorporated the creole into the defense system to a degree unparalleled elsewhere in New Granada. The creole of Quito and Guayaquil had come to view the military as a vehicle for power, economic opportunity, and public honor. In that important regard he sharply differed from his counterparts in Santa Fe, Popayán, and Cartagena.

66. Governor García Pizarro was also responsible for a vigorous expansion of Guayaquil's commerce, especially through the development of the cacao industry. Ibid., pp. 220–21, 248–53; León Borja and Nagy, "El comercio del cacao," pp. 39–40; expediente on the conduct of R. García Pizarro, 1787–89.

67. Fernández de Moure to Valdés, with documents, Cartagena, March 6, 1788; Castillo, *Los gobernadores*, pp. 248–52.

68. Castillo, *Los gobernadores*, pp. 248–52; expediente on the residencia of R. García Pizarro, 1789–91, AGI: Quito, legajo 271; Villalengua became regent of the audiencia of Guatemala following his tenure in Quito. R. García Pizarro eventually became president of Charcas, only to be overthrown in the abortive uprising of 1809, which many have viewed as the opening scene in the wars for independence. See Charles W. Arnade, *The Emergence of the Republic of Bolivia*, chap. 1. Arnade, p. 10, portrays Ramon García Pizarro far differently from the figure that appears in Guayaquil. "He was neither haughty nor stern. . . . He disliked rough talk or anything that even resembled a fight. Pizarro abhorred war and was very proud that he had never fought in a battle; he was a pacifist, the sight of any weapon nauseated him." The present writer is at a loss to explain the contrast unless, perhaps, the governor mellowed with age.

In 1787 Viceroy Caballero y Góngora finally moved to correct the condition of the militia of the southwest of New Granada. The crown on February 13 of the previous year had reduced jurisdictional confusion concerning military privileges by declaring that members of all units classified as urban were not entitled to the fuero militar unless mobilized.[69] The royal order of February 13 created little difficulty in provinces such as Cartagena and Panama, which possessed clearly authorized disciplined establishments, but it caused much uncertainty in Guayaquil and Quito where the militia still awaited formal completion and approval. For that matter, even the units of southern Popayán, in Pasto and Barbacoas, were doubtful about their status. These units lacked proper maintenance, and following the dismal failure of the Pasto militia to protect Deputy Governor José Ignacio Peredo in 1781, Caballero y Góngora conspicuously declined to sustain its fuero in judicial proceedings, although those units clearly had been classified originally as disciplined.[70]

Caballero y Góngora, whose attention rarely focused on the Presidency of Quito or its militia, seems to have been uncertain himself about the exact legal status of its various establishments. He indiscriminantly dispatched copies of the February order to all the upland provinces and Guayaquil without indicating whether it should be treated as a point of general information or as a judgment directly affecting the recipient's own status. Most provincial authorities took the order in the latter sense and obediently issued statements of compliance without question or protest. Two exceptions, however, were the governor of Guayaquil and Corregidor José del Corral y Narro of Guaranda, both of whom suspended publication of the law pending clarification from higher authority. Governor García Pizarro accurately reminded the viceroy of the original royal orders creating and approving the Guayaquil militia, and he won a reaffirmation of the disciplined status of those units. Despite strong support from his close friend President Villalengua, Corregidor and Colonel Corral y Narro, who it will be remembered had uniformed over half of his battalion at considerable personal expense, was unable to do likewise because of the hazy status of the upland militia. Caballero y Góngora ruled that the Guaranda militia, as well as the other units of interior Quito, lacked a clearly disciplined standing and were therefore subject to the royal order.[71]

The uncertainty caused by the royal order of February 13, 1786, dramatized the general lack of coordination and supervision which had resulted from New Granada's piecemeal approach to military reform. Outside the mainstream of the military reorganization, numerous units had sprung up through

69. Royal order, February 13, 1786, ANC: MM, vol. 2, fols. 327–36.
70. Expedientes on jurisdictional disputes in Pasto, 1782–84, ANC: MM,vol. 43, fols. 944–67, and vol. 52, fols. 749–62; expediente on a jurisdictional dispute in Barbacoas, 1784–85, ANC: Cabildos, vol. 10, fols. 958–74.
71. Expediente on the royal order of February 13, 1786, ANE: Pres., vol. 234, fols. 77–95.

the initiative and sponsorship of ambitious provincial authorities or interested parties, but usually, as in the example of upland Quito, without proper support or direction. Certainly, the extension of the military reform to strategic coastal provinces such as Santa Marta and Riohacha during the eighties could be justified by reason of external security, and the extension of the reform to the interior of Quito and Santa Fe could be justified by domestic considerations. But the sizes of these establishments were usually inflated and when taken together exceeded what the population and resources of New Granada could realistically sustain. In addition, this marginal militia was often the source of damaging jurisdictional disputes or other evils. With the royal order of 1786, the time clearly had arrived to impose a sense of order and direction on the disciplined militia of New Granada.

To achieve this objective, Viceroy Caballero y Góngora called upon his trusted military advisor, Colonel Anastasio Zejudo. Zejudo had recently returned from Darién where severe illness had forced him to relinquish command of an expeditionary force battling the Cuna Indians (see chapter 6). With royal approval, Caballero y Góngora vested him with the title of *subinspector general*, with the authority to review and reform the military establishments of Popayán, Quito, Guayaquil, and Panama, and thereafter to maintain a general supervision of the army of New Granada. The viceroy urged Zejudo to conduct a strict review, eliminating all marginal units but preserving those best suited to the needs and resources of the viceroyalty. Reflecting the importance attached to his mission, Zejudo was assigned a salary of 6,000 pesos, making him one of the highest paid officials in New Granada.[72]

With a cadre of four officers and two corporals as well as a number of servants and guides, Zejudo departed Santa Fe for Popayán in January 1788, but he did not complete his long, exhausting commission until March 1789. The tour itself is a vivid reminder of the immense difficulty in attempting a general coordination of the reform. Traveling time proved enormous and physical perils were great. Among his ordeals, Zejudo was obliged to scale the Quindío Pass of the Central Cordillera, traverse the "bloody" Patía and Mira valleys between Popayán and Quito, and, after descending to the tropical coast, navigate from Guayaquil to Panama and from there to Cartagena. Zejudo nearly perished on his way to Cuenca in the snows of the Lasuay Pass, where he incurred temporary blindness and baldness, and two of his Indian guides died. Moreover, at every step of the way the subinspector general encountered

72. The viceroy enjoyed an annual salary of 40,000 pesos, the governor of Cartagena 7,500, the governor of Panama 6,637, and the president of Quito 6,435. Officials such as the oidores of the audiencias and the governors of important provinces such as Popayán and Guayaquil were paid around 3,000 a year. Relación of the annual salaries of the officials of the Viceroyalty of New Granada, Santa Fe, December 12, 1788, AGI: Santa Fe, legajo 561; expediente on the subinspectorship of Zejudo, 1787–89.

hostile local officials, who were wary of the distant authority of Santa Fe and jealous of his commission.

As Anastasio Zejudo advanced his inspection of the troops of the southwest and Panama, a viceroyalty-wide militia policy at last began to take shape. In each province he introduced the standard organization observed in Cartagena and Santa Fe and rather abruptly disbanded those units which contributed little or nothing to the security of the realm. In Popayán he consolidated the numerous separate infantry companies into a ten-company regiment of all colors but added a squadron of white dragoons for purposes of mobility. In the uplands of Quito he disbanded all the units created by García Pizarro and Villalengua except the regiments of infantry and dragoons of Quito and the infantry regiment of Cuenca, all of which he officially placed on a disciplined footing. This action eliminated the largely decorative battalions of Ibarra, Riobamba, and Guaranda with their honorific officerships, but did retain units for the capital of the presidency and its principal inland governorship. In Guayaquil Zejudo continued his policy of reducing the militia to the bare minimum demanded by necessity. There he dissolved the pardo infantry battalion and the pardo artillery company; he joined the remaining artillery company to the battalion of whites while consolidating the four dragoon companies into a squadron of three companies. Zejudo had left the number of troops approximately the same in Popayán, but he reduced the authorized forces of Quito and Guayaquil by thirty per cent and the number of major units by nearly one-half.[73]

In Panama Zejudo found that the fixed battalion had withered to merely 140 men but that the militia, although understrength, did exhibit some military skill. He disbanded one of the original two pardo battalions, preserved the white infantry battalion, and abolished the various separate infantry companies of Panama, except the artillery unit. In Portobelo he combined the four infantry companies into a single corps but eliminated the artillery company. Elsewhere in the Commandancy General of Panama, Zejudo found that the governor of Veragua had won during the expansive period following the Comunero Rebellion a disciplined classification for a militia of one battalion of whites and four separate companies of pardos, which that province had raised in the previous decade. Like most of the new establishments created during that period, however, these units lacked the necessary equipment and veteran cadres, and Zejudo consolidated them into a battalion of seven companies.[74]

73. Expediente on the subinspectorship of Zejudo, 1787–89. It should be noted that while reducing the number of battalions, and hence officerships, Zejudo increased the authorized strengths of the individual units.

74. Ibid.; expediente on the insubordination of the governor of Veragua, 1773–75, ANC: MM, vol. 16, fols. 949–71, vol. 77, fols. 653–55, 847–50, 973–79, and vol. 92, fols. 882–83; Carbonell to Flores, Panama, December 12, 1776, ANC: MM, vol. 75, fols. 710–14; royal order, March 27, 1784, ANC: MM, fols. 307–11.

When Colonel Zejudo arrived in Cartagena in March 1789, the authorized strength of the disciplined militia of New Granada totaled 14,595 men, a force roughly equal to that claimed in 1779 (see Tables 4 and 6). Yet the capacity of the defense system to meet the security needs of New Granada had undoubtedly been increased through both a broader geographic troop distribution and generally improved organizational levels. After a decade and one-half of a drift, an attempt had finally been made to introduce some semblance of viceroyalty-wide coordination to the military reform. The more controversial issues concerning the feasibility of sustaining an elaborate military establishment in the interior of the kingdom, first raised by the cabildo of Popayán but now forcefully voiced in Santa Fe, and the proper relationship of the creole to the defense system both still remained.

6. The Military on the Frontier

ANOTHER DIMENSION of the military's expanding role in colonial life developed on New Granada's frontiers in the form of a new, militarized policy toward non-pacified Indians. During the period of the reform, the viceroyalty departed from traditional, mission-oriented operations in its strategic Caribbean frontier areas and came increasingly to depend on the military as its primary instrument for expanding and enforcing royal authority. Beginning in Riohacha during the 1770s, this development reached its climax under Viceroy Antonio Caballero y Góngora, who in 1785 sent into action on the Darién frontier, Isthmus of Panama, a force which came to total nearly 1,000 regulars and militiamen, most of whom were products of the military reform. Whereas in times past the missionary had been the government's chief agent in frontier expansion, now, in a time of an increased militarization of government policy, the soldier emerged in the foreground; the winning of souls, previously an important consideration along with extending government control, became almost an afterthought, eclipsed by the desire for a rapid and effective occupation. When coupled with the expansion of the reform to the interior of New Granada for reasons of internal security, the extension of armed action to the viceroyalty's frontiers represented a substantial growth in the responsibility, activity, and importance of the emerging military.

The frontier campaigns in New Granada were only part of a general intensification of militarized pacification and colonization operations throughout the

130

empire under Charles III and his aggressive minister, José de Gálvez. In New Spain, for example, where the missionary, though necessarily supported by the military, had traditionally dominated frontier policy, the crown promulgated a reglamento in 1772 for the northern frontier which thrust the military into the pacification foreground both administratively and tactically. To implement the new policy, Lieutenant Colonel Hugo Oconor, acting in the newly created post of inspector general with military authority over the entire frontier, made war on the ubiquitous Apache Indians and shaped a coherent line of heavily garrisoned *presidios* to protect newly encouraged colonization centers. In 1776 the crown furthered this process by establishing an autonomous military command for the region, the Commandancy General of the Interior Provinces, an institutional arrangement that endured until the close of the colonial period.[1] Frontier expansion followed a similar pattern in the Viceroyalty of Río de la Plata, where the authorities conducted an extensive series of military operations against the plains Indians during this same period and also created lines of fortifications in Mendoza, Córdoba, and Buenos Aires as the basis for colonization and frontier expansion.[2] And in the Captaincy General of Guatemala, following the English withdrawal from the Honduran coast in 1786, the government attempted a pacification-colonization campaign against the Sambo-Miskitos, which depended primarily upon a line of strategically positioned coastal strongholds.[3] Although the missionary could and did participate in these actions, his role was clearly a secondary one at best.

The shift in frontier policy stemmed from both the increasingly secular orientation of the Spanish government and a general dissatisfaction with the slow rate of missionary expansion into the vast unpacified and undeveloped regions of the empire. Under the enlightened regime of Charles III, the traditional status of the Church as a coequal partner of the state gave way to one of definite subordination; ecclesiastical power was reduced, and the numerous functions of the Church that encroached on the secular realm were subjected to unsympathetic scrutiny. At the same time that the military fuero was embellished to underpin the enlargement of Spain's armies, the once sacrosanct ecclesiastical fuero faced harsh criticism and sharp curtailment.[4] The expulsion of the Society of Jesus from America in 1767, although applauded in some sectors of the clerical hierarchy, nevertheless represented an additional setback for the power and influence of the Church. This was especially true on the frontiers of the empire where the Jesuits had long acted as the shock troops

1. John Francis Bannon, *The Spanish Borderlands Frontier, 1513–1821*, particularly chaps. 8 and 10; Alfred B. Thomas, *Teodoro de Croix and the Northern Frontier of New Spain, 1776–1783*; and David M. Vigness, "Don Hugo Oconor and New Spain's Northeastern Frontier, 1764–1776."
2. Jorge Comadrán Ruiz, "En torno al problema del Indio en el Río de la Plata"; Alfred J. Tapson, "Indian Warfare on the Pampa during the Colonial Period."
3. Troy S. Floyd, *The Anglo-Spanish Struggle for Mosquitia*, chap. 11.
4. N. M. Farriss, *Crown and Clergy in Colonial Mexico, 1759–1821*.

of the missionary struggle.[5] Indeed, no clearer expression can be found of the new search for secular solutions to those affairs of state traditionally assigned to the purview of the Church than the militarized frontier campaigns of the 1770s and the 1780s.

Disillusionment with the traditional, mission-oriented frontier policy predated the military reform in New Granada, reaching its first full expression as a result of mission failures in the coastal Province of Riohacha. In 1769, the Guajiro Indians, a stubborn tribe which inhabited the Guajira Peninsula to the northeast of the city of Riohacha and which had long resisted Spanish authority, destroyed in a single uprising the results of over seventy years of Capuchin missionary labors. They demolished nearly all the missions, massacred settlers, and drove Spanish influence back to the capital city of Riohacha itself on the western fringe of the province.

This devastating reverse crystallized a growing sense of frustration concerning the viceroyalty's unpacified frontiers. By 1772 both outgoing Viceroy Messía de la Cerda and the *fiscal protector de indios* of the royal audiencia, Francisco Antonio Moreno y Escandón, reinforced by a chorus of local officials, complained bitterly about an alleged history of mission ineffectiveness and called for a greater employment of military force in coping with recalcitrant aboriginals, especially those suspected of consorting with foreign enemies of the crown.[6] On the latter count, both the Guajiros of Riohacha and the aboriginals of Darién, the Cunas, were unquestionably guilty, at least in a commercial sense, and their acquisition of British firearms added further weight to urgent cries for action.[7] Incoming Viceroy Manuel Guirior, Messía de la Cerda's successor, responded to the dilemma with a fresh frontier approach which de-emphasized the mission and entailed a new, expanded role for the armed forces of New Granada. He fashioned this program to contend with the urgent problem posed by the Guajiros of Riohacha, but it was substantially the same approach that the viceroyalty would later extend to Darién. For that reason, and for the fact that the Riohacha experience ultimately stimulated an expansion of the military reform in its own right, it requires brief consideration.[8]

In formulating a program for the Riohacha frontier, Guirior had to contend

---

5. For a variety of views on the expulsion of the Jesuits, see Magnus Morner, ed., *The Expulsion of the Jesuits from Latin America*.

6. Moreno y Escandón, "Estado . . . 1772," pp. 559–60, 575–77; Messía de la Cerda, in *Relaciones de mando*, pp. 97–98.

7. Moreno y Escandón, "Estado . . . 1772," pp. 564–67, 572–77; Narváez to Flores, Riohacha, August 26, 1779, in José Félix Blanco and Ramón Azpurua, comps., *Documentos para la historia de la vida pública del Libertador . . .* , 1:187–88.

8. A detailed analysis and account of the Riohacha experience can be found in Allan J. Kuethe, "The Pacification Campaign on the Riohacha Frontier, 1772–1779."

not only with mission stagnation but with military paralysis as well. His predecessor had overreacted to the 1769 uprising by organizing an expedition of over 1,000 troops, only to discover, when the force assembled in Riohacha in 1771, that it was too small to achieve a military victory, and to learn further that New Granada could never hope to marshall a force equal to the task. Therefore, Guirior adopted a more limited and gradual approach commensurate to existent military resources, which at that time had not yet been appreciably affected by the reform. His program featured the establishment of fortified settlements at three strategic points: Bahía Honda on the northern point of the Guajira Peninsula, Sinamaica on the eastern side, and Pedraza in the interior midway between Sinamaica and the capital city of Riohacha in the west. Later, under Viceroy Flores, a fourth base, Sabana del Valle, was established between Sinamaica and Bahía Honda.

Three kinds of frontier agents acted from these newly established bases. Recently returned Capuchin missionaries propagandized the faith; several hundred colonists worked to develop the land and served as a counterbalance to the aboriginals; and military forces shielded the colonists and missionaries and exerted pressure on the Indians to remain at peace and to adopt an acceptable mode of living. To accomplish their mission, the armed forces had to function cautiously, both avoiding direct confrontations and awaiting opportunities to assert royal authority. The government hoped by a continued, forceful presence to gradually wear down Guajiro independence and thereby bring this vital area into the effective dominion of the Spanish crown. Under this pacification-colonization system, the military function was paramount, with the success or failure of the entire venture depending upon its fortune (see Table 7).

Despite the vital mission of the military in Riohacha, manpower and morale always posed serious problems; and although a partial solution to the dilemma eventually came through an implementation of militia reform, it arrived too late to be of much consequence in the conquest of the Guajiros. The basic problem was that the pacification campaign in Riohacha, provoked by the Guajiro uprising, materialized before the military reorganization could produce the wealth of trained personnel necessary for such an ambitious undertaking. The authorities were always reluctant to commit for a prolonged period of time large numbers of regulars from the key base of Cartagena. Even when Messía de la Cerda sent the 1771 expedition—which incidentally was only possible because of the arrival of the rotating Battalion of Savoy—he did so with the understanding that it would act with all dispatch to insure a prompt return. And although troop flexibility increased somewhat at Cartagena with the implementation of the reform there, the number of regulars committed to the pacification-colonization campaign seldom surpassed two hundred.

Furthermore, these troops were usually the poorest that Cartagena had to offer.[9]

To make matters worse, the militia employed in Riohacha was unsatisfactory because of both a low performance rate and recruitment difficulties. Although the local authorities maintained lists of able-bodied men, the method of recruitment in time of need from Santa Marta and Riohacha appears to have been outright impressment since the men were untrained, displayed little if any inclination for service, and fled at the first sign of a new levy. For example, in 1776 the governor of Santa Marta, when called upon to deliver one hundred men, could produce only fifty-five, and in the south of that province,

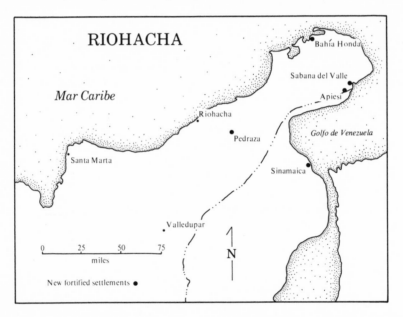

in the jurisdiction of Valledupar, the authorities met with even less success.[10] Moreover, this contingent, when subsequently assigned to Sabana del Valle, behaved so viciously that it constituted a permanent source of disruption, and many of its members deserted at the first opportunity.[11] This unhappy group was soon dismissed and further recruitment efforts in the Province of Santa Marta failed completely. Most of the militiamen from Riohacha itself had served without relief from the initiation of the colonization enterprise, and, consequently, irate wives and relatives besieged officials with a barrage of

9. Ibid.

10. Díaz de Perea to Flores, Santa Marta, March 19, 1776, ANC: MM, vol. 95, fols. 332–37.

11. Arévalo to Messía de la Cerda, Cartagena, September 11, 1776, ANC: MM, vol. 140, fol. 659.

petitions for their release.[12] These problems were not unique to the year 1776 but characterized the earlier phases of the venture as well.[13]

In pleas to the viceroy concerning the manpower problem, local officials invariably argued for more regular troops, but Flores firmly held the troop limit from Cartagena at two hundred.[14] For a solution he turned instead to a formalization of the militia structure along new, reformed lines. Apparently such action had not been attempted earlier because most able-bodied men were already on duty, and consequently it appeared to be unnecessary. However, Antonio de Narváez y la Torre, who in early 1777 became governor of Santa Marta—to which Riohacha was joined under his common governorship

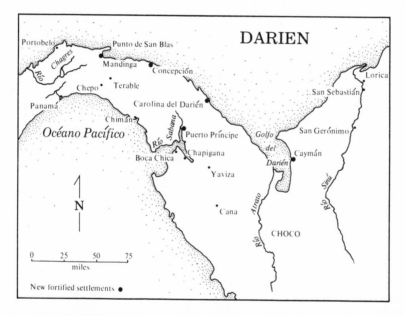

by royal order of November 18 of the same year—called for a reassessment of the entire system.[15] He postulated that a formalized, structured militia, in which conscripts who had a direct stake in the future of the province received quality preparation and proper corporate incentives, would produce

12. Díaz de Perea to Flores, Santa Marta, December 4, 1776, ANC: MM, vol. 99, fols. 912–14; Narváez to Flores, Santa Marta, April 19, 1777, ANC: MM, vol. 95, fols. 276–82; R. García Pizarro to Flores, Riohacha, July 12, 26, 1777, ANC: MM, vol. 99, fols. 294–96, 298, 301.

13. Mendoza to Messía de la Cerda, Riohacha, June 10, 1769, and August 1769, ANC: MM, vol. 138, fols. 868–69, 968–72, respectively.

14. R. García Pizarro to Flores, Riohacha, July 12, 26, 1777.

15. Antonio Caballero y Góngora, "Relación del estado del Nuevo Reino de Granada . . . ," in José Manuel Pérez Ayala, *Antonio Caballero y Góngora, virrey y arzobispo de Santa Fe, 1723–96*, pp. 369–88.

better results than the practice of merely dragging people at random out of their homes.[16]

Flores responded on July 15, 1778, to the Narváez recommendation by ordering the creation of a disciplined 126-man company of pardo dragoons. Following the outbreak of war with Great Britain in 1779, he ordered the formation of a second company.[17] The subsequent record of these units appears to have been surprisingly good despite their remaining on active duty almost continually. Significantly, on two occasions when they were called upon for service outside of their immediate locality—once for border action against the Comuneros in 1781 and later for action in Darién—they responded by mass desertion.[18] These dragoon companies were only the beginning of military reform in Riohacha; under the crisis of war, additional disciplined militia was rapidly organized on a separate company basis in both Riohacha and Santa Marta under the special command of Francisco Pérez Dávila, ayudante of militia from Cartagena.[19] In the postwar era a viceregal order of June 12, 1784, formally organized these units into regiments.[20]

The Riohacha experiment, in spite of the effort and resources invested in it, was not destined to succeed. In late 1775, even before the establishment of the fourth settlement at Sabana del Valle, Guajiro warriors inflicted a serious defeat on the expeditionary force at a site called Apiesi in the eastern portion of the peninsula. Subsequent efforts to restore the prestige of Spanish arms and to quiet the newly aroused aboriginals failed, and, as a consequence, many of the missionaries and colonists departed the area, never again to return. An even more serious blow to the expedition came with the outbreak of war with Great Britain in 1779 and the accompanying shift of defense priorities back to the main bases. Forced to withdraw most of the expedition's regular forces to Cartagena, the authorities disbanded Bahía Honda and Sabana del Valle, and concentrated the remaining troops, largely militia, along the base of the peninsula in the line running from Sinamaica to Pedraza to Riohacha.

In the postwar era, because of a growing crisis in the more strategic Darién area, Riohacha failed to regain its earlier prominent place in the frontier plans of the viceroyalty. As a result, its needs were usually neglected, and the Guajiros soon reasserted uninhibited sovereignty over most of the peninsula. Yet, despite a lack of much conspicuous lasting success, the Riohacha frontier campaign opened the way for an expanded military role in New Granada's

16. Narváez to Flores, Santa Marta, April 19, 1777.

17. Troop inspection reports, Santa Marta and Riohacha, Narváez, August 4, 1784, ANC: MM, vol. 99, fols. 445–46; Narváez to Flores, Santa Marta, October 26, 1784, ANC: MM, vol. 124, fols. 229–30.

18. Narváez to Caballero y Góngora, Riohacha, November 22, 1785, ANC: MM, vol. 93, fols. 653–56.

19. F. Pérez Dávila to Flores, Santa Marta, September 19, 1780, ANC: MM, vol. 99, fols. 779–81; Narváez to Flores, Santa Marta, January 27, 1780, ANC: MM, vol. 76, fols. 846–47.

20. Troop inspection reports, Santa Marta and Riohacha, Narváez, August 4, 1784.

frontiers and provided a model to answer the needs of a rapidly deteriorating situation in Darién.[21]

The Province of Darién had a deeply troubled history in the eighteenth century. Its civilized inhabitants, scattered in small settlements in the south central and Pacific portions of the isthmus, declined in number from some 20,000 in 1712 to a mere 1,000 in 1780. This depopulation resulted from a steady battering by British invaders, pirates, and Indians, including the sacking of the capital, Santa Cruz de Cana, in 1712. A peaceful interlude followed the War of Jenkins' Ear, but by 1760 hostilities with the Cuna Indians, who dwelt along the inland rivers and the Caribbean coast of Darién, resumed. To contain new invasions, a series of four forts was constructed along the southern Pacific frontier, beginning in 1762 at Yaviza, the newly named provincial capital, and continuing into the following decade with establishments at Cana, Chapigana, and Boca Chica. These strongholds were initially garrisoned by twenty regulars from Panama supplemented by roughly ninety local pardos. A similar company under the jurisdiction of Panama was maintained along Darién's western frontier to garrison three populated outposts at Chepo, Terable, and Chimán.[22] By the 1780s these units had emerged as separate pardo segments of the regular army.[23] The Cunas, however, remained secure in their population centers on the Caribbean side of the isthmus, and by 1772 they were conducting raids beyond the Gulf of Darién as far east as the Sinú River and on into the Province of Cartagena.[24] This latter development was an important consideration behind the formation of numerous companies of disciplined militia in the district of Lorica during the 1773 reform.[25]

The incidences of Indian assaults continued to mount during the 1770s, reaching crisis proportions during the North American Revolution.[26] In the past, the Cunas had limited themselves to small raiding parties, but in 1780 they mustered sufficient strength to besiege a fortified military detachment, which was one of several patrols in the region designed to frustrate anticipated British penetration.[27] This act was followed by the massacre in 1782 of more than two companies of regulars from the Regiment of the Crown that had been shipwrecked on the Darién coast en route to New Granada from Havana. Needless to say, that brutal outrage further aroused the ire of the viceroyalty's leadership against the Cunas. Moreover, in 1783 a raiding party crossed the Sinú River and attacked San Gerónimo de Buena Vista, an important western

21. Kuethe, "The Pacification Campaign."
22. Manuel Luengo Muñoz, "Génesis de las expediciones militares al Darién en 1785–86," pp. 345–56, 361–68.
23. Troop inspection report, Panama, July 5, 1783, ANC: MM, vol. 64, fols. 1035–38.
24. Moreno y Escandón, "Estado . . . 1772," p. 572.
25. Report on the militia of Cartagena, Pimienta, March 26, 1778, ANC: MM, vol. 40, fols. 152–65.
26. Luengo Muñoz, "Génesis," pp. 371–77.
27. Carvajal to Flores, Panama, November 22, 1780, ANC: MM, vol. 118, fols. 154–60.

frontier settlement in the Province of Cartagena. Serious enough in their own right, the implications of these bold actions were compounded by intelligence reports that the British were once again planning to occupy the Bay of Caledonia, which had been the site of an unsuccessful venture by the Scotch Merchant Company in 1697–99.[28]

The crown, concerned about the Darién problem throughout the eighteenth century, issued a series of orders commanding various sorts of remedial action. Among these was one in 1729, repeated in 1731, for a colonization project along the coast; another in 1761 for the construction of a fortress on the Caimán River in the Gulf of Darién; another in 1762 for the fortification of the Bay of Caledonia; and an order in 1778 commanding Viceroy Flores to conduct investigations and preparations for sending an armed expedition to the region. None of these was executed. In response to a royal order of 1760, however, Viceroy Messía de la Cerda did dispatch Antonio de Arévalo, colonel of engineers at Cartagena and one of the viceroyalty's most capable public servants, to map the coast of Darién. In view of the alarming developments during the North American Revolution, the crown issued another order dated August 15, 1783, that the Darién coast must positively be pacified by either the reduction or the extinction of the Cuna Indians. This decree came when Archbishop-Viceroy Antonio Caballero y Góngora was viceroy.[29]

Despite the crown's genuine concern and perhaps the best of intentions, it is clear in retrospect that a major action in Darién had little chance of success prior to the introduction of the military reform. Because of the small size of the prereform establishment, nearly all of the armed forces would have had to come from Spain on an unprecedented scale. On those occasions when Spain did send reinforcements to the viceroyalty, they were immediately siphoned off to bolster sagging defenses in the established coastal strongholds. In any case, local forces would be required to sustain any venture entailing prolonged action. Riohacha, for its part, contained a small non-Indian population which could and did function as a militia to complement the regular forces which could be spared from Cartagena, but in Darién such a reserve was almost nonexistent. Because the military reform had only begun to take effect prior to the North American Revolution, any major action by Guirior or Flores requiring the use of the viceroyalty's new disciplined militia would have been premature. Moreover, although both viceroys did display a profound concern with Darién, they fell heir to the Riohacha dilemma with a commitment already in existence.

By 1783 circumstances had changed. The Cunas' bold hostility, the newly

28. Luengo Muñoz, "Génesis," pp. 351, 359–60, 378–79; Caballero y Góngora, in *Relaciones de mando*, p. 752; Caballero y Góngora to Gálvez, Cartagena, January 31, 1784, AGI: Panama, legajo 307.

29. Luengo Muñoz, pp. 369, 375–76; Caballero y Góngora, in *Relaciones de mando*, pp. 752–54.

anticipated British aggression, and the latest royal order all combined to give Darién precedence over Riohacha. With a reformed military force now capable of meeting the challenge, the archbishop-viceroy responded accordingly.

In complying with the 1783 royal order for the occupation of Darién, Caballero y Góngora first solicited the counsel of the military and political officials of the viceroyalty who possessed specialized knowledge relating to the problem. These included Sargento Mayor Antonio Vázquez, currently serving in the Chocó Province; Ramón de Carvajal, commandant general of Panama; Félix Martínez Malo, governor of Portobelo; Andrés de Ariza, governor of Darién; Captain Antonio de la Torre, a man with an exceptionally distinguished record in conducting pacification and colonization projects in the Chocó; and Antonio de Arévalo, who had commanded the Riohacha expedition and had since briefly served as governor of Cartagena. Arévalo had the additional qualification of having personally charted the region in question. The viceroy issued the inquiries on January 8, 1784, expressing a personal preference for an all-out invasion.

The six officers formulated their replies almost immediately, the last dated April 8. They all envisioned an extensive role for the military, thus reflecting the new, tougher mood; but they differed on how best to apply this force. Opinions on the latter divided into two general groups: those advocating the removal and extermination of the Cunas by massive military sweeps through the isthmus, and those favoring the establishment of strongholds staffed with troops and colonists, with the assertion of pacificatory pressure from those bases. The representatives of the major defense centers, Carvajal, Martínez Malo, and Arévalo, were all of the former mind.[30] That consensus probably reflected a desire to insure a prompt return of their garrisons through rapid rather than gradual action.

Arévalo's declaration departed from the restrained policy with which he was earlier associated in Riohacha and indicated a deep disillusionment and bitterness from that experience. He had first been converted to extreme action by the 1775 massacre of expeditionary forces at Apiesi. At that time, he suggested a campaign of systematic extermination through Guajira, taking the precaution that no one should escape to spread the alarm.[31] Arévalo now proposed a Darién invasion from both ends of the isthmus, converging toward the center to secure an unconditional surrender. All resisting elements should be annihilated, the remainder taken away in chains. He advocated the use of Chocó Indians for mopping-up operations to dispose of those who escaped the invasion net. Once military operations had eliminated all the aboriginals,

30. Luengo Muñoz, pp. 360–81.
31. Antonio de Alcácer, *Las misiones capuchinas en el Nuevo Reino de Granada, hoy Colombia (1648–1820)*, pp. 215–16.

he concluded, the region could be safely settled and its wealth developed. A fourth proponent of extermination was Sargento Mayor Vázquez, who differed in that he did not believe that the regular army could operate effectively in the jungle. He urged an extensive employment of Chocó Indians adept at jungle maneuvering, who in the dark of night could creep up to Cuna settlements to accomplish their objectives.[32]

Ariza and de la Torre favored more gradual approaches, which resembled the program earlier attempted in Riohacha. As governor of Darién, Ariza had supervised the patrols conducted through Cuna country during the war, and from that experience he concluded that the Indians could easily elude any mass invasion because of the sheer impossibility of effectively using troops on large-scale sweeps through the jungle.[33] Consequently, he advocated the establishment of colonies at strategic points both in the interior of the isthmus and along the coast, particularly where potential transisthmian crossings existed. Fortified garrisons to combat the Indians would support these establishments. De la Torre proposed a vague but similar plan whose main distinction was a restriction of fortified settlements to nine enclaves, all on the coast, a strategy which would simplify logistics. Patrols conducted from such bases, he believed, could divorce the Indians from their foreign contacts, the main source of their corruption, and simultaneously work toward their reduction.[34]

Caballero y Góngora submitted these proposals to the Junta Superior de Tribunales in Santa Fe. With the Riohacha precedent still fresh, it selected the proposal of de la Torre, and the viceroy approved, although he narrowed its scope to four potential settlement sites. These sites were the mouths of the Caimán River in the Gulf of Darién and of the Mandinga River below the Punta de San Blas in the west; the Bay of Caledonia, situated midway along the coast and the site of the former Scotch colony; and the Bay of Concepción, located roughly halfway between Caledonia Bay and the Mandinga River mouth.[35] Caballero y Góngora then forwarded the proposal to the crown for a final decision. However, owing to an incredible communications snarl with inquiries, orders, reports, and replies crisscrossing each other to and from Spain, the viceroy was eventually forced to proceed on his own authority if action were ever to be taken. When he launched the expedition in 1785, he had still not received final approval from Spain.[36]

The viceroy's first choice as commander of the expedition was Captain de la Torre, author of the chosen plan, but in the preparatory operations he quickly proved more of a liability than an asset. Apparently seeking promotion

32. Luengo Muñoz, "Génesis," pp. 380–81, 388, 393.
33. Ariza to Carvajal, Yavisa, October 28, 1780, ANC: MM, vol. 118, fols. 15–52; Ariza to Caballero y Góngora, Yavisa, March 27, 1784, ANC: MM, vol. 118, fols. 15–19.
34. Luengo Muñoz, "Génesis," pp. 386–97.
35. Ibid., pp. 398–99.
36. Ibid., pp. 381–84.

to a higher rank before proceeding, his execution of the office was fraught with excuses and delays. Finally, annoyed and impatient, Caballero y Góngora journeyed to Cartagena himself to expedite matters and remained there until 1787. Finding that de la Torre had accomplished little, the viceroy replaced him with Arévalo, although retaining the agreed-upon plan of operations.[37] Under their joint leadership, preparations were concluded by January 1785, at which time they dispatched the first of two expeditionary forces from Cartagena. It made amphibious landings at Caimán, Concepción, and Mandinga. The second departed in July and occupied Caledonia, which was rechristened "Carolina del Darién."[38]

The armed forces which the viceroyalty employed in the Darién campaign were almost entirely drawn from the reformed military. Normally totaling around 1,000 men, the garrisons of the four fortified settlements were much larger than their earlier counterparts in Riohacha, although the number of regulars was about the same (see Table 8). The increment came from the disciplined militia of the Caribbean provinces, all of which except Santa Marta contributed components. Pardo units bore a disproportionate share of the burden, usually well over 50 per cent of the militia contingent in comparison to a total pardo enlistment in the affected provinces of approximately 45 per cent.[39] This imbalance obviously occurred in part because pardos were regarded as more expendable than other vassals, but also because Negroes adapted better to jungle conditions than whites and because of their recognized propensity for wielding machetes, a valuable asset for jungle action. Although some overlapping did occur, units from the Commandancy General of Cartagena normally supplied most of the personnel for Caimán and Carolina, while Panama assumed responsibility for staffing Concepción and Mandinga.[40]

The extensive employment of militia units in Darién could be construed with some validity as evidence of the government's confidence in their military capacity. This practice also, however, reflected the determination of the authorities to retain maximum regular forces in the key defense bases of Panama and Cartagena, which continued to take priority over all other concerns except Santa Fe. Significantly, the crown increased the capability of the regular army at this time by dispatching to New Granada two battalions from the Regiment of the Princess. Cartagena retained most of these troops, however, to compensate for the previous transfer of a battalion to Santa Fe and

37. Ibid., pp. 399–404; Caballero y Góngora to Gálvez, Cartagena, December 15, 1784, AGI: Panama, legajo 307.

38. Luengo Muñoz, "Génesis," pp. 414–15; Caballero y Góngora, in *Relaciones de mando*, pp. 754–55.

39. For the forces of the Commandancy General of Panama during this period, see Table 4, but note that a battalion of whites and four separate pardo companies were organized in 1784 in Veragua. For the forces of the Commandancy General of Cartagena, see Table 6.

40. Arévalo to Caballero y Góngora, Cartagena, October 2, 1788, ANC: MM, vol. 136, fols. 708–9.

to offset the drain of regulars to Darién and Riohacha. Panama also acquired three companies from these units to compensate for its component in Darién.[41] In effect, then, the Spanish troops, which normally were regarded as higher in quality, were retained in the defense bases while the burden of combat was passed on to the sons of the viceroyalty. To ameliorate the ordeal of the militia as well as to maintain fresh troops, the authorities endeavored to relieve the garrisons frequently, and in 1788 Caballero y Góngora formally limited the term of active duty to three months.[42]

Gradually the system of fortified settlements began to assume a definite shape and character. Carolina served as the expeditionary command and supply headquarters. In addition to its central location, this base possessed the geographic advantage of having to its rear a potential transisthmian route discovered in 1781. Shortly after the establishment of Carolina, a colony supported by the regular garrison of Darién was also founded on the Pacific side of this link on the Sabana River at Puerto Príncipe.[43] While Arévalo coordinated operations from Cartagena, a deputy commander (segundo comandante general) directed action in Darién. Residing in Carolina, various officers briefly held this position, including Anastasio Zejudo, but the ravages of disease necessitated a rapid turnover.[44]

In addition to colonists, the civilian personnel for the establishment included an array of technicians, particularly physicians, carpenters, and bureaucrats, as well as Chocó Indian laborers. During the course of the campaign, as new homes were constructed, the authorities transferred additional colonists to Darién. By April 1787 the civilian personnel in Caimán and Carolina totaled 169 individuals and 256 families.[45] Initially, missionary activity amounted to only a minor aspect of the enterprise, although a number of Capuchin friars did go to Darién to work within the fortified cities, and several also worked directly with the Indians outside of Concepción.[46]

The Darién enterprise placed an extraordinarily large demand on the vice-

41. Troop inspection report, Cartagena, April 1787, ANC: MM, vol. 71, fols. 24–54.

42. Arévalo to Caballero y Góngora, Cartagena, October 2, 1788; petition by the component from Mompós, Caimán, October 3, 1788, ANC: MM, vol. 116, fols. 319–22.

43. Caballero y Góngora, in Relaciones de mando, p. 755; Ariza report, Cartagena, April 12, 1785, AGI: Panama, legajo 381.

44. Caballero y Góngora to Zejudo, Turbaco, October 16, 1785, and to Commander of Carolina Francisco de Fersen, Cartagena, February 3, 1786, AGI: Panama, legajo 381.

45. Report on Carolina, April 1, 1787, ANC: MM, vol. 122, fol. 314; report on Caimán, April 1, 1787, ANC: MM, vol. 122, fol. 316. Data on the civilians of the other two establishments for 1787 have not come to the attention of this writer. Perhaps this information was siphoned off through Panama and never reached Santa Fe, or perhaps large-scale settlement was not yet advanced to these localities. By January 1789, Mandinga and Concepción possessed 184 colonists. However, disease had ravaged the Darién settlements and Carolina and Caimán's number had fallen to 236 colonists between them. See the expense report for the Darién expedition, Cartagena, January 24, 1789, AGI: Santa Fe, legajo 573.

46. Report on Carolina, December 19, 1787, ANC: MM, vol. 123, fols. 352–57; Alcácer, Las misiones capuchinas, pp. 230–31.

royalty's resources.[47] Merely to cope with the problem of logistics, which included the supply of foodstuffs, other necessities, and the movement of troops, the archbishop-viceroy found it necessary to augment an almost non-existent local fleet to thirty-two functional vessels by repairing old ships, purchasing and constructing new ones, and chartering others.[48] Moreover, because local production failed to meet food requirements, he imported flour by opening the port of Cartagena to merchants from the United States and neighboring colonies. The viceroyalty defrayed part of the flour expense by granting special concessions to those foreign merchants for the extraction of brazilwood from Santa Marta and Riohacha.[49]

Until the summer of 1787, a state of war existed between the Cuna Indians and the expeditionary forces. The initial January landings met sporadic resistance on the beaches and the ensuing period was characterized by mutual harassment, including a number of limited offensive thrusts from the fortified bases.[50] Events climaxed with an unsuccessful Cuna attack on Carolina in the summer of 1786, followed by harsh retaliatory assaults upon Indian settlements, which the viceregal forces systematically destroyed along with crops, boats, and other means of livelihood.[51] By mid-1787, military pressure had produced the desired effect: Cuna leadership through the mediation of Enrique Hooper, an English merchant in the region for some twenty years, expressed a desire to come to terms.[52] Following a preliminary conference with Commander Arévalo in Carolina, five local leaders and General Chief Bernardo, together representing most of the Cuna nation, journeyed to Cartagena to meet with Viceroy Caballero y Góngora in the nearby town of Turbaco. There, on July 21, 1787, after a preliminary display of firepower by the local military establishment, the belligerents signed a treaty of peace.[53]

The Treaty of Turbaco opened Darién to free colonization and development. The Cunas recognized the sovereignty of the crown, asked pardon for their past misdeeds, vowed to live as loyal vassals, and promised to discontinue

47. Caballero y Góngora, in *Relaciones de mando*, p. 756.

48. Ibid., p. 273.

49. José Ezpeleta, in *Relaciones de mando*, pp. 279–80; Francisco Gil y Lemos, "Gil y Lemos y su memoria sobre el Nuevo Reino de Granada," pp. 186–87.

50. Diary of the expedition, March 12–April 26, 1785, ANC: MM, vol. 123, fols. 1–16; Commander of Carolina Francisco de Fersen to Caballero y Góngora, Carolina, March 29, April 7, 1786, ANC: MM, vol. 122, fols. 679–82, and vol. 140, fols. 324–48; Caballero y Góngora, in *Relaciones de mando*, p. 755.

51. Fersen to Caballero y Góngora, Carolina, September 5, 1786, ANC: MM, vol. 118, fols. 267–71; Commander of Carolina Antonio Vásquez to Caballero y Góngora, Carolina, December 29, 1786, ANC: MM, vol. 122, fols. 606–10; Caballero y Góngora to Gálvez, Turbaco, June 30, 1786, AGI: Panama, legajo 307; Caballero y Góngora, in *Relaciones de mando*, p. 755.

52. Governor José Carrión y Andrade to Caballero y Góngora, Cartagena, June 28, 1787, ANC: MM, vol. 118, fol. 294; diary of the Commander of Darién, Carolina, June 1787, ANC: MM, vol. 122, fols. 495–509; Caballero y Góngora, in *Relaciones de mando*, pp. 755–56.

53. Caballero y Góngora, in *Relaciones de mando*, p. 756; Silvestre, *Descripción*, p. 121; "Pacificación general de los indios del Darién, celebrada el 21 de julio, 1787."

their relations with foreigners. They in turn were promised protection for their homes, property, and persons. The Cunas formally recognized the Spanish right to dispense justice and agreed to surrender accused Indians to the local authorities. All vassals of the crown, now including the Cunas, had the right of free settlement on unoccupied land and the right to move freely throughout the region.[54] To enforce the treaty, Caballero y Góngora maintained the expeditionary force at full strength in the region.

Relations with the Cunas appear to have improved somewhat after the peace treaty.[55] Indeed, the archbishop-viceroy was so encouraged by progress in Darién that he created a commission to recruit North Americans to advance the colonization of the region. Roughly 1,500 settlers were obtained from the non-Spanish West Indies and the United States. Few of them ever advanced beyond Cartagena, however, because of a serious epidemic which broke out in Darién, causing the viceroy to suspend their transfer.[56] Affairs were in this state when Francisco Gil y Lemos replaced Caballero y Góngora in January 1789. Although later events would prove his claims of success premature, the archbishop-viceroy was satisfied that he had successfully achieved the desired conquest, and in his relación de mando he suggested that Riohacha be reopened as the next arena of conquest and colonization.[57]

When viewed together, the Riohacha and Darién campaigns signalled a further expansion of major military activity and responsibility. These actions drew large numbers of militiamen into active duty, and new militia units were raised to assist in meeting the challenge. This new, vigorous frontier activity was one more example of the general growth in the military's role in the changing colonial scene of the late eighteenth century. By 1789 the army had emerged as a major and complex entity. Of all the organs of the state, it ranked as the single largest consumer of royal revenues, which in itself is a clear indication of the change produced by the reform.[58] Compared to the anemic little force which clung to the coastal defense bases of the viceroyalty in 1772, the reformed army of 1789 was a thriving giant. It had moved beyond its original geographical confines up into the interior and out onto the coastal frontiers. It now acted not only as a defender against foreigners, but as an agent in the interior for the preservation of the state and on the frontiers for the pacification of savage Indians.

54. "Pacificación general de los indios."
55. Ariza to Caballero y Góngora, Yavisa, October 24, 1788, ANC: MM, vol. 120, fols. 402–3.
56. Silvestre, *Descripción*, p. 122; Caballero y Góngora, in *Relaciones de mando*, pp. 756–57.
57. Caballero y Góngora, in *Relaciones de mando*, p. 759. Following his service in New Granada, Caballero y Góngora returned to Spain where he became archbishop of Córdoba. He occupied this position until his death in 1796.
58. Ibid., p. 268.

7. Reaction and Readjustment

THE FLOWERING of the military reform, with the growth of both the size and the function of the army of New Granada, was not destined to endure. The accession of Rear Admiral Francisco Gil y Lemos to the viceregency on January 8, 1789, severed the continuity of a military development spanning the administrations of Guirior, Flores, Pimienta, and Caballero y Góngora. During Gil y Lemos' rule, which lasted slightly less than seven months before his transfer to Peru, and during that of his successor, José de Ezpeleta (1789–97), the government in Santa Fe, backed by the crown, abruptly curtailed the extensive and varied domain of the reformed military. It sharply reduced the size of the disciplined militia, abridged the scope of general military responsibility, and reoriented the army back to the coast, where it was isolated from the cultural heartland of the colony, and where its impact upon existing social and political institutions was, at most, marginal.

The readjustments executed during the period 1789–96 are largely attributable to inherent weaknesses stemming from the haphazard, piecemeal nature of the earlier reform; but equally important, they derived from a changing scene in which new leadership reassessed the assumptions of the Caballero y Góngora era and reached substantially different conclusions. Viceroy Gil y Lemos recommended most of the forthcoming revisions, and after subsequent royal approval his successor, José Ezpeleta, executed them, although at times reluctantly. Together, their administrations blend to form a period of reassessment and reaction, bringing an abrupt end to the expansion and development of the reformed military in the Viceroyalty of New Granada.

Important leadership changes in Spain preceded the abrupt turnabout in New Granada. In 1787 death claimed the dynamic minister of the Indies, José de Gálvez, and on December 14, 1788, Charles III died, leaving the throne to his unimaginative and lackluster son, Charles IV. The succession of ministers which followed Gálvez failed to match his strength and commitment to reform, and this change of mood quickly found its way to New Granada through Gil y Lemos. The new viceroy owed his appointment to Gálvez' immediate successor, Antonio Valdés, one of his former navy comrades and a man with whom he enjoyed close personal rapport.[1]

As viceroy, Gil y Lemos lacked the disposition to carry through the ambitious programs of Caballero y Góngora. Although the Enlightenment influenced him on certain issues, especially those affecting the dispersion of scientific knowledge, he was strongly conservative in his broader views. He firmly adhered to the old-fashioned divine right theory of absolutism; he exalted the traditional role of the Church, including the Inquisition; and he advocated the strict observance of mercantilistic commercial policies.[2] Socially, Gil y Lemos instinctively mistrusted any action which might encourage the castas to question or to abandon their accustomed station in life. Moreover, his high self-esteem often led him to make quick, sometimes unwise, decisions which might have benefited from more careful deliberation.

When Gil y Lemos arrived in New Granada in 1789 he found what he perceived to be fiscal chaos. Despite increased income, the far-flung projects of Caballero y Góngora had placed a considerable strain on the treasury, with the viceregal debt mushrooming from some 900,000 pesos to nearly 2 million during his administration.[3] Gil y Lemos originally underestimated the magnitude of the deficit, but he was, nevertheless, deeply concerned by what he found, and he responded by suspending those of his predecessor's undertakings which lacked specific royal sanction.[4] By order of April 2, 1789, the crown, now acting through Valdés, approved his actions; it also authorized Gil y Lemos to formulate recommendations for reducing expenditures within confirmed programs.[5]

Although Gil y Lemos effected immediate but small savings by suspending the mining reform mission and by reducing the inflated staff of the viceregal secretariat, the expanded military, as the largest single consumer of revenues in New Granada, offered the most promising target for his economy drive.[6]

1. Rubén Vargas Ugarte, S. J., *Historia del Perú: Virreinato (siglo XVIII)*, p. 11.
2. Richard Konetzke, "Ideas políticas del Virrey Francisco Gil de Taboada."
3. Caballero y Góngora, in *Relaciones de mando*, p. 263; Ezpeleta, in *Relaciones de mando*, p. 279.
4. Gil y Lemos, "Memoria," p. 185.
5. Royal order, April 2, 1789, AGI: Santa Fe, legajo 573.
6. Gil y Lemos reduced the number of clerks in the secretariat, which had grown to fifteen under Caballero y Góngora, to merely nine. Gil y Lemos, "Memoria," pp. 177, 186.

The salaries of the fixed regular army and the veteran cadres assigned to the disciplined militia reached 727,315 pesos annually according to Gil y Lemos. That figure included the permanently activated dragoons of Riohacha but not the salaries of the personnel of the Regiment of the Princess, which returned to Spain in 1789, leaving behind a manpower deficit of at least one battalion in Cartagena.[7] The creation of a fixed battalion to fill that gap would add over 100,000 pesos a year to the military payroll.[8] Furthermore, the Darién expedition, with its activated militia forces and other salaried personnel, added another 356,000 pesos a year in costs.[9]

Therefore, in the name of economy, Gil y Lemos proposed the curtailment of much of Caballero y Góngora's military program. Specifically, he recommended a withdrawal from the Riohacha and Darién frontiers, a termination of the disciplined militia system in the interior, and the transfer of a battalion from the Auxiliary Regiment of Santa Fe to Cartagena.[10] Gil y Lemos regarded both the garrisoning of the interior and the conquest of the frontiers as ventures of marginal and in some respects clearly negative utility, unworthy of continuation on their own merits and certainly not justifying the immense investment required to sustain them. Indeed, his eagerness to reduce expenditures in these areas reflected a deep dissatisfaction with Caballero y Góngora's overall strategy for sustaining and expanding effective royal authority in the viceroyalty.

With regard to the frontiers, expressly the Darién expedition, there were a number of important reasons besides finances for terminating action. Both Gil y Lemos and his successor, Ezpeleta, were inclined toward the traditional frontier policy and they questioned the fundamental assumption of Caballero y Góngora that a secularized, crash program of frontier penetration would work, and if so that the results would justify the investment. When later commenting on the subject, Viceroy Ezpeleta postulated that a more gradual approach, consisting of a push by settlers from the peripheries, with military forces employed only in specific, limited missions, would work just as well with less expense.[11] "Perhaps the patience required for this approach will not satisfy fiery temperaments imbued with the martial spirit; but when it is considered that military forces cannot operate against Indians concealed in highly rugged, impervious mountains as with cultured nations dwelling in open country, and when the futility of the endeavors of the archbishop-viceroy is comprehended—as it too clearly is already—it will be understood that these slower but surer methods are preferable. They cannot bear results in one administration; they are works of time and constancy which in the end will

7. Ibid., pp. 205–12.
8. Ibid., p. 192.
9. Gil y Lemos to Valdés, Cartagena, January 30, 1789, AGI: Santa Fe, legajo 573.
10. Gil y Lemos, "Memoria," pp. 191–92, 202–3.
11. Ezpeleta, in *Relaciones de mando*, pp. 361–62.

conquer all."[12] A curtailment of the frontier enterprises would also relieve the chronic manpower shortages in the coastal defense bases.[13]

To traditionalists, the most alarming aspect of Caballero y Góngora's frontier policy was the colonization of conquered territory with North Americans, many of whom were Protestants, a measure incidentally which the crown had never expressly approved.[14] In the words of Francisco Silvestre, a former viceregal secretary and governor of Antioquia, who was one of the harshest contemporary critics of the archbishop-viceroy: "Under the administration of Mr. Góngora an attempt has been made to open a road from north to south, and to populate [Darién] with Anglo-Saxon colonists and other foreigners. God has not permitted this to take effect because it was the same as placing the region in the hands of our enemies and making them masters of both seas."[15] The conservative Gil y Lemos emphatically concurred in that judgment.[16]

On another level, the importation of foreign flour, largely from the United States, to supply the Darién expedition adversely affected grain production in the interior of New Granada. During the administration of José de Solís (1753–60), the government had cleared a road from Vélez to the Magdalena River to facilitate the marketing of wheat from the Tunja district, hoping to stimulate local production. Because of the opening of Cartagena to foreign carriers during wartime and again during the Darién campaign, however, native growers were chronically undersold and production remained stagnant, the road falling into disuse. Furthermore, grain commerce from the Santa Fe area suffered in a similar fashion.[17] Gil y Lemos supported the interests of these disadvantaged local producers, protesting that the flour concession worked at cross purposes with the need to develop the interior; this consideration added further weight to his argument for an end to the frontier campaigns and their related programs.[18] Finally, the viceroy suspected that the various commercial concessions granted to foreign merchants because of the Darién expedition were the source of extensive contraband trade, which undercut Spain's mercantilistic position in the colony.[19]

As a consequence of the mounting arguments against continuing the Darién campaign, the viceroyalty liquidated all of its fortified settlements on the isthmus and returned the garrisons to their home bases, although the process proceeded gradually, passing through several phases before reaching comple-

12. Ibid., p. 362.
13. Gil y Lemos, "Memoria," p. 192.
14. Ibid., p. 191.
15. Silvestre, *Descripción*, p. 87.
16. Gil y Lemos, "Memoria," p. 191.
17. Pedro Fermín de Vargas, *Pensamientos políticos y memoria sobre la población del Nuevo Reino de Granada*, pp. 21–26, 38–39.
18. Gil y Lemos, "Memoria," p. 194.
19. Ibid., pp. 186–87.

tion. Gil y Lemos initially urged the abandonment of only the three northern Darién settlements, with the retention of Caimán in the Gulf of Darién as a base for the protection of newly legalized commerce on the Atrato River. That recommendation, however, was superseded by a second plan formulated by a special junta convoked by Gil y Lemos while he awaited transportation from Cartagena to Peru. The junta decided to transfer the Caimán establishment to a nearby, healthier, more convenient location. Although the crown approved each of these schemes in turn, difficulties developed over arranging military security for the settlement. Ezpeleta refused to promise military protection for more than one year, and the colonists were reluctant to relocate with such limited support. Finally, a junta summoned in October 1791 recommended that security on the Atrato River be assigned to the coast guard and that the fourth settlement also be abandoned. Ezpeleta approved and the militarized pacification campaign on the Darién frontier came to an end.[20]

Meanwhile, the viceroyalty also acted to liquidate the non-military aspects of the frontier campaigns. Before leaving office, Gil y Lemos himself cancelled the various special trade concessions. He also began relocating the foreign colonists, most of whom were still waiting on the coast of Cartagena, and Ezpeleta finished that task.[21] Under Ezpeleta these colonists were given the option of settlement in safe, suitable locations in the interior or of transportation back to the United States. Most of them chose the latter alternative, and the viceroyalty provided them with passage to Charleston and Philadelphia.[22] The departing colonists included at least thirty-two individuals who under the tolerant regime of the archbishop-viceroy had managed to find their way into the Auxiliary Regiment of Santa Fe, where they had caused much scandal because of their heretical religious beliefs.[23]

To compensate for the withdrawal from the Darién coast, the viceroyalty established a new defense line back along the Sinú River. Two new disciplined militia companies were formed in the frontier outposts of San Gerónimo and San Bernardo, Province of Cartagena, and some of the colonists from Caimán, most assuredly native-born, were resettled in the latter location. The new companies received royal approval as disciplined on August 28, 1792.[24]

As for Riohacha, the government abandoned and destroyed the fortified

20. Cañaveral to Ezpeleta, including a copy of junta proceedings of December 2, Cartagena, December 9, 1791, ANC: MM, vol. 136, fols. 953–57; royal order, May 23, 1791, ANC: MM, vol. 117, fols. 82–86; Ezpeleta, in *Relaciones de mando*, pp. 359–62; Gil y Lemos, "Memoria," pp. 191–92.

21. Ezpeleta, in *Relaciones de mando*, pp. 360–61; Gil y Lemos, "Memoria," pp. 186–87, 191.

22. Gil y Lemos, p. 191; Allan J. Kuethe, "Un interesante caso de tolerancia religiosa en la época colonial."

23. Kuethe, "Un interesante caso."

24. Zejudo to Mendinueta, Cartagena, November 19, 1798, ANC: MM, vol. 12, fol. 757; Ezpeleta, in *Relaciones de mando*, p. 362.

city of Pedraza in 1790, and a royal order of August 13 of the same year, in response to a recommendation by Ezpeleta, transferred Sinamaica to the jurisdiction of the Captaincy General of Caracas.[25] The withdrawal from Pedraza amounted to the last step in returning the Guajira Peninsula to the aboriginals and their British allies. Thereafter, the city of Riohacha with its disciplined militia became the western barrier against Guajiro penetration.[26]

The army of New Granada never again assumed an offensive posture on the frontiers of either Riohacha or Darién. Following the withdrawals, both regions returned to full Indian sovereignty under strong British influence. As early as 1792 southern Darién from Chimán to Boca Chica began experiencing heavy Cuna attacks.[27] By 1803 the hope that a frontier policy based on understanding and commercial development would achieve a measure of Spanish influence in the Darién and Riohacha areas had all but disappeared.[28] Whether the maintenance of a permanent military presence within these hostile regions might have produced more favorable results is a matter of conjecture. Certainly, as events developed, all the costly endeavors of the two preceding decades were for naught, and a major area of military responsibility had been eliminated.

Even more significant for the future of the military in New Granada were Viceroy Gil y Lemos' policies for the interior of the viceroyalty. From the outset of his administration, Gil y Lemos seemed skeptical about the effectiveness of the defense system fashioned by the archbishop-viceroy and Colonel Anastasio Zejudo. When he arrived in Cartagena on January 6, 1789, he found the military leadership of New Granada in an uproar. Zejudo's inspection tour of 1788–89, which was still in progress, had stirred a wave of protests from those parties injured by his decisions and especially from the three commandants general, Juan José Villalengua of Quito, José Domás y Valle of Panama (1786–93), and José Carrión y Andrade of Cartagena (1785–89). All three resented Zejudo's viceroyalty-wide superior authority as subinspector general.[29] Especially influential was Governor Carrión y Andrade, who had developed a bitter antipathy for Caballero y Góngora and his favorites during the viceroy's lengthy stay on the coast while directing the Darién campaign.[30]

25. Narváez to the governor of Maracaibo, Riohacha, March 16, 1791, in José Félix Blanco and Ramón Azpurua, comps., *Documentos para la historia de la vida pública del Libertador* . . . , 1: 233; Antonio de Alcácer, *Las misiones capuchinas en el Nuevo Reino de Granada, hoy Colombia (1648– 1820)*, p. 236.

26. Pedro Mendinueta, in *Relaciones de mando*, p. 559.

27. Governor José Domás y Valle to Ezpeleta, Panama, March 8, 1792, ANC: MM, vol. 136, fols. 988, 1007–11.

28. Mendinueta, in *Relaciones de mando*, pp. 559–60, 563–66.

29. Domás y Valle to Valdés, Panama, December 1, 1789, AGS: GM, legajo 7089; Carrión y Andrade to Valdés, Cartagena, September 28, October 24, 1787, AGS: GM, legajo 7089; expediente on the visit of Zejudo to the Commandancy General of Quito, 1788–89, AGS: GM, legajo 7089. Carrión y Andrade was the former governor of Vera Cruz. Domás y Valle eventually became captain general of Guatemala.

30. According to Carrión y Andrade, Caballero y Góngora usurped most of his military and

Carrión y Andrade, as field marshal, argued that his subordination to a mere colonel subverted the proper system of military authority. He particularly opposed the subjection of the prestigious governorship of Cartagena to any military authority other than the viceroy's. Needless to say, as commander of Cartagena he also hoped for a reorientation of the defense system to benefit that stronghold, at least to the degree of strengthening its regular garrison. Gil y Lemos conferred at length with Carrión y Andrade in Cartagena before finally beginning his ascent to the capital.[31] Not surprisingly, the viceroy unceremoniously relieved Zejudo of his position when the latter reached Cartagena from Panama, reducing him to colonel of the Fijo. He then petitioned the crown for its approval and proceeded to map out yet another reorganization of the defense system of the Viceroyalty of New Granada.[32]

The most abrupt departure of Gil y Lemos from the defense policies of his predecessor involved the upland militia. In a communication of May 15 he urged the reduction of the entire interior militia to an urban status, including the establishments of Santa Fe, Popayán, Quito, and Cuenca. This measure would deprive the militia of its veteran advisors, much of its equipment, its systematic training, its peacetime fuero, and, in effect, its meaningful existence. As in the case of the frontier expeditions, Gil y Lemos urged this measure in the name of economy; but he also had other significant reasons derived from a new perspective on the proper strategy for sustaining order and royal authority.[33]

Gil y Lemos estimated that his militia proposal would reduce military expenditures annually by some 20,000 pesos. Flores and Caballero y Góngora regarded this as a modest cost considering the political leverage they obtained from the militia. Indeed, Gil y Lemos' own actions indicate that cost was not an immensely important factor in his decision either, despite his claims to the contrary. Shortly after advocating a reduction of the militia, he proposed the reestablishment at half-company strength of the halberdier unit of the viceregal guard, which had been disbanded following its disgrace during the Comunero Rebellion, as well as an expansion of the cavalry company from forty to fifty-six men. The cost in new salaries for these two units alone would amount to roughly 10,000 pesos, which was two-thirds of the expense in salaries of the entire Santa Fe veteran militia cadre![34] If such increases in ex-

political functions and prerogatives, reducing him to a mere "orderly." Petition of Carrión y Andrade, San Lorenzo, November 2, 1790, AGI: Santa Fe, legajo 1011.

31. Gil y Lemos to Minister of Grace and Justice Antonio Porlier, Cartagena, February 28, 1789, AGI: Santa Fe, legajo 578; Gil y Lemos to Valdés, Cartagena, March 14, 1789, AGS: GM, legajo 7089.

32. Gil y Lemos to Zejudo, Cartagena, March 13, 1789, AGS: GM, legajo 7053; expediente on the subinspectorship of Zejudo, 1787–89, AGS: GM, legajo 7053.

33. Expediente on the subinspectorship of Zejudo in Quito, 1788–89, AGS: GM, legajo 7089.

34. Expediente on the reestablishment of the viceregal guard, 1789–91, AGS: GM, legajo 7081; Gil y Lemos, "Memoria," p. 205.

penditures merely for ceremonial purposes were possible, then the sum of 20,000 pesos for the militia should not have been prohibitive, provided that Gil y Lemos had retained Caballero y Góngora's confidence in the value of the militia system.[35]

Gil y Lemos had, in fact, come to believe that the interior militia was not only largely useless, but that it could pose a real threat to the social and political stability of the colony. Now a safe distance from the mass upheaval which his predecessor had witnessed, he argued both in his May 15 letter and in his recommendations to Ezpeleta that the implications of the Comunero movement had been vastly exaggerated and that a prudent, humane leader could depend on the fidelity of the people. A careful investigation, which had benefited from "reliable accounts" (*seguros informes*), had shown, he believed, that the inhabitants were docile and without seditious intentions; even if by chance there were exceptions, they lacked the means to be dangerous.[36] Consequently, he saw no compelling reason to maintain either a large disciplined militia in the interior or, for that matter, a regular force of the present size.

Gil y Lemos, moreover, carried his arguments much further. He predicted that the interior militia program itself, if continued, might become a menace, for although the local citizenry was not yet dangerous, providing it with arms and military training might make it so.[37] In his words to Ezpeleta: "To have them live among veterans, fortify the capital, and be maintained in a constant state of war, is to teach them what they do not know; it is to make them think about that which otherwise would not occur to them; it is to force upon them an appreciation for their own power, and on the occasion in which they employ it, they may comprehend their advantage. Therefore, if in addition to the indispensable appropriations which the King must make for the security of these domains against the exterior enemy, the interior defense is placed on a comparable footing, its maintenance will not only become useless but dangerous."[38] This line of thought was much the same as that advanced by the cabildos of Santa Fe and Popayán, whose opposition after six years in the former location and over a decade in the latter remained as vigorous as ever. It was also essentially the same argument as that articulated by Regent-Visitor Gutiérrez de Piñeres in his criticism of the Popayán reform in the period preceding the Comunero Rebellion. Although Gil y Lemos never specifically identified the source of the "reliable accounts" in which he placed so much

35. Although the viceregal guard had some combat value, it served largely a decorative, ceremonial function. Captain Veremundo Ramírez de Arellano of the cavalry company, for example, spent much of the Ezpeleta administration on leave escorting an unusual parrot to the court in Spain along with a young giant from Vélez who had attracted royal curiosity. AGS: GM, legajos 7058 and 7079.

36. Gil y Lemos, "Memoria," pp. 201–2.

37. Gil y Lemos to Valdés, Santa Fe, May 15, 1789, AGS: GM, legajo 7089.

38. Gil y Lemos, "Memoria," p. 202.

faith and which provided the justification for his skepticism about the disciplined militia, they were presumably the same elements—fearful creole aristocrats, harried cabildos, and jealous commandants general—that for various reasons had stubbornly opposed the initiatives of the archbishop-viceroy.

One such powerful voice which emerged in opposition to the interior military reform during this period was that of Juan José Villalengua, the president of Quito, who, it will be recalled, was the son-in-law of José García de León y Pizarro, now of the Council of the Indies. Until the *subinspección general* of Colonel Anastasio Zejudo, Villalengua had been a staunch supporter of the Quito militia. When, for example, the circulation of the royal order of February 13, 1786, threatened the fuero militar of the upland establishment, he vigorously defended both the legitimacy and necessity of the fuero. He was especially strong in support of Colonel José del Corral y Narro and his unsuccessful attempt to preserve the privileges of the Guaranda militia (see chapter 5). Yet when Zejudo restructured the upland militia at the expense of the self-serving system devised by García Pizarro and perpetuated by Villalengua—eliminating the units of presidential cronies such as Corral y Narro and José Renxijo but declaring the fuero militar for those he deemed worthy of preservation—Villalengua quickly emerged as a forceful adversary of a disciplined status for the upland militia. In so doing, he strengthened those forces which would eventually eliminate the system from the entire interior of New Granada.

President Villalengua focused his overt opposition to the work of Zejudo on the minor question of whether the commandancy general required a military judicial advisor. When Zejudo officially informed Villalengua of the changes he had effected in the Quito militia system, he also instructed him to select an assessor to aid in the disposition of military causes.[39] The use of an assessor was a standard procedure outlined in the Cuban reglamento, but the president claimed uncertainty and used it as an excuse to withhold indefinitely the fuero and therefore to obstruct the new militia system.[40] In an appeal to Spain dated August 18, 1788, accompanied by petitions from Corral y Narro and Renxijo, which accused Zejudo of high-handed and unjust tactics, Villalengua protested Zejudo's order and viciously attacked the work of the subinspector general. Moreover, he denounced the disciplined status of the surviving militia as both an unnecessary expense and a menace to the political and social stability of the region.[41] This protest, which reached Spain in time for the royal deliberations on the fate of the interior militia, was a complete reversal of the stand Villalengua had taken two years earlier, and is a

39. Zejudo to Villalengua, Quito, July 8, 1788, ANE: Pres., vol. 252, fol. 119.
40. *Reglamento . . . de Cuba,* chap. 10, art. 8; Villalengua to Oidor Decano Lucas Muñoz y Cubero, Quito, July 13, 1788, ANE: Pres., vol. 252, fols. 122.
41. Petition by Villalengua, Quito, August 18, 1788, AGS: GM, legajo 7089.

striking example of the facility with which public functionaries embroiled in the militia controversy could switch positions when it suited their personal purposes.

To the viceregency, which was then still occupied by Caballero y Góngora, Villalengua merely communicated notice of an appeal to Spain, ostensibly to contest the creation of the assessorship. His message reached Cartagena during the transfer of authority to Gil y Lemos, and, although it did not disclose the broader protest to Spain, it did provide support for those seeking to undo the work of Caballero y Góngora and Anastasio Zejudo. In all likelihood Villalengua's protest influenced Gil y Lemos in his decision to advocate a general reduction of the disciplined militia of the interior.[42]

While the viceregal authorities awaited a royal decision on the fate of the interior militia, they also worked to reduce the size of the regular garrison of Santa Fe. With some semblance of order now restored to the interior, the leadership of New Granada generally agreed that the Auxiliary Regiment, with its standard battalion and six attached companies, was excessive in size, especially given the limited resources of the viceroyalty and the manpower needs of Cartagena. Among those expressing doubts about the existing arrangement was Francisco Silvestre, who argued that at least part of the resources consumed for the defense of Santa Fe could more wisely be expended in Cartagena. Physiocrat Pedro Fermín de Vargas betrayed a creole distaste for the security force, daring to suggest that the Auxiliary Regiment be assigned to road building projects so that the viceroyalty might in some way benefit from its troop expenditure.[43] Significantly, Colonel Juan Antonio Mata, who had become commander of the Auxiliary Regiment, himself declared in July that the size of the regiment was extravagant, given its responsibilities, and he recommended a substantial reduction.[44]

Although Gil y Lemos indicated a desire to reduce the size of the Auxiliary Regiment early in his administration, he awaited an opportunity to discuss the matter with his successor before forwarding his recommendations to Spain. Ezpeleta arrived in Santa Fe on July 30, assuming office the following day; he and Gil y Lemos conferred some two weeks before the latter departed for Cartagena.[45] As a consequence of their deliberations, they jointly urged a reduction of the Auxiliary Regiment by six companies and a reestablishment of the fixed unit of Cartagena at regiment strength. The second battalion in Cartagena would be formed from the six companies of the Auxiliary Regiment and by recruitment from the Regiment of the Princess, which was preparing

42. Villalengua to Caballero y Góngora, Quito, August 18, 1788, ANC: MM, vol. 36, fols. 786–91; Gil y Lemos to Villalengua, February 26, 1789, ANE: Pres., vol. 252, fols. 125–26.
43. Vargas, *Pensamientos políticos*, pp. 36–37; Silvestre, *Descripción*, pp. 116–17.
44. ANC: MM, vol. 31, fol. 396, and vol. 66, fols. 442–44.
45. Gil y Lemos to Porlier, Santa Fe, August 15, 1789, AGI: Santa Fe, legajo 578.

to depart for Spain.[46] Considering the expense of maintaining a regular garrison, the peaceful record of the uplands since 1781, and the unsatisfied manpower demands of Cartagena, this recommendation was certainly prudent and timely.

The crown responded favorably to the proposals of Gil y Lemos concerning both the restructuring of the interior defense and the system of militia inspection. Regarding the latter, the monarchy, barraged by hysterical protests from the commandants general, had resolved to remove Zejudo from the subinspectorship even before Gil y Lemos reported his provisional action in the matter. Hopeful of quieting the issue, it attached the position to the governorship of Cartagena, then occupied by Joaquín de Cañaveral (1789–96).[47] The crown also promptly approved the transfer of regular troops from the interior to the coast and the expansion of the Fijo into a regiment. During mid-1790, Ezpeleta combined personnel from the six extinguished companies of the Auxiliary Regiment with some 449 men recruited from the Regiment of the Princess to form the second battalion. He also successfully proposed the incorporation of the regular companies of Santa Marta into the Fixed Regiment. These units were chronically undermanned and underdisciplined, a problem which Ezpeleta hoped to solve by rotating fresh troops to that base from Cartagena in an arrangement similar to the one traditionally observed between Panama and Portobelo.[48]

In by far the most important of its decisions, the crown, acting through Valdés, approved on January 11, 1790, the recommendation of Gil y Lemos concerning the interior militia and thereby reduced the units of Santa Fe, Popayán, Quito, and Cuenca to an urban status. It ordered the viceroy to reassign their veteran cadres either to coastal units or to the regular army. To reward the volunteer officers of the demoted units, some of whom had made considerable personal and financial sacrifices, the crown elected to extend permanently their fuero militar, although enlisted men, by virtue of their urban status, lost their military privileges.

This royal order, which seemingly accepted the arguments of Gil y Lemos at face value, cited as considerations only cost and a conviction that relief from the military burden would inspire greater "love and loyalty" from the citizenry. The minutes of the crown's deliberations reveal, however, that it was also concerned about the abuse and exploitation of laboring militiamen, which had become a widespread feature of the militia system in New Granada, especially in the interior, and which had been denounced not only by Gil y Lemos but earlier by Anastasio Zejudo and Caballero y Góngora. Moreover, the

46. Expediente on the reorganization of the regular garrisons of Santa Fe and Cartagena, 1789–90, AGS: GM, legajo 7054.

47. Royal order, January 20, 1789, AGS: GM, legajo 7089.

48. Expediente on the reorganization of the regular garrisons of Santa Fe and Cartagena, 1789–90.

monarch pronounced himself "completely convinced of the perfect fidelity" of his subjects; this piece of wishful thinking presumably made it possible to correct abuses and defects in the interior defense structure by simply abolishing it.[49] Thus, with one regal stroke of the pen, the crown curtailed and effectively destroyed the internal defense system devised amidst such heated controversy by Manuel Flores and Antonio Caballero y Góngora as a political weapon for the enforcement of royal authority against the interests of the entrenched creole aristocracy. The monarchy of Charles IV had in effect retreated from the policy of confrontation, which had characterized the orientation of Charles III's struggle for reform.

Although José Ezpeleta endorsed many of the initiatives of Gil y Lemos, especially those involving significant fiscal consideration, he differed sharply on the question of the disciplined militia. A field marshal of the army, he had served as captain general of Cuba before his appointment to New Granada. An imaginative, energetic leader, Ezpeleta was one of the ablest viceroys to serve in New Granada.[50] His perceptive thought and his ability to manipulate the bulky administrative system of New Granada were particularly praiseworthy. He now found himself confronted by a royal decision which, he believed, was ill advised and potentially harmful to the political stability of the viceroyalty.

Viceroy Ezpeleta responded to the January 1790 order by suspending its execution pending a carefully reasoned appeal to Spain. Although he recognized the shortcomings of the existing militia system, including the abuses resulting from the personal ambition of those shaping many of the units, he argued that the interior militia could be salvaged if further reduced in size and properly supported, and he asserted that there was in fact no viable alternative to its continuation. The limited resources of New Granada made it impossible, he argued, to maintain sufficient regular troops in the interior to sustain royal authority, and transportation difficulties made unrealistic any hope that coastal garrisons could deal effectively with further upland disorders. Ezpeleta expressed some sympathy for Gil y Lemos' apprehensions over the reliability of an armed citizenry, but he did not see this concern as an insurmountable obstacle. He contended that in a vast country a rebellion never reached all sections at the same time. Therefore, in the event of insurrection, the colonial leadership could exploit regional differences in bringing

49. Expediente on the organization of regular and militia forces in Santa Fe, 1783–90, AGS: GM, legajo 7089.

50. Given the present lack of exhaustive analyses for the various aspects of their administrations, it is hazardous to attempt to rate the viceroys of New Granada, and for that reason present judgments ought to be considered tentative. It would seem, however, that both Flores and Ezpeleta were outstanding in providing strong, lucid leadership. Caballero y Góngora, although inspiring sympathy for his enlightened views and initiatives, was only a mediocre administrator. Messía de la Cerda, Guirior, Gil y Lemos, Mendinueta, and Amar y Borbón all appear to have been lesser men.

force to bear. Similarly, unanimity would probably not exist even within the rebel areas, where internal divisions might also be exploited. However, a successful strategy of divide and conquer required that loyal vassals receive solid military preparation, a need that could best be satisfied through the existing disciplined militia system. To eliminate remaining abuses in the militia, Ezpeleta renewed an earlier offer to develop a viceroyalty-wide defense plan, which would, once and for all, standardize militia organization and procedure.

In his proposal, Ezpeleta was vague on just how the reliable persons would be distinguished from the unreliable in recruiting militiamen, which no doubt would be the crucial step in effecting his scheme. Presumably, the traditional tactic of favoring Spanish officers would be fundamental, although he did not directly advocate this; in fact, he indicated disenchantment with the current practice of employing revenue officials in the militia because of residence difficulties and excessive absenteeism. He bluntly warned the monarchy, however, that it should entertain no illusions about the effectiveness of urban militia, which he characterized as worse than useless because the viceregal leadership might one day make the mistake of depending on it.[51]

Ezpeleta's position on the retention of the interior militia was certainly more carefully considered than that of Gil y Lemos. The latter had acted hastily, riding the crest of a wave of anti–Caballero y Góngora resentment that had emerged with the departure of the archbishop-viceroy. But his perception of what had happened in 1781 was shallow and his political assessment of 1789 was naïve. Gil y Lemos never explained how he intended to cope with mass insurgency, simply arguing that it would never happen. This was a short-sighted assumption indeed, but one which was accepted by the crown. True, the general slowing of the impetus for reform would tend to lessen tensions; yet, the basic conflict between the creole aristocracy and the monarchy remained, as events would soon demonstrate. For the time being, however, Gil y Lemos had the ear of the monarchy. On November 26, 1790, the crown in a one-sentence statement ordered Ezpeleta to execute the order of January 11, his reservations notwithstanding.[52]

Unfortunately, the records of the royal deliberation on the fate of the interior militia provide no additional insights into the reasoning of the crown or, more specifically, an explanation as to why Ezpeleta's arguments failed to achieve positive results. It is, nevertheless, possible to speculate about additional reasons for the royal steadfastness. By this time, the massive Villalengua challenge to the interior militia of Quito had arrived in Spain.[53] Villalengua's father-in-law, José García Pizarro, the former president of Quito, undoubtedly had considerable influence from his position on the Council of the Indies.

51. Ezpeleta to Valdés, Santa Fe, April 19, 1790, AGS: GM, legajo 7089.
52. Ibid.
53. Villalengua to Valdés, Quito, August 18, 1788, AGS: GM, legajo 7089.

Moreover, Pedro Valencia, the strong-man of Popayán who had opposed the reform from the beginning, had a well-married son in the Ministry of the Indies, where he also most likely acted as a transmitter of anti-reform sentiment. Probably most significant, however, was the close personal relationship between Valdés and Gil y Lemos, as exemplified by the uncritical manner with which the former accepted report after report from the latter. Direct documentation for the precise effect of these factors obviously does not exist, but, in accounting for such an abrupt reversal of royal policy, they cannot be ignored.

Finally, there was royal displeasure with the disruptive impact of the fuero militar. During the preceding decade, as seemingly endless litigation clogged the channels of royal justice and as military prerogatives worked to undercut the institutions of municipal government, the crown had become exasperated. Frequent admonitions to colonial authorities to dampen such conflicts reflected this increased impatience, but its most graphic expression was the order of February 13, 1786, which flatly denied the fuero to urban units. Two circular orders issued for the empire in 1791 indicate that this sentiment bridged the change of administration in both Spain and New Granada. The first order stated that units formed by viceroys but not enjoying explicit royal approval could not claim the fuero militar. The second declared that all militia units must be classified as either urban or disciplined, the latter being defined as those possessing veteran cadres, systematic training, and the corresponding equipment. It also clarified ambiguities in militia terminology by specifying that the term "provincial" was no longer synonymous with either classification.[54] In New Granada, the reduction of the interior militia to an urban status had the administrative advantage of denying the fuero to those very units that were the major source of jurisdictional disputes.[55]

The reduction of the army's size and responsibilities diminished royal expenditures, as sought by Gil y Lemos and Ezpeleta, but revenue collections declined as well. Under Ezpeleta, annual income slumped to approximately 3 million pesos and remained near that level for the duration of the colonial period. In both the aguardiente monopoly and in Cartagena's customs receipts, sharp decreases occurred, and modest gains in the tobacco monopoly could offset them only partially. Reduced customs receipts resulted from the disruptive effect of the international turbulence upon commerce; the reduction also reflected the loss of trade with concessionaires from neighboring foreign colonies and the United States, which had been permitted by Caballero y Góngora but halted by Gil y Lemos. The aguardiente monopoly

54. Royal orders, April 8, August 22, 1791, in Colón y Larriátegui Ximénez de Embún, *Juzgados militares*, 2: 252–55.
55. Viceroy Pedro Mendinueta, when reflecting upon the question of an interior militia, attributed to the fuero a large measure of responsibility for the hostility that existed toward the system. Mendinueta, in *Relaciones de mando*, p. 543.

suffered from competition from both authorized Spanish imports and extensive illegal local sales.[56] Following the departure of Caballero y Góngora and the subsequent curtailment of the interior army, the royal administration simply did not—and probably could not—display the earlier vigor in advancing revenues. Although the cultivation of tobacco was relatively easy to regulate, as reflected by the increase in monopoly profits, the manufacture of liquor was not, especially without a full administrative commitment and the power to sustain it.

On the other side of the coin, the reduction of military costs and, especially, the elimination of the expensive frontier campaigns, when combined with the savings resulting from the abandonment of other Caballero y Góngora programs, brought the viceregal budget back into equilibrium. By the end of his administration, Ezpeleta not only paid off the massive debts left by the archbishop-viceroy but actually built a surplus of some 400,000 pesos. Despite wartime demands, his successor, Pedro Mendinueta (1797–1803), increased that sum to 1.5 million pesos, which were duly transported to Spain.[57] Thus, although revenue collection stagnated under Caballero y Góngora's successors, reduced government expenditures and careful management more than compensated for the change.

With the reorganization of the regular army completed and the question of the interior militia resolved, the royal administration finally turned its attention to the task of defining a comprehensive militia system for New Granada. Viceroy Ezpeleta had originally offered to structure such a plan in September 1789, when hope still remained for the interior militia. In May 1790, the crown ordered him to proceed with this undertaking and later persisted in that judgment despite its November rejection of his proposal for the upland militia.[58] Ezpeleta completed his work in November 1793, at which time he submitted a militia reglamento or code to Spain for royal consideration.[59] On July 13, 1794, the crown granted its approval, thereby giving New Granada a formally coordinated militia system after a twenty-year history of piecemeal, provincially oriented reform.[60]

56. Ezpeleta, in *Relaciones de mando*, pp. 379–84; Mendinueta, in *Relaciones de mando*, pp. 525–31; Restrepo, *Historia de la revolución*, 1: xxxi. There are some indications that the consumption of chicha became a form of protest against the aguardiente monopoly, even in upper class homes.

57. Mendinueta, pp. 525–31. The replacement of the Regiment of the Princess with a second battalion for the Fijo, which was largely created from the six extinguished companies of the Auxiliary Regiment and the garrison of Santa Marta, cut costs by roughly 100,000 pesos a year. When this sum is combined with the savings from the dissolution of the Darién and Riohacha frontier campaigns, they alone account for a reduction in expenditures by roughly 500,000 pesos annually.

58. Ezpeleta to Valdés, Santa Fe, September 15, 1789, and royal order of May 28, 1790, AGS: GM, legajo 7089.

59. Ezpeleta to Alange, Santa Fe, November 19, 1793, AGS: GM, legajo 7080.

60. Royal order, July 13, 1794, AGS: GM, legajo 7080.

The *Reglamento para las milicias disciplinadas . . . del Nuevo Reyno de Granada . . .* amounted largely to a codification of the work of Colonel Anastasio Zejudo, minus the interior militia (compare Tables 6 and 9). Coastal troop distribution remained essentially the same, although with a number of readjustments. On the one hand, Ezpeleta trimmed the size of the militia by standardizing battalion strengths at 800 men, eliminating the infantry battalion of Veragua, and replacing the infantry regiment and two dragoon companies of Riohacha with a four-company corps of light infantry and cavalry. On the other hand, he established two separate companies each in Barbacoas, Loja, and Jaén de Bracamoros. The two latter locations, which had originally pertained to the now extinguished regiment of Cuenca, received these companies because of their position on the uneasy Amazon frontier with Portugal and because of the government's concern over local Indian difficulties.[61] Barbacoas had experienced yet another rebellion in 1791 over the aguardiente monopoly, which prompted Ezpeleta to resurrect its militia for want of any alternative, given its great distance from the regular garrison in Popayán. The location of Barbacoas near the Pacific Ocean also permitted justification of militia there by reason of coastal defense.[62] Elsewhere on the coast, Ezpeleta replaced the two nine-company regiments of whites and all colors of Cartagena with a single regiment of two battalions. As far as the newly classified urban militia of the interior was concerned, Ezpeleta simply omitted any reference to it in the reglamento, explaining that he found no value in perpetuating it.[63]

In drafting militia policy for the new code, Ezpeleta employed the Cuban reglamento as his guide, preserving much of it but also incorporating subsequent royal decisions, such as the exemption of wholesale merchants, and effecting those adjustments demanded by local conditions. The most striking characteristic of the new reglamento was its persistent, underlying insistence on quality training and its carefully devised set of checks and safeguards to prevent the lapses in discipline that were so common during the early reform. The reglamento also sought to prevent specific abuses such as the sale of offices, the exploitation of troops by provincial authorities, and the award of officerships to revenue officials or others with conflicting interests.[64] Needless to say, the actual enforcement of such provisions would be another matter, but at least the institutional machinery was available.

61. Troop inspection report, Cuenca, March 11, 1789, ANC: MM, vol. 107, fols. 112–16; Ezpeleta to Alange, Santa Fe, November 19, 1793.

62. Ezpeleta to Alange, Santa Fe, November 19, 1793; expediente on the disorders in Barbacoas, 1791–92, AGS: GM, legajo 7078. Because of its proximity to the South Sea, the viceroyalty customarily organized emergency urban militia forces in Barbacoas during time of war. Beccaria to Caballero y Góngora, Popayán, November 17, 1782, ANC: Virreyes, vol. 16, fols. 22–30.

63. Ezpeleta to Alange, Santa Fe, November 19, 1793. In the various coastal establishments, he also effected minor shifts at the company level in unit location, presumably to enhance recruitment prospects.

64. *Reglamento . . . del Nuevo Reyno de Granada,* especially chap. 2.

Except for the emphasis on discipline, most of Ezpeleta's revisions of militia policy were modest, although there were a number of important changes. Ezpeleta officially eliminated, for example, the position of veteran lieutenant, which, it will be recalled, was an innovation first introduced by Guirior in Guayaquil and generalized by Anastasio Zejudo. All things considered, this was a practical provision. Even with the reduced number of units, the militia of New Granada would have required some sixty-three lieutenants at the rate of one per company under the previous system, not including pardo and artillery units. This would have posed a serious drain both on the regular army and the royal treasury. To compensate for the deletion, Ezpeleta simply increased the number of ayudantes on the battalion command and staff groups from one to three, with the stipulation that they rotate among the various companies to supervise the performances of the veteran enlisted men serving as sergeants and corporals.[65] Because the position of veteran lieutenant had in actuality disappeared anyway, the enlarged number of ayudantes represented an increase in the amount of veteran input into the militia. Moreover, this action resolved once and for all the lingering uncertainty over the proper size of the veteran cadres for the disciplined militia.

One particularly revealing adjustment to local conditions was the elimination of the "white" and "all color" classifications in the militia, although pardo units retained their social designation. This abolition amounted to an admission that the membership of "white" units was no longer white, if indeed it had ever really been so. In the continuing struggle to sustain enlistment quotas, the authorities had become increasingly lax in upholding social distinctions, which, given the extent of miscegenation along the coast, was probably a futile objective anyway. When Anastasio Zejudo reorganized the militia of Guayaquil in 1788, for example, he officially abolished the pardo battalion but then proceeded to incorporate that unit's enlisted men into the regiment of whites.[66] And service records for Guayaquil's Squadron of Militia Dragoons for the same year reveal that all the first sergeants were free pardos.[67]

Circumstantial evidence suggests that when Ezpeleta organized the new militia regiment in Cartagena he also incorporated many pardos, because the companies of the second battalion came from many of the same municipalities that had supported companies in the now defunct regiment of all colors. Furthermore, there was a high incidence of direct continuity in the officer corps of the two units. The transition was even less subtle in Santa Marta, where the Infantry Regiment of Disciplined Militia of All Colors of Santa Marta simply changed names and became the Regiment of Infantry Volun-

65. Ezpeleta to Alange, Santa Fe, November 19, 1793.

66. Petition of the pardo officers of Guayaquil, Guayaquil, November 19, 1788, AGS: GM, legajo 7089.

67. Service records, Squadron of Militia Dragoons of Guayaquil, ANC: MM, vol. 47, fols. 10–34.

teers of Santa Marta.[68] Significantly, Viceroy Pedro Mendinueta confirmed that most of the enlisted men in the non-pardo coastal units were in fact men of color, except for the officers.[69] In effect, then, by 1794 units classified as "pardo" can still be presumed pardo in membership; but units lacking a specific social label might be anything. The reglamento also eliminated the fiction concerning the command of pardo units, with the head of the white command and staff group formally receiving the title of commander.[70]

Finally, one of the most important modifications of militia policy concerned the fuero militar, but that change originated in Spain, not in New Granada. When Ezpeleta forwarded his proposal to the crown, he left the basic fuero unaltered, including the provision that the fuero of officers might be active as well as passive. As indicated earlier, however, royal impatience with the disruptive impact of military privilege had increased. This attitude was reflected by the various efforts to limit eligibility for the fuero and had influenced the decision to reduce the interior militia. The crown now challenged the advisability of perpetuating an active fuero in New Granada, explaining that its use should be reserved for only the most special occasions—its twenty-year history in New Granada apparently notwithstanding—and went on to delete that traditional prerogative of the militia officer corps of New Granada from the reglamento.[71] This step was another blow to the corporate prestige of the militia and represented a further decline in the status and influence of the army of New Granada under the administration of Charles IV.

The deepest significance of the new reglamento, however, lay not in the changes that it introduced into unit distribution and militia procedure, but in its role as the first royal attempt to define a viceroyalty-wide militia program for New Granada. The reglamento had the effect of solidifying the previously fluid experiment into a system that would endure without major alterations until the end of the colonial period. This stabilization and coordination of militia operations paved the way for a standardization of unit support, including the areas of equipment, veteran cadres, and instruction. As a result, the quality of the disciplined militia of New Granada improved appreciably in the following period.

As part of its attempt to define military procedures in New Granada, the royal administration also clarified and institutionalized the supra-provincial structure of troop inspection and supervision. When Viceroy Ezpeleta re-

68. *Reglamento . . . del Nuevo Reyno de Granada*, relaciones 1 and 3; troop inspection report, Militia Infantry Regiment of All Colors, Cartagena, July 1, 1784, AGI: Santa Fe, legajo 1156; service records, Regiment of Infantry Volunteers, Santa Marta, December 1797, ANC: MM, vol. 27, fols. 672–719, and December 1800, AGS: GM, legajo 7282.

69. Mendinueta to Secretary of War Juan Manuel Alvarez, Santa Fe, June 19, 1798, AGS: GM, legajo 7069.

70. *Reglamento . . . del Nuevo Reyno de Granada*, chap. 2, art. 18.

71. Royal order, July 13, 1794.

ceived the royal decision to attach the office of subinspector general to the governorship of Cartagena, he reminded the crown that it would be utterly impossible for the governor of Cartagena to inspect personally an area as vast as coastal New Granada and still discharge his responsibilities as governor. He suggested that the defense system might be better served by simply returning the task of inspection to the full discretion of the provincial governors.[72] By royal order of February 19, 1790, however, the crown established a mechanism for supra-provincial inspectional authority through the traditional structure of the commandancies general.

Under this order, the commandants general of Quito and Panama officially acquired the title of *subinspector particular* (regional subinspector), while the governor of Cartagena remained subinspector general. Each subinspector possessed supervisory authority in military affairs over the subordinate provinces of his commandancy general, but with the governor of Cartagena exercising full command over the other two.[73] The governor of Panama had customarily exercised this kind of prerogative in his dependent provinces; on the other hand, this concession appreciably strengthened the authority of the commandants general of Cartagena and Quito in Santa Marta and Guayaquil respectively, where the local governors had traditionally functioned with near independence (see chapter 1). The Governorship of Popayán, by contrast, had as a matter of practice largely gone its own way, and by the 1790s its subordination to Quito was purely nominal.

For militia inspection, the reglamento of 1794 provided further clarification. Under its provisions, the two subinspectores particulares assumed direct authority over most matters of militia administration in their dependent provinces, including the regulation of units, the correction of illicit practices, and the proposals for volunteer appointments. They channelled this material through the office of the subinspector general, who then directed it to Santa Fe with his own recommendations. The subinspector general himself initiated all proposals for veteran and other salaried positions in the militia, and he possessed authority to conduct inspections as necessary.[74] The thrust of this system was to curtail abuses by provincial authorities, which had become so common, especially in Guayaquil.

The lines of authority for the supervision and review of the regular army paralleled those for the militia, with an additional strengthening of the role of the commandant general. The governor of Panama had traditionally controlled directly the garrisons of his subordinate provinces, which depended upon him for men and equipment. The incorporation of the companies of Santa Marta into the Fixed Infantry Regiment of Cartagena in 1790 accom-

72. Ezpeleta to Valdés, Santa Fe, September 15, 1789.
73. Royal order, February 19, 1790, AGS: GM, legajo 7089.
74. *Reglamento . . . del Nuevo Reyno de Granada*, chaps. 2, 6.

plished the same effect in the Commandancy General of Cartagena. In 1793–94, Ezpeleta extended this concept to the Commandancy General of Quito, where he combined the regular garrisons of Quito and Guayaquil into a corps of four companies. The commandant general, thereafter, rotated companies by twos between Quito and Guayaquil, a procedure which had the effect of making Guayaquil directly dependent upon Quito, and which, incidentally, also represented a further reduction of interior troop strength.[75] As a consequence of these readjustments, all the regular troops of New Granada except those of Popayán and Santa Fe came under the direct control of the three commandants general, or subinspectores, and all troops were at least nominally subject to the authority of the governor of Cartagena as subinspector general.

While on the surface the new structure of inspection promised to centralize and coordinate the lines of authority, actual change was often more apparent than real. The role of subinspector strengthened the hands of the commandants general in their subordinate jurisdictions, where they commanded the regular troops and directly managed militia operations, but the subinspectores particulares themselves remained largely autonomous from effective supervision. It was impossible to exercise any real inspectional authority from Cartagena and, despite a provision in the February 19 order permitting governors of Cartagena to vest their powers in the lieutenant governor while on inspection, not one governor of Cartagena ever ventured beyond his commandancy general to examine the work of the subinspectores particulares. Unless the subinspección general became a separate office, as had been the case under Anastasio Zejudo, it in effect amounted to another layer of bureaucracy that had little practical value. Ezpeleta recognized this difficulty and petitioned the crown to redefine the position as independent of the governorship.[76] The monarchy, however, no doubt mindful of the uproar caused in the commandancies general by the inspection tour of Anastasio Zejudo, declined action.[77] Thus, despite a definite movement in the direction of centralization and coordination, the royal administration never managed to overcome fully the essentially regional orientation of the military reform.

75. Ezpeleta believed that the rotation of units between Quito and Guayaquil would improve discipline and morale. Because the standard size of a company of regulars was seventy-seven men, it was necessary to increase the number deployed in Guayaquil from one company to two. The former company had operated at the strength of 100 men, and Ezpeleta believed that Guayaquil should have first priority because of its coastal location. Expediente on the reorganization of the veteran garrisons of Guayaquil and Quito, 1793–98, AGS: GM, legajo 7069.

76. Ezpeleta to Alange, Santa Fe, July 19, 1795, AGS: GM, legajo 7064.

77. Royal order, December 17, 1795, AGS: GM, legajo 7064.

8. The Final Challenge

IT IS REMARKABLE in retrospect that Gil y Lemos could have unhesitatingly proclaimed the innocence and loyalty of the vassals of New Granada and could have acted upon that assumption in reshaping the viceroyalty's defenses. None of his immediate predecessors nor any of his successors would have dared to do so. Gil y Lemos ruled during the brief interlude between the relaxation of the tensions generated by the Comunero Rebellion and the advent of the French Revolution in the summer of 1789. Events in France soon sent shock waves across the Western world, however, and the authorities of New Granada found themselves confronted by increasingly restless, often rebellious elements of the creole population that found in the principles of revolutionary France answers to many of their own points of dissatisfaction. As relations between creole and Spaniard degenerated into an ugly hostility, the army of New Granada once again found itself asked to sustain the authority of the Bourbon monarchy through force and intimidation. But whereas a decade earlier it had acted merely to support controversial reform initiatives, it was now summoned to defend the very existence of the regime.

In late 1791, Pedro Fermín de Vargas, a distinguished creole from San Gil, Province of Tunja, abruptly shattered the momentary political tranquillity of New Granada when he suddenly slipped out of the viceroyalty for the avowed purpose of soliciting support for the liberation of his homeland. Vargas, a graduate of the Colegio del Rosario in Santa Fe, had been an intimate of royal government, having served as an employee of the viceregal secretariat under Caballero y Góngora, as an associate of the Botanical Expedition, and, at the time of his departure, as interim corregidor of Zipaquirá, an appointment he had received from Viceroy José Ezpeleta.[1]

Other grave incidents soon followed. In 1794 the authorities discovered that Antonio Nariño, another distinguished creole and a close acquaintance of Vargas, had dared to print some 100 copies of the *Declaration of the Rights of Man and the Citizen*, along with favorable editorial comment. Nariño, a former alcalde of Santa Fe, was a personal friend of Ezpeleta and had access to the official government printing press. He had also held positions as treasurer of tithes and export monopolist for the royal quinine industry, and he had even served briefly as standard-bearer of the militia infantry regiment. Nariño had encountered the *Declaration of the Rights of Man* in a history of the Constituent Assembly written by Salart de Montjoie, which he had procured from Captain Cayetano Ramírez de Arellano of the viceregal guard. Ramírez, as it turned out, had himself obtained the book from the private library of his uncle, the viceroy![2] Although only two copies of Nariño's work ever entered circulation, his deed and that of Vargas were by implication most alarming, for they exposed the extent to which revolutionary publications had penetrated the colony and revealed the impossibility of determining who could or who could not be held in confidence. Nariño was quickly arrested, tried and convicted, and sentenced to ten years of imprisonment in Africa.

A rash of other seditious activities also surfaced in 1794. An informer in Santa Fe declared that a clique of revolutionaries, including Sinforoso Mutis, nephew of José Celestino Mutis of the Botanical Expedition, José María Lozano, former lieutenant colonel in the disciplined militia, and a number of other young creoles, among them students from the Colegio del Rosario and Nariño himself, were plotting to seize the barracks of the Auxiliary Battalion and initiate an insurrection while the troops attended Sunday Mass. Moreover, a Spaniard, Francisco Carrasco, revealed that a fellow countryman, José Arellano, had confided in him that he and three young creoles, also from the Colegio del Rosario, had authored and posted a number of seditious lampoons in Santa Fe. This latter revelation quickly brought arrests, torture, convictions, and stiff prison sentences in Africa. Both the viceroy and the audiencia had doubts, however, about the authenticity of the plot to seize the Santa Fe barracks. Nevertheless, the crown brought most of the accused to Spain for further investigation, detaining them there until 1799.[3] Meanwhile, the authorities in Quito arrested Francisco de Santa Cruz y Espejo, the direc-

1. Tisnes, *Movimientos*, pp. 97–115.
2. Thomas Blossom, *Nariño: Hero of Colombian Independence*, pp. 2–3, 8–21; Raimundo Rivas, *El andante caballero don Antonio Nariño: La juventud (1765–1803)*, pp. 19–23.
3. Tisnes, *Movimientos*, pp. 147–61.

tor of the public library of Quito, for plotting the independence of America from Spain. Espejo had earlier made the acquaintance of Nariño in Santa Fe and had attended *tertulias* (social intellectual gatherings) at his home.[4]

The reactions that these incidents inspired in the creole community were as disturbing as the incidents themselves. José Antonio Ricaurte, Nariño's brother-in-law and a defense lawyer, so skillfully defended Nariño by attacking alleged injustices in the regime that the manuscript of the trial itself became censored material and Ricaurte followed Nariño to prison.[5] In the case of the lampoons, deep public sympathy emerged for the three convicted students. Rather than denounce their acts as outrageous or shameful, the cabildo of Santa Fe harshly criticized the handling of the case by the viceroy and the audiencia. The cabildo, which during recent times had become increasingly uninhibited in the statement of its views, expressed skepticism as to the guilt of the imprisoned and chose to interpret the affair as an unwarranted persecution of creoles. What emerged at this juncture was something more than a simple disagreement over the enforcement of policy; the tone of the cabildo protest was blunt, harsh, and indeed defiant at times of royal authority.[6]

The case of José María Lozano provides another revealing illustration of this deterioration of respect for the crown's authority. Lozano was among those named in the suspected plot to seize the barracks of the Auxiliary Regiment; he had also been labeled a conspirator by Arellano, the Spaniard, who sought unsuccessfully to extricate himself by implicating others. For reasons not entirely clear, the authorities elected not to proceed against Lozano directly, but they did feel compelled to suspend his shocking election by the cabildo in January 1795 as alcalde of the first vote, ordering him to retire to one of his country estates. His brother, Jorge Tadeo, who had served as *alférez* in the militia cavalry regiment of Santa Fe and later as alférez in the Royal Corps of Spanish Guards in Spain, and who was destined to become the first president of revolutionary Cundinamarca, demanded with the support of the cabildo that his brother be permitted to assume his office since no charges had been proven against him. In so doing, both Jorge Tadeo and the municipal government chided the crown for its political indiscretion in sending José María back to an hacienda, where he commanded over 1,000 dependents who could readily be converted into a private army! The implication of Jorge Tadeo's statement was that the crown must not really believe his brother seditiously oriented or it must have taken leave of its political and military

4. Ibid., pp. 312–19; Blossom, *Nariño*, pp. 7–8.
5. Blossom, pp. 14–21.
6. Petition of the cabildo of Santa Fe through Juan Antonio Rubio Plaza, Madrid, May 11, 1795, AGI: Estado, legajo 55; see also cabildo petitions, October 19, 1794, and December 8, 1795, in José Manuel Pérez Sarmiento and Luis Martínez Delgado, comps., *Causas célebres a los precursores . . .* , 1: 274–82, 431–54.

senses. This incident served as a stark warning of creole power and it betrayed a deep alienation of New Granada's creole patriciate from Bourbon Spain.[7]

When confronting this restless, often rebellious, population, the authorities faced a difficult if not impossible situation. The enlightened despot Charles III, in attempting the colonial reorganization, had shattered customary colonial inertia by forcing administrative and fiscal reforms down to the provincial and municipal levels on the one hand, while whetting appetites through the promise of expanded commerce or improved social status on the other. The social and political ideals of the Enlightenment inevitably followed, whether through contraband, agencies such as the Botanical Expedition, or simply the personal libraries of viceroys such as Caballero y Góngora and Ezpeleta, whose books found their way into the hands of men like Vargas and Nariño. Ironically, the primary victim of the new learning was the Bourbon regime itself, which had first aroused and challenged the creole patriciate by its attempt at reform and which now provided the first target for the sharpened creole political consciousness. Disenchanted colonists were particularly attracted to the idea of collective sovereignty, which offered an alternative to an authoritarian regime that too often confronted them with unwelcome policies. In the principle of equality before the law, they found a substitute for a hierarchical system that accorded a special virtue to European birth, particularly in the recruitment of tax collectors and high administrative officials. Thus, Charles III's attempt to reform and to revitalize his American empire entailed the inherent liability of unleashing forces which in the long run threatened its existence.

The creole hostility that surfaced in the 1790s has often been attributed, with some validity, to the repressive nature of the colonial regime. Certainly, the clumsy and at times brutal—not to mention unproductive—methods employed by the audiencia in handling the judicial processes of the various conspirators exacerbated hostilities, tending to sustain that interpretation. It should be remembered, however, that Gil y Lemos had shown none of this attitude when he argued in 1789 against the maintenance of a large military force in the interior of New Granada. Even more significant, Ezpeleta had extended personal and political confidence to men such as Vargas and Nariño, naming them to important and lucrative positions in the government. That Ezpeleta felt betrayed and embarrassed by their actions is indisputable, especially after Nariño reached into his own personal library to find a copy of the *Declaration of the Rights of Man*. In shaping a response to the new threat of subversion, the viceregal authorities would not dare to extend such confidence again.

Although the authorities made feeble attempts to tighten censorship, it was clearly too late by 1794 to seal off the ideological challenge from Europe.

7. Petition of Jorge Tadeo Lozano, Aranjuez, May 25, 1795, AGI: Estado, legajo 55.

On the one hand, the secular spirit of the Enlightenment had greatly weakened the strength of the Inquisition and its capacity to regulate popular thought.[8] On the other hand, outside sources of subversive ideas were so numerous, and the amount of seditious material that had already penetrated the colony so large, that it is unlikely that any system of censorship could have contained them. As a consequence, the primary response of the colonial authorities, including the audiencia, was to turn to the military—principally the regular army—with the hope that if all else failed it would sustain the regime.

Viceroy Ezpeleta, however, found the army poorly suited to meet the responsibilities of maintaining domestic peace and preserving the regime. Lagging recruitment combined with personnel erosion through death and desertion had left the Fixed Infantry Regiment of Cartagena undermanned even for peacetime, and Spain presently found herself at war with France. Moreover, local recruits were usually taken from the depressed area around Socorro, Corregimiento of Tunja, or from the coastal lowlands.[9] The former were politically suspect; the latter were normally pardos and hence by social stigma of dubious value.

Elsewhere, the upheaval in Barbacoas in 1791 had forced the authorities to reduce the size of the Auxiliary Battalion to compensate for a reestablishment of a veteran company in Popayán. Ezpeleta had sought an expansion of Popayán's twenty-five-man detachment into a full company after he lost his battle with Spain to retain a disciplined militia in the interior, arguing that the generally successful advancement of revenue reform had depended directly on the army for support. When the population of Barbacoas rebelled against an attempt to establish the aguardiente monopoly in September 1791, his argument seemed vindicated. Without awaiting royal authorization, he increased the garrison of Popayán to eighty men and dispatched Carlos Ciaurriz, a lieutenant from the Auxiliary Battalion, to Barbacoas as deputy governor. To compensate for the cost and manpower of the garrison in Popayán, Ezpeleta proposed a reorganization of the Auxiliary Battalion along lines recently developed in Toledo and Vitoria in Spain, which defined a battalion as four companies of fusileers at 120 men and one 63-man company of grenadiers. Five additional second lieutenants would assist with the larger companies.[10]

8. José Toribio Medina, *Historia del tribunal del Santo Oficio de la Inquisición de Cartagena de Indias*, chaps. 15–16.

9. Ezpeleta to Alange, Santa Fe, September 9, 1794, AGS: GM, legajo 7063; *memoria*, Audiencia of Santa Fe, Santa Fe, March 30, 1796, AGI: Estado, legajo 52; Ezpeleta to the Príncipe de la Paz, Santa Fe, May 19, 1796, AGI: Estado, legajo 52; Zejudo to Ezpeleta, Cartagena, November 9, 1796, AGI: Santa Fe, legajo 1016; Mendinueta to Alvarez, Santa Fe, June 19, 1798, AGS: GM, legajo 7069; troop inspection report, Fixed Infantry Regiment of Cartagena, April 1801, ANC: MM, vol. 70, fols. 1198–1204.

10. *Reglamento que El Rey ha mandado expedir para el nuevo pie y establecimiento de los Regimientos de Infantería de Toledo y Vitoria*, arts. 4–5. Tuquerres, Pasto, Tumaco, and Barbacoas were the only districts in the Governorship of Popayán which still had not been subjected to the aguardiente monopoly. Expediente on the disorders in Barbacoas, 1791–92, AGS: GM, legajo 7080.

Although the local authorities in Barbacoas restored order without outside assistance, the crown approved Ezpeleta's measures, including the reorganization of the Auxiliary Battalion. The net effect of this action was to strengthen appreciably royal authority in Popayán, but it reduced the Auxiliary Battalion by more than 130 men.[11] Ezpeleta, who acted in this matter before Nariño's exploits revealed the extent of creole disaffection in the viceregal capital, argued that the new arrangement would prove sufficient to satisfy the purposes of the unit. Although he never officially reversed that position, Viceroy Ezpeleta obviously had second thoughts after 1794.

In the Commandancy General of Quito there were also difficulties with the domestic defense system. Ezpeleta's scheme to combine the garrisons of Guayaquil and Quito into a single corps of four companies, periodically rotated in pairs between the two cities to enhance morale and to improve performances, had amounted to the loss of one company for the capital of the presidency. The continued growth of Guayaquil as a Pacific port, moreover, and the advent of an almost continuous series of wars effectively eliminated any chance that Quito would ever recover its troops. As a consequence of the liquidation of the interior militia, the president also lost the services of a 30-man detachment of militia dragoons that had been maintained on salary since the tense days of 1781. The troops that remained stationed in Quito were nearly all native born, which was an additional worry, especially after the Espejo incident. President Luis Muñoz de Guzmán, complaining of new restlessness both in the capital and in outlying Indian villages, petitioned for a battalion of five 100-man companies for the commandancy general and a restoration of the dragoon detachment, but he received no support from the authorities in Santa Fe, who had more immediate concerns.[12] On the brighter side, Panama reported no security difficulties, and thus it could support Quito by sea with its veteran force should complications arise.

Less critical, at least in an immediate sense, was the condition of the regular army's officer corps. Spaniards outnumbered creoles in all the important units and held wide margins at the levels of captain and above (see Table 10). This superiority resulted in large measure from the prominent role that Europeans had played in newly created fixed units. Many men who began as second lieutenants or lieutenants in the 1770s had risen to the rank of captain or higher by the 1790s. There was, moreover, a legitimate tendency on the part of the royal administration to place men with combat experience in positions of command, something that few creoles acquired unless they had participated in the Riohacha or Darién Indian wars. Large numbers of creole cadets had

11. Expediente on the disorders in Barbacoas, 1791–92.
12. Expediente on the reorganization of the veteran garrisons of Guayaquil and Quito, 1793–98, AGS: GM, legajo 7069; expediente on the garrison of Quito, 1793–98, AGS: GM, legajo 7070.

entered military service during the seventies and eighties, however, and by the mid-nineties they were gradually working their way up in the officer corps, where they reinforced other creoles who had simply purchased commissions.[13] By the mid-nineties, therefore, creoles dominated the junior officerships in all units except the Auxiliary Battalion, which was a younger unit and more carefully structured socially. Since promotions were normally based on seniority—unless some overriding consideration intervened—this situation promised future political difficulty unless major assistance was soon provided by Spain.

To cope effectively with the political crisis in New Granada, Ezpeleta believed that substantial numbers of crack European troops were absolutely essential for key units of the army. Spanish regulars should comprise at least 50 per cent of the Fijo and, it was hoped, 100 per cent of the Auxiliary Battalion.[14] Since the Comunero Rebellion, the government had generally aimed to sustain a high percentage of European troops in the regular garrison of Santa Fe, believing them to be more politically reliable than the American-born, but this was a difficult goal to attain.[15] The last major influx of Spanish troops into the fixed army of New Granada came with the departure of the Regiment of the Princess in 1789; in 1793 Spain was again at war, this time with France, which necessarily placed priority demands on troops and officers for Europe. Ezpeleta, nevertheless, formally requested 1,000 Spanish reinforcements as an immediate necessity given the domestic crisis.[16] Meanwhile, he ordered 150 Spanish troops from Cartagena to Santa Fe to fill vacancies in the Auxiliary Battalion and to strengthen his hand politically.[17]

To emphasize his concern for domestic security, Ezpeleta elected to remain in Santa Fe during the war with France, 1793–95.[18] This decision broke a

13. The purchase of officerships was not unusual. Moreover, these purchases could contain special arrangements. When the father of Pedro Domínguez, for example, paid 5,000 pesos to place his son, age sixteen, in a captainship of the Auxiliary Battalion, he did so with the understanding that Pedro would serve only in that unit. The reorganization of 1792 eliminated four captainships, however, including Pedro's, which had the lowest seniority. His father thus petitioned the crown that it not reassign his son to Panama or Cartagena and that it return his money. The crown acceded to his request by reassigning Captain Domínguez to the Auxiliary Battalion. Expediente on the officership of Pedro Domínguez, 1792, AGS: GM, legajo 7078.

14. Ezpeleta to Secretary of State Duque de la Alcudia (Manuel Godoy), Santa Fe, June 19, 1795, AGI: Estado, legajo 55.

15. Troop plan, Caballero y Góngora, AGS: GM, legajo 7089; Caballero y Góngora to Gálvez, Cartagena, December 15, 1784, AGI: Santa Fe, legajo 950; Ezpeleta to Valdés, Santa Fe, October 19, 1789, AGS: GM, legajo 7081. Gil y Lemos is an exception to this rule. He believed that there were plenty of vagabonds in the viceroyalty to fill the army and saw no good reason to solicit recruits from Spain. Gil y Lemos to Valdés, Santa Fe, July 26, 1789, AGS: GM, legajo 7054.

16. Ezpeleta to Alcudia, Santa Fe, June 19, 1795.

17. Ezpeleta to Alange, Santa Fe, October 19, 1794, AGS: GM, legajo 7063.

18. Ezpeleta to Alange, Santa Fe, July 19, 1793, and reply, February 15, 1794, AGS: GM, legajo 7083. The immediate challenge that France posed to New Granada certainly was minor.

tradition established by his wartime predecessors—Eslava, Messía de la Cerda, and Flores, all of whom took residence in Cartagena—and it is in itself testimony to the gravity with which he viewed the danger of domestic insurgency. Indeed, the transfer of highly esteemed Spanish troops from Cartagena to Santa Fe during wartime also dramatically demonstrates that the authorities had come to fear domestic insurgency more than foreign invasion. The new orientation can in part be explained by the fact that France was less of an invasion threat than Spain's traditional foe, Great Britain, but this practice continued in subsequent years when Spain and Britain renewed their rivalry. Finally, Ezpeleta also adopted the policy of systematically employing retired veteran troops as revenue security guards to create an additional military reserve for the regime.[19]

When Spain settled her differences with revolutionary France in the Peace of Basle, July 1795, the crown was free to cope with the crisis in New Granada. To revitalize the Auxiliary Battalion and the Fijo, it ordered 1,000 regulars drafted from the veteran regiments of southern Spain.[20] A troop injection of this proportion was unprecedented, but the crown showed itself every bit as concerned about potential revolution as the viceregal leadership. After a number of delays the first 700 of these men along with extensive arms and supplies, including some for Trinidad, departed Cádiz on August 4, 1796.[21] Two days earlier, Lieutenant General Pedro Mendinueta had departed Spain to relieve José Ezpeleta as viceroy.[22]

New Granada, however, was not destined to receive the military reinforcements it awaited. Even as the relief expedition left Cádiz, war again threatened the empire, this time with Great Britain, and hostilities began in October. When the troop convoy reached Trinidad, Governor José María Chacón, who believed that his island was in imminent danger of attack, invoked emergency authority to requisition for its defense all of the ships, weapons, and troops. His premonition proved correct. In February 1797, the British under Admiral Henry Harvey appeared with vastly superior forces and effortlessly seized the island and its defenders, inflicting yet another humiliation upon the empire, and, in the process, depriving New Granada of the Spanish troops

---

Nevertheless, given the circumstances under which the viceroyalty was created during the advent of the War of Jenkins' Ear, and the behavior of New Granada's leaders during later conflicts, the decision to remain in Santa Fe amounted to more than a practical decision to dismiss the French threat.

19. Ezpeleta to the Príncipe de la Paz, Santa Fe, May 19, 1796.

20. Ezpeleta to Minister of War Miguel José Azanza, Santa Fe, May 19, 1796, AGS: GM, legajo 7064.

21. Josefina Pérez Aparicio, *Pérdida de la Isla de Trinidad*, pp. 65–66.

22. Mendinueta, in *Relaciones de mando*, p. 534; Mendinueta to Azanza, Cádiz, August 1, 1796, AGS: GM, legajo 7084. This was a routine transfer of authority. Actually, Ezpeleta ruled one year longer than normal because the first man selected to succeed him, the Marqués de Casares, died before he could leave for New Granada.

it needed so badly.[23] Moreover, the domestic crisis soon worsened; Antonio Nariño had escaped his captors in Cádiz and was making his way back to New Granada via France and Great Britain, where he sought aid for the liberation of his homeland.

Pedro Mendinueta, who had journeyed to New Granada by way of Puerto Rico rather than Trinidad, reached Cartagena in September 1796. Before continuing on to Santa Fe, he conducted an extensive survey of the military preparations in Cartagena in conjunction with Anastasio Zejudo, with whom he quickly developed close rapport. Since losing the subinspector generalship through the actions of Gil y Lemos, Zejudo had functioned as commander of the Fijo, earning promotion to brigadier in 1791. In 1795 he was elevated to the rank of field marshal and appointed governor of Cartagena, which, incidentally, made him subinspector general again. Mendinueta remained in Cartagena until Ezpeleta descended from the capital to effect the transfer of viceregal authority, January 3, 1797; shortly thereafter, despite the fact that the empire was again at war, he departed for Santa Fe in deference to domestic imperatives, leaving the able Anastasio Zejudo to command the coast.[24]

As a leader, Mendinueta was a man of moderate to good ability reinforced by considerable colonial experience, which he had acquired as troop inspector of New Spain. Over the course of his administration in New Granada, he performed competently, exercising basically sound judgment. Temperamentally, however, he was somewhat given to histrionics, and when the news of the troop loss in Trinidad reached him, followed by word that Nariño had secretly slipped back into New Granada, his state of mind could only be described as sheer panic.

Even before he learned of Nariño's latest movements, Mendinueta saw far-reaching implications in the capture of Trinidad. He feared that the British intended to use the island as a base to penetrate the Orinoco River system, attack through Guayana into the Province of Los Llanos de Casanare, and from there strike into the heartland of New Granada.[25] When the viceroy and the audiencia discovered that Nariño had reentered New Granada, they immediately concluded that he was preparing a popular uprising in support of such a British invasion. Further, they feared that Vargas and perhaps other conspirators had accompanied him.[26] The British, operating through the famous Venezuelan precursor, Francisco Miranda, along with Nariño, Var-

23. Pérez Aparicio, *Pérdida de . . . Trinidad*, pp. 65 ff.; Eric Williams, *History of the People of Trinidad and Tobago*, pp. 49–50.

24. Restrepo Tirado, *Gobernantes*, pp. 118–19; Mendinueta to Azanza, Cartagena, January 30, 1797, AGS: GM, legajo 7084; expediente on the appointment of Zejudo, 1794–95, AGS: GM, legajo 7085. Zejudo did not formally assume the governorship until February 18, 1796.

25. Mendinueta to the Príncipe de la Paz, Santa Fe, June 19, 1797, AGI: Estado, legajo 52.

26. Mendinueta to the Príncipe de la Paz, Santa Fe, July 19, 1797, and the Royal Audiencia of Santa Fe to the Príncipe de la Paz, July 19, 1797, in Pérez Sarmiento, *Causas célebres*, 1: 159–62, 170–73.

gas, and others, did consider such a plan, but developments in Europe soon derailed it.[27]

To prepare for possible insurgency and British invasion, Mendinueta placed the provincial authorities and the military on special alert; he ordered 200 veteran troops from Cartagena to Santa Fe; and he petitioned the governors of Havana and Puerto Rico for military assistance, a gesture that predictably proved fruitless. He also sent an officer from the Auxiliary Battalion to the Province of Los Llanos, the anticipated invasion route, to act as a military governor. Finally, he organized secret lists of vassals who might be trustworthy in crisis, although he dared not formally organize them into a militia for fear of arming enemies by misjudgment or alienating loyal vassals by excluding them.[28] Much to the relief of the authorities, however, the immediate crisis abruptly ended in July when Nariño, apparently discovering that his plans lacked any real popular support, negotiated a peaceful surrender.[29]

Yet the broader crisis continued despite the apprehension of Nariño. His failure, as well as a similar failure at this time by the revolutionaries Manuel Gual and José María España in Caracas, revealed that the authorities had overestimated the immediate danger of popular rebellion, but the basic mistrust between the royal administration and the creole aristocracy remained intense.[30] As Viceroy Mendinueta observed in May 1798: "Although there presently are no indications in this viceroyalty that the seditious projects that were afoot still continue, I will never be persuaded that these municipalities sustain in them the most dutiful submission and obedience that they should; they will continue their superficial tranquillity until an opportunity arises to throw off the gentle yoke that governs them. The truth is that in the interior of the Kingdom and among the common people there are not all the necessary prerequisites or the disposition for such an unhappy occurrence; but they are very vulnerable to persuasion and seduction, and because that is what the enemies of domestic peace have planned for them, the indispensable need arises for a vigilance capable of curtailing such schemes."[31]

Spain did manage to reinforce the army of New Granada in 1799 with twelve officers and four hundred men from the Regiment of the Queen, and eighteen separate officers at the ranks of second lieutenant and lieutenant to bolster sagging veteran militia cadres.[32] Because extensive transfers of Spanish

27. Blossom, Nariño, pp. xxii–xxiv, 36–43.
28. Mendinueta to the Príncipe de la Paz, Santa Fe, July 19, 1797.
29. Blossom, Nariño, pp. 42–45.
30. For the conspiracy in Caracas, see Pedro Grases, La conspiración de Gual y España y el ideario de la independencia.
31. Mendinueta to the Príncipe de la Paz, Santa Fe, May 19, 1798, AGI: Estado, legajo 52.
32. Relación of Spanish troops for New Granada, January 25, 1799, AGS: GM, legajo 7069; Zejudo to Alvarez, Cartagena, February 1, 1799, AGI: Santa Fe, legajo 1016; militia service records for Panama, Cartagena, and Valledupar, AGS: GM, legajo 7082 and ANC: MM, vol. 26, fol. 694, vol. 31, fol. 336, vol. 40, fols. 10–11, and vol. 45, fols. 67, 365, 671.

troops from the coast to the interior had already been effected, Mendinueta called only thirty of the new troops to Santa Fe, assigning the main force to Cartagena.[33] These reinforcements, although few in number, relieved much of Viceroy Mendinueta's anguish until the war ended in 1802, when Spain ordered the unit back to Europe. Before the troops departed, however, Mendinueta acted on his own authority to recruit eighty of the men for his personal guard and other fixed units of the viceroyalty.[34] To say the very least, Spanish troops remained a rare, coveted commodity in New Granada as the viceroyalty entered the nineteenth century.

The disciplined militia during this period was primarily oriented toward external defense, although not exclusively so. No serious attempt occurred to reestablish a disciplined militia in the interior provinces. Ironically, the interior militia had been dismantled as unnecessary because of the presumed tranquillity in the uplands; now, after Nariño, it remained dismantled because the authorities came to view the upland vassals as too dangerous politically to be armed. As Viceroy Mendinueta observed during the crisis of 1797: "I have prepared lists [of loyal vassals] that because this is a delicate situation have been made and continue to be made in secrecy; in this sort of situation most people hide their true convictions and one runs as much risk of arming an enemy as attracting those who would be loyal, or by excluding the latter making them hostile; that is why I have not proceeded to make an enlistment and a formal organization. . . ."[35]

The combat reputation of disciplined militia did, however, improve greatly at this time. Admiral Harvey, after his easy triumph in Trinidad in early 1797, had tried his fortune at San Juan, Puerto Rico, where the feeble regular garrison numbered only 200 men. Puerto Rico, however, still had a functioning disciplined militia which dated from the visit of Alejandro O'Reilly to the island in 1765. That force and the regular army, with substantial spontaneous popular support, decisively repelled the British invaders, who barely managed to escape from the island.[36] The militia fought well in the encounter, and word of its accomplishment soon reached New Granada, where Viceroy Mendinueta, who was harshly critical of the reduction in the size of the army of New Granada, both veteran and militia, raised a series of additional militia units on an urban basis. As customary during wartime, the authorities also mobilized portions of the disciplined militia to complete and reinforce the coastal garrisons.[37]

33. Zejudo to Mendinueta, Cartagena, October 9, 1801, ANC: MM, vol. 88, fols. 110–21.
34. Mendinueta, in *Relaciones de mando*, pp. 533–34. Spain customarily authorized such recruitment but for reasons not clear had not done so in this instance.
35. Mendinueta to the Príncipe de la Paz, Santa Fe, July 19, 1797.
36. R. A. Van Middeldyk, *The History of Puerto Rico*, pp. 139–40.
37. The urban units included a corps of 480 infantrymen in Mompós, 270 others elsewhere in the backlands, three companies of dragoons in Mahates and Barranca, and two companies of

Viceroy Mendinueta also expanded the disciplined militia during the war, because of an invasion scare. This incident occurred in early 1798, when intelligence sources in Jamaica warned the governor of Cartagena of a possible attempt to punch through New Granada's coastal defenses by invading Riohacha and joining forces with the Guajiro Indians, who had remained virtually sovereign since the collapse of the pacification campaign. Such a development would present the deeper danger of a British link-up with insurgent elements in Socorro, Province of Tunja, which was only a three-week march from Riohacha. Although Mendinueta generally discounted the probability of such an invasion, he did view the danger as serious enough to justify the emergency formation of additional disciplined militia. In conjunction with the governor of Santa Marta, he raised a 600-man force in Valledupar south of Riohacha to block the invasion route into the interior. He drew extensively on personnel from the recently extinguished Infantry Regiment of Riohacha, which had sustained a number of companies in that region, and he incorporated a number of officers from those recently received from Spain. Finding Mendinueta's action an inexpensive precaution, the crown quickly approved the militia, although it refused to grant disciplined status for his other creations.[38]

Despite its orientation toward external defense, the coastal militia still related to the compelling question of domestic security. In 1781, it will be remembered, half of the 500-man force that Cartagena sent to the interior was disciplined militia, which demonstrated the value of coastal units for long-range pacification maneuvers. Moreover, during the turbulent nineties, the lowlands generally remained tranquil and thus seemingly offered a reservoir of faithful political support if properly utilized. In late 1797, when describing to the crown the perils of arming the upland population, Viceroy Mendinueta went on to assert: "there is more confidence in the loyalty of the inhabitants of the provinces of Cartagena, Santa Marta, and Riohacha, and those of all of the coast in general, who until now—and despite the fact that there are some perverted spirits—have in all instances shown themselves loyal vassals, diligent for Royal Service, including the colored people whose number is very considerable, [and] it has been necessary to count on their support. . . ."[39]

By the mid- to late nineties creoles had come to dominate the officer corps of the coastal militia, but the authorities did not seem greatly concerned about

---

artillery in Cartagena; Panama had one cavalry company and an infantry battalion in Veragua. Moreover, in response to a severe Indian upheaval in Riobamba, Mendinueta raised a regiment of dragoons in Quito. Mendinueta, in *Relaciones de mando*, pp. 532–48; Mendinueta to Alvarez, Santa Fe, October 13, 1797, AGS: GM, legajo 7068; troop inspection report, Fixed Infantry Regiment of Cartagena, September 1803, ANC: MM, vol. 66, fols. 678–84.

38. Expediente on the creation of the disciplined militia of Valledupar, 1798–99, AGS: GM, legajo 7082.

39. Mendinueta to Alvarez, Santa Fe, October 13, 1797.

this development and in reality had few alternatives. Spaniards were rarely found in remote locations such as Riohacha, Valledupar, Barbacoas, Jaén, and to a degree even Guayaquil. In Panama, Santa Marta, and especially Cartagena, where there was a substantial European element, most Spaniards were wholesale merchants, who were exempted from militia duty, or revenue officers, who were prohibited from service under the 1794 reglamento. This situation left few available candidates, and those who did serve tended to change locations more frequently than creoles, thus leaving the way open for men who could steadily advance through seniority (see Table 12).

Potentially, the most important militia units for purposes of domestic security were those of Cartagena, which was the best positioned and best equipped stronghold to relieve Santa Fe. In recognition of that fact, Ezpeleta, when shaping the Cartagena militia under the 1794 reglamento, departed from the policy he had just established by selecting a veteran officer, Captain Manuel Prada, rather than a volunteer as colonel of the infantry regiment.[40] The previous colonel, the quarrelsome Juan Fernández de Moure, who so belligerently asserted the fuero militar, had been retired with uniform and fuero shortly before, only to lose the latter in 1794 when his continuing litigation finally alienated the authorities in Spain.[41] Prada, a Spaniard, was sustained by a solid veteran cadre composed largely of European officers, which helped to compensate for the increasing number of creole volunteers.[42] By way of contrast, the colonels of the infantry regiments of Panama, Santa Marta, and Guayaquil were all volunteers, the latter two creoles.[43]

In any outright confrontation between the creole aristocracy and the royal administration, an element of major significance in the coastal militia would be the pardo. Governor Anastasio Zejudo stressed the importance of this class to Viceroy Mendinueta during the 1797 crisis, and the latter, who drew upon his own considerable experience on the coast, fully agreed. They saw in the pardo not only the preponderant component of that region demographically, but a class whose interests diverged substantially from those of the colonial aristocracy. A lowland pardo, properly motivated, could become a decisive weapon against the upland creole. Both Zejudo and Mendinueta respected the strength and endurance of the coastal pardo and his record of political fidelity. Pardo militiamen had served in the 1781 relief expedition to Santa Fe, and Mendinueta believed that they would perform better than whites in any simi-

40. Ezpeleta to Alange, Santa Fe, June 19, 1795, AGS: GM, legajo 7080.
41. Minutes, June 4, 1794, and June 1802, AGS: GM, legajos 7062 and 7066.
42. In addition to Captain Prada, who acted as militia colonel, the unit had seven officers attached to it, six Spanish, the other from Vera Cruz. Significantly, the lieutenant colonel, Inocencio Agrasot, although a native of Cartagena, was a retired lieutenant from the Fijo, who had been attached to the port's command staff. Service records, Volunteer Infantry Regiment, Cartagena, December 31, 1797, AGS: GM, legajo 7281.
43. Service records, the volunteer infantry regiments of Panama, Santa Marta, and Guayaquil, 1797, AGS: GM, legajo 7281.

lar crisis in the future; "[it is] indisputable that the white inhabitants of Cartagena or any other city of the coast would be quick to defend their own land and homes in the case of an invasion, but if it becomes necessary to summon them to service in the interior, or perhaps to assist another distant place on the same coast that might be attacked by the enemy, in most instances insuperable difficulties would arise that not even the government with its authority could overcome; [it is] not that way with the pardos, people who by the nature of their condition and other mentioned qualities are quick to lend themselves with distinct facility to whatever kind of service arises."[44]

An incident concerning the insignia of pardo officers illustrates the great importance which Zejudo and Mendinueta attached to that class. Under the reglamento of 1794, pardo, but not white, officers lost their customary right to wear the same insignia as veteran officers. This provision resulted from a short-sighted policy decision in Spain, which aimed at expressing more fully the distinction between pardos and members of the white estate. When the pardo officers of Cartagena bitterly complained about the innovation, both Governor Zejudo and Viceroy Mendinueta came to their defense. They reminded the crown that the unnecessary humiliation of men of color might bear dangerously bitter fruit. Not only was high morale essential during time of war and danger of invasion, but for purposes of domestic security the only suitable substitute for the pardo soldier was the Spanish soldier, who was currently in very short supply. Consequently, Mendinueta acceded to the pardo petition and provisionally suspended the new policy; he justified his initiative on the defensible grounds that communications with Europe were very irregular and that military imperatives did not permit delay for consultation.[45]

Unlike leaders such as Flores, Caballero y Góngora, and Ezpeleta, Anastasio Zejudo and Pedro Mendinueta were not strongly associated with the Enlightenment. As practical soldiers their concern was less with the inherent dignity of man or his natural rights than with military realities on the coast. Not only did pardo units comprise an important segment of the coastal defenses, but men of color also were prominent in the enlisted ranks of the "white" militia and indeed the regular army. In both Riohacha and Portobelo it had even been necessary to combine white and pardo companies into the same units under the reglamento of 1794.[46] When originally framing militia policy in Cuba, Alejandro O'Reilly had authorized extensive privileges for pardos in practical recognition of the immense importance of that class, and the authorities in New Granada had been compelled to adapt to the same reality. Moreover, since the Darién Indian pacification campaign, New Granada had repeatedly faced war and had called extensively upon the militia. Personal sacrifices,

44. Mendinueta to Alvarez, Santa Fe, June 19, 1798, AGS: GM, legajo 7069.
45. Ibid.; *Reglamento . . . del Nuevo Reyno de Granada*, chap. 8, art. 1.
46. *Reglamento . . . del Nuevo Reyno de Granada*, relación 4.

whether in the Darién jungles or in the fortifications of Cartagena, were immense. An abrupt decline during this period of jurisdictional challenges to the fuero militar, most notably that of the pardo, reflected this reality, and Zejudo and Mendinueta did not wish to reawaken social tensions over a question such as officers' insignia. When confronted by Mendinueta's challenge, the crown elected not to interfere further, for it "neither approved, nor disapproved" his action.[47]

Viceroy Mendinueta's prudent gesture on behalf of the pardo proved timely indeed. Within the broader framework of revolutionary ferment in the late eighteenth century, the well-known Negro slave uprising in the French colony of Saint Domingue (modern-day Haiti) had erupted in 1791, accompanied by the brutal destruction of the planter aristocracy and a massive political upheaval, which eventually resulted in the independence of the colony. This rebellion, which spilled over into Santo Domingo, sent a shudder through the Caribbean, including New Granada. The slave in New Granada was a much smaller factor than in the French colony, but the example from the north nevertheless could—and indeed would—lead to difficulties.

In 1795 the district of Coro, Captaincy General of Caracas, experienced a violent but unsuccessful rebellion by Negro slaves and freemen, who seemingly had been influenced by the example of Saint Domingue.[48] Similar difficulties reached Cartagena in 1799 when a small group of French slaves, apparently acquired from Saint Domingue, plotted the seizure of the Castle of San Felipe de Barajas and other strong points, the raising of the Negro population and the destruction of whites, the plunder of the city, and the acquisition of their personal freedom. Although the conspirators won over at least one militia artillery sergeant in an attempt to gain military support, the scheme failed when a pardo militia corporal refused to collaborate and alerted Governor Zejudo on the eve of the planned uprising. Had Zejudo and Mendinueta not taken careful pains to cultivate the free pardo, this event might have had a far different outcome. As it was, the pardo units remained loyal and Zejudo easily smashed the conspiracy.[49] Moreover, in the following years he continued to treat the pardo as a major pillar of the defense structure.

It should also be noted that within non-pardo militia units, numerous vassals of obscure status continued to function along with "nobles" or "hidalgos" as white or creole officers. Social descriptions such as "distinguished," "honorable," "decent," or simply "good" remained common in the units of Guayaquil, Santa Marta, and Valledupar; this was also the case in Cartagena, especially in the companies of the backlands, where these labels predominated, and in

47. Minute, royal order, December 20, 1798, AGS: GM, legajo 7070.
48. Tisnes, *Movimientos*, pp. 237–45.
49. Mendinueta to Minister of Finance for the Indies Francisco de Saavedra, Santa Fe, May 19, 1799, with copy of Zejudo to Mendinueta, Cartagena, April 9, 1799, AGI: Estado, legajo 52.

Panama, where no one rated so high as "noble" after 1797.[50] As will be recalled, there were no precise definitions for these usages, and their application varied widely; it will also be remembered that the status associated with them could depend on culture and wealth, or the lack thereof, as much as on birthright. The general reduction of the size of the militia in the several provinces, dating from the work of Anastasio Zejudo in the mid-eighties and on through the reglamento of 1794, relieved some of the necessity for recruiting vassals who did not fully meet the social excellence envisioned by militia policy; but the seemingly endless succession of wars from Darién on, together with the danger of combat or the drudgery of garrison duty, must have done much to discourage the faint-hearted from seeking commissions. For those with clouded social backgrounds, however, an officership in the militia offered a white status, extensive corporate privileges, and a vehicle to validate claims of honor and social quality.

In 1803 the crown replaced Pedro Mendinueta with Antonio Amar y Borbón, who upon his selection as viceroy received a promotion to lieutenant general. Anastasio Zejudo, who had enthusiastic support from the audiencia because of his thirty-year record of zealous, forthright leadership, narrowly missed the appointment. Zejudo's strong record actually weakened his candidacy, the irresolute authorities in Spain fearing that he might have made too many enemies in the execution of his numerous commissions. Amar, who took possession of his office on September 17, 1803, was one of New Granada's weaker viceroys.[51] He was indecisive, unimaginative, and probably too old for the job. Zejudo himself, however, was sixty-two at this time and his many years of service in Cartagena were beginning to take their toll.

The defense system that Amar inherited, including troop distribution and strengths, remained essentially unaltered until the end of the colonial period. Nevertheless, a number of important changes did occur in the internal composition of the various units, especially those of the regular army. The ratio of Spanish to creole officers, which had been shifting in the previous decade, tilted decidedly in favor of the native-born, as Spaniards died or retired and junior creole officers advanced through seniority (see Tables 10 and 12). In 1804 Spain once more found herself at war with Great Britain and was therefore again unable to infuse into the army of New Granada the number of European reinforcements demanded by domestic considerations. As a consequence, creoles assumed sizeable majorities in the officer corps of the veteran garrisons of Panama and Cartagena during the administration of Amar, even

50. Service records, the Volunteer Infantry Regiment, Panama and Natá, 1797 and 1800, the infantry regiments of Santa Marta, Guayaquil, and Cartagena, 1800, and the dragoon regiment of Valledupar and dragoon squadrons of Corozal and Guayaquil, 1800, AGS: GM, legajos 7281 and 7282.

51. Expediente on the succession to the viceregency of New Granada, 1802–3, AGS: GM, legajo 7084.

at the senior level, although the commanding officers remained Spanish. Creoles also continued to dominate the volunteer offices of the coastal militia, significantly including the Regiment of Infantry Volunteers of Cartagena.

The one notable exception to this pattern was the Auxiliary Battalion of Santa Fe, which received extraordinary attention because of its particularly sensitive location and function. It was the only major unit to preserve a strong European majority both at the enlisted level and in its officer corps. The Auxiliary Battalion was of more recent creation than the other veteran units, and a sizeable portion of the original membership, which was largely Spanish, still remained at the time of Amar.[52] Moreover, the two reorganizations of the unit by Gil y Lemos and Ezpeleta had afforded additional opportunities for manipulation to insure a favorable ethnic composition. Finally, when small numbers of replacements from time to time managed to reach New Granada from Spain, including some 190 who arrived in 1803, most were assigned to the Auxiliary Battalion as a matter of course to strengthen further the Spanish contingent.[53] Indeed, with creole participation effectively curtailed, the Auxiliary Battalion came to resemble a foreign army of occupation more than an authentic expression of the colonial community.

Significantly, the unique nature of the regular garrison in Santa Fe worked to widen still further the gulf between the upland creole and the army of New Granada, while the continued absence of a disciplined militia closed yet another avenue that might have led to a measure of local involvement. The creole community was, of course, fully cognizant of the purpose and orientation of the internal defense system. Politically, this awareness could only have deepened creole suspicions toward the regime and, in a broader sense, intensified a long-standing antipathy toward the institution of the military itself. To many, certainly, the Auxiliary Battalion was the hated symbol of all that was unjust and oppressive in the colonial regime. Yet the authorities for their part could not afford to relax their domestic vigilance without concrete evidence of a changed political climate in New Granada. Furthermore, intelligence reports warned that the insurgent Francisco Miranda, along with Pedro Fermín de Vargas and Manuel Gual, was preparing for a rising of the population of northern South America. Miranda's unsuccessful assault in 1806 upon Coro, Captaincy General of Caracas, confirmed those fears.[54]

The defense system in Popayán at the close of the colonial period closely resembled that of Santa Fe, but on a much smaller and less conspicuous scale. On the one hand, the lack of a disciplined militia eliminated an important

52. Service records, Auxiliary Infantry Battalion, 1809, ANC: MM, vol. 13, fols. 4–43.
53. Zejudo to Mendinueta, Cartagena, June 19, 1803, ANC: MM, vol. 102, fols. 1027–29.
54. Petition of the cabildo of Santa Fe through Juan Antonio Rubio Plaza, Madrid, May 11, 1795; Mendinueta to Secretary of State and War Pedro Ceballos, Santa Fe, October 19, 1801, AGI: Estado, legajo 52; Amar to the Príncipe de la Paz, Santa Fe, May 19, 1806, AGI: Panama, legajo 380.

vehicle for significant community participation in the military. On the other, the veteran company, reestablished in 1792 as a consequence of the Barbacoas uprising, consisted principally of European troops drawn from the Auxiliary Battalion under Spanish officers. The Infantry Company of Popayán was not an institution closely connected to the local community, therefore, nor one that enjoyed much public esteem, although in subsequent years the garrison of Popayán depended much more upon local recruitment than did the Auxiliary Battalion.[55]

Under Amar, the Commandancy General of Quito remained the most neglected military jurisdiction in New Granada. Quito's difficulty derived partly from its isolation from Santa Fe, but a continuing antipathy between the viceroys in Santa Fe and the presidents in Quito was also a contributing factor. A number of presidents, most notably José García Pizarro, had attempted to make themselves captains general and hence acquire autonomy from viceregal authority; not surprisingly, therefore, attempts to enlarge the Quito garrison and with it the military prestige of the president aroused much skepticism in Santa Fe.[56] A massive Indian uprising in the Province of Riobamba in 1803 caused outgoing Viceroy Mendinueta second thoughts, however. Because the two companies in Quito were unable to cope with the rebellion, Mendinueta was forced to order regular troops from Guayaquil to the interior and to move the veteran company of Popayán toward Riobamba. He covered the latter transfer by sending fifty troops from Santa Fe to Popayán, and, in order to protect Santa Fe, deployed three companies from Cartagena in Mompós on the Magdalena, where they could quickly reach the viceregal capital or return to the coast in the event of British attack. These awkward, inconvenient troop movements convinced the viceroy that an augmentation of the garrison of Quito might be in order after all.[57]

Despite the Riobamba uprising and Mendinueta's recommendations, however, the royal authorities did not expand the veteran garrison of Quito, although the city received authorization to establish an urban—but not disciplined—regiment of dragoons.[58] With Spain again at war in 1804, pressing demands elsewhere for manpower and finances effectively precluded any real consideration of Quito's needs. Meanwhile, the four-company veteran

55. Expediente on the disorders in Barbacoas, 1791–92; Mendinueta, in *Relaciones de mando*, p. 541.

56. García Pizarro was instructed that earlier uses of the title captain general by a number of presidents had simply been the result of special favors for the individuals involved, not the institutional integration of the function of captain general into the office of president. Expediente on the command of the troops of Quito, 1779, AGI: Quito, legajo 573. Significantly, Rear Admiral Luis Muñoz de Guzmán, who proposed the expansion of the Quito garrison, had conducted a running feud with Ezpeleta over his prerogatives as president and commandant general. Muñoz to Alange, Quito, February 20, 1795, AGS: GM, legajo 7087.

57. Mendinueta, in *Relaciones de mando*, pp. 536, 539–40.

58. Ibid., p. 545.

infantry corps of Quito and Guayaquil, for want of any practical alternative, continued to recruit locally to fill its ranks, and creoles had become predominant in the officer corps.[59] By royal order of July 7, 1803, the crown did move, nevertheless, to improve support for the external defense of Guayaquil by severing that governorship from New Granada and attaching it to the Viceroyalty of Peru.[60] This action undoubtedly reflected an appreciation of the growing importance of Guayaquil and a realistic judgment that Lima was far better equipped strategically to sustain that Pacific jurisdiction than was Santa Fe.

At the time of Guayaquil's transfer to Peru, the intimate, traditional relationship among the business community, the municipal government, and the militia leadership remained intact, although without the despotic overtones that had characterized the period of Governor Ramón García Pizarro. Of all the major coastal militia establishments, that of Guayaquil featured the creole most prominently. Only a small fraction of the officer corps was European, and Colonel Jacinto Bejarano, Guayaquil's leading cacao exporter, frequent public servant, and former crony of Governor García Pizarro, remained in command of the infantry regiment.[61] By the end of the century, the creole officials almost universally claimed a "noble" or "distinguished" social status, which was in large measure a reflection of their success in sharing in the prosperity of the colony.[62] Many continued to come from families that were active in local politics, some serving in the municipal government themselves.[63] In the absence of significant revolutionary ferment in Guayaquil,

59. Ibid., p. 541; service records, Veteran Infantry Corps of Quito, December 1800, AGS: GM, legajo 7282. Creoles outnumbered Spaniards six to five and presumably strengthened that margin in subsequent years since seven of eight cadets were Americans. Significantly, Captain Juan Salinas, one of the principal conspirators in the 1809 movement in Quito, was the lowest ranking lieutenant in the corps at this time.

60. Also transferred to Peru were the provinces of Mainas and Quijos. Royal cédula, July 15, 1802, and royal order, July 7, 1803, with related correspondence, in Cornelio Escipión Vernaza, comp., *Recopilación de documentos oficiales de la época colonial, con un apéndice relativo a la independencia de Guayaquil . . .* , pp. 181–202; Hamerly, "A Social and Economic History of . . . Guayaquil," pp. 4–6.

61. Bejarano was the brother-in-law and business associate of Juan Antonio Rocafuerte, who served for a time as captain in the militia, and was therefore the uncle of Vicente Rocafuerte Bejarano, who later became president of Ecuador. The highest ranking infantry captain was Agustín Oramas, another wealthy associate of former Governor Ramón García Pizarro; Oramas had represented the latter in his residencia. Castillo, *Los gobernadores*, pp. 201, 249–51, 266–67, 288. It will be remembered that dragoon squadrons had no volunteer command and staff group.

62. Service records, volunteer infantry regiment and dragoon squadron of Guayaquil, 1800, AGS: GM, legajo 7282. Interestingly, the squadron of dragoons contained a number of officers, including Captain Juan Ponce and Captain José Juan Echevarría, who had earlier only managed a "good" social rating. Their ascent to "distinguished" probably reflected increased family fortune, successful militia service, and a tolerant ayudante. Echevarría, incidentally, had earlier served as alcalde ordinario of Guayaquil.

63. Castillo, *Los gobernadores*, pp. 210–29, 245–51, 266–67, 285, 316–32.

the close connection between the creole elite and the military was accepted as a matter of course by both the royal administration and the community.

When news reached New Granada in 1808 of the French invasion of Spain, and of the seizure of the Spanish throne and the constitutional crisis that was destined to plunge the empire into chaos, the army of New Granada was certainly no better prepared to underpin the royal administration than it had been when Nariño first jolted the authorities with the publication of the *Declaration of the Rights of Man* a decade and a half before. If anything, it was less so. The succession of wars beginning in the 1790s had denied the regular army of New Granada the European reinforcements that all agreed were vital, while the exemption of merchants and the banning of revenue officers from militia service resulted in a creole domination of the disciplined militia. Given the fear of creole sedition, the only unit which seemed politically safe was the Auxiliary Battalion of Santa Fe with its large Spanish majority both at the officer and enlisted levels. That unit, however, as a symbol of Spanish oppression, probably did as much to alienate native loyalty as to gain subservience through intimidation. This very difficult situation called for strong, imaginative viceregal leadership, but during the years of Amar, New Granada experienced quite the opposite.[64] And Lieutenant General Anastasio Zejudo, the man who through thirty-five years of service in New Granada knew the colony better than anyone else in a position of authority, died in January 1808, leaving a massive void not only in Cartagena but in the entire viceroyalty as it encountered its fateful crisis.[65]

In the end, domestic security planning in New Granada proved hopelessly unequal to the bewildering political and legal situation that developed. In the chaotic events that unfolded in 1809 and 1810, allegiances and responsibilities became confused in ways that could not have been anticipated. Despite claims by the patriotic Supreme Central Junta in Seville and its successor, the Council of the Regency, that they and the royal bureaucracy in America spoke for the deposed monarch, unit after unit of the reformed army in New Granada, including the Auxiliary Battalion, actively or passively supported the local juntas that sprang up in their districts. The fate of the army of New Granada during the course of those events and later, when the colonial juntas became open vehicles for revolutionary ambitions, is beyond the scope of this study. It is, however, a topic most worthy of the attention of some future student of the revolutionary era.

64. In fairness to Viceroy Amar, he performed competently during the Quito rebellion of 1809. In the words of Robert L. Gilmore, "the viceroy [Amar] proved to be a vigorous discreet official who understood his mission and used intelligently the limited means at his disposal." In "The Imperial Crisis, Rebellion and the Viceroy: Nueva Granada in 1809," p. 1.

65. Governor Blas de Soria to Miguel Cayetano Soler, Cartagena, January 28, 1808, AGI: Santa Fe, legajo 1017.

9. Consequences of the Military Reform

In final analysis, the military reform made substantial progress toward achieving its original objective of strengthening New Granada's external defenses. The regular army was expanded considerably in size, and, as a result of better leadership and organization, also seems to have improved in quality. The disciplined militia system, despite nagging problems such as empty companies, lazy officers, and weapon shortages, was clearly superior to what preceded it. Through a systematic training program, it acquainted large numbers of coastal subjects with the rudiments of the military art, thereby making them a creditable reserve force. Furthermore, the quality of the militia improved as the viceroyalty gained in experience and as it developed a coordinated system of supervision. The inspectional visit of Anastasio Zejudo between 1788 and 1789 and the 1794 reglamento of José Ezpeleta highlighted the government's efforts to eliminate useless militia units and to upgrade the quality of those retained. It is, of course, impossible to determine precisely the extent of the improvements in colonial defense because the army of New Granada was never tested by foreign invasion, but perhaps this fact in itself is a tribute to the success of the reform.

Less clear-cut were the results of the attempt to use the army to strengthen the domestic authority of royal government, which to the viceregal leadership became an important, and at times the paramount, objective of the reform. Certainly, the reformed army, which did much to contain the Comunero

185

Rebellion, was a major force in the reestablishment of royal authority during the nullification of the Capitulations and during Caballero y Góngora's administration in the strained aftermath of that action. Moreover, the archbishop-viceroy, confident of the military force supporting him, made extensive advances in revenue reform during his administration. In the long run, nevertheless, the reformed military proved an uncertain pillar of royal authority. First, the machinations of Gil y Lemos in 1789 led to the dissolution of the upland militia establishment. Then, during the 1790s and after, Spain's preoccupation with the nearly constant warfare in Europe denied New Granada's regular army the Spanish reinforcements it so desperately needed, while Spanish enlistment also dwindled in the militia. The result was a strong shift toward creole domination of the officer corps of both the regular army and the militia at the very time that the native population was increasingly influenced by the revolutionary currents unleashed in France. The Auxiliary Battalion stood as a vivid exception to this rule, but even it could not guarantee domestic security as the foundation of Spanish dominion in New Granada slowly crumbled.

Of comparable, perhaps superior, significance were the social and political side effects of the military reform. Throughout its history, the reformed army acted at a number of levels as an important vehicle for social mobility in the colony. The personal immunities and the extensive judicial prerogatives attached to military service elevated the social status of thousands of militiamen, many of them pardos, who in return accepted the drudgery of Sunday drills and risked the danger of possible mobilization. Although creoles suffered discrimination in competition for officerships both in the militia and in the regular army, many were able to validate or reinforce claims of honor by the acquisition of commissions, often through purchase, especially during the latter period of the reform. The social impact of the military reorganization was uneven, however. Its smallest effect came in the uplands, where the militia's duration was brief; its greatest effect occurred on the coast, where the militia was largest and where it enjoyed a continuous existence.

There were also immediate consequences implicit in the history of the military reform which are less tangible and which will become clearer only when further research is completed on other aspects of the late eighteenth century. The primary example is that the reformed military, particularly during the 1780s when the army was largest and when the frontier campaigns peaked, devoured immense quantities of royal revenues and other resources. This drain was definitely linked to the financial crisis unveiled by Gil y Lemos in 1789, and it must surely have produced contingent consequences, the implications of which are still uncertain. In addition, military affairs consumed much of the attention of the viceregal leadership, especially during the Darién campaign when Caballero y Góngora took up residence at Turbaco on the Caribbean coast. This fact suggests a partial explanation for the weak bureaucratic management which afflicted his regime and opened the way for the conservative reaction under Gil y Lemos.

The principal question that arises in assessing the consequences of the military reorganization in New Granada is whether or not it had any permanent effect upon civil-military relations. It is evident that outside of the Presidency of Quito an elitist military tradition did not take firm hold in New Granada. To be sure, the military reform did lay the legal foundation for such a heritage by conceding to the militia extensive corporate privileges as defined by the reglamento of Cuba and as reaffirmed for the most part by the 1794 reglamento for New Granada. And, during the early years of the reform, these military privileges posed a significant challenge to established political institutions and threatened to subvert existing lines of civilian authority. In the long run, nevertheless, the missing element was a successful marriage between the emerging military institution and the creole aristocracy of the institutional, demographic, and cultural heartland of New Granada. In the Province of Popayán and in the region around Santa Fe, the military, as the instrument of enlightened despotism, was viewed with hostility and scorn by the local aristocracy; the exercise of its privileges was vigorously challenged; and the militia's existence was brief—some fourteen years in Popayán and six in Santa Fe. Furthermore, as a consequence of the suspicions aroused by the Comunero Rebellion, the viceregal authorities never extended the military reform to other key upland provinces such as Antioquia, Mariquita, Tunja, and Pamplona. Finally, silent restrictions upon the creole's role in the upland army, both militia and regular, further reduced the chance that a significant sector of the creole population would embrace the military corporation.

The Caribbean lowlands, by contrast, absorbed the reform well, aside from such short-term problems as pardo privileges. The coast had long been accustomed to a prominent military presence, and the role of the military as defender of the colony was accepted as a matter of course. Moreover, with the evolution toward a smaller militia, even the explosive pardo issue diminished in importance. As a consequence, the hostility toward the reform that appeared in the interior provinces did not develop in Panama, Cartagena, Santa Marta, or Riohacha, and the creole in his quest for honors and privileges sought, and in time found, a prominent place in the armed forces. The coastal army was directed primarily toward external defense rather than internal political order, however, and hence the danger of the establishment of a praetorian tradition was correspondingly diminished. Furthermore, the coast, with its garrison mentality, was only a small if significant part of New Granada; in most of the viceroyalty the reform had either no lasting effect or evoked a negative reaction. When the area that is now Colombia entered the independence period, therefore, it did so without an established tradition of military elitism.

Looking ahead, Colombia emerged as one of the few Latin American countries without an authentic praetorian tradition. Military dictatorships in Colombia occurred rarely and were generally unpopular, and its army never gained the prestige and independence generally associated with the Latin American military. The colonial experience of New Granada does not in itself, of course, explain the unique character of Colombian civil-military relations, but it adds significantly to an understanding of the larger picture. When Colombia moved toward independence, creole elements in the colonial army did in fact patriotically assert themselves, and they thus gained for the military corporation a momentary degree of respectability. During the Spanish reconquest, however, these same elements were nearly all liquidated, a development which simultaneously left an important leadership void and nearly severed the revolution's link to the colonial military.

When liberation finally came in 1819, it was the achievement of Simón Bolívar and an army whose officer corps was composed largely of Venezuelan outsiders, many of whom were uncultured plainsmen. This army was at first viewed with mistrust, then with the traditional heartland hostility toward the military. When the Venezuelans were finally expelled during the 1830s, there were few authentic Colombian war heroes remaining who could claim prestige for the army; and there was little if any residue of pro-military sentiment to draw upon in the principal families of Colombia, which sought to monopolize political authority through means other than the shaping of a prestigious, elite army. The colonial heritage had simply not prepared the creole aristocracy for a militaristic tradition. It left them instead with a deep mistrust, indeed hostility, toward the army. As a consequence, military recruitment came from other, less esteemed social sectors during the following decades. Civilian authority prevailed, and the fate of the Colombian army was one of subjugation, at times humiliation, and, on a number of occasions, near dismemberment.[1] Indeed, the military in Colombia remains to this day distinctly subordinate to civilian institutions.

The Presidency of Quito, excluding Popayán, presents a differing picture. From the time of Víctor Salcedo y Somodevilla and the García Pizarros, the reformed military was closely implicated in the social, economic, and political designs of the creole aristocracy and the opportunistic bureaucrats who descended upon that jurisdiction. The elites of both Quito and Guayaquil quickly accommodated themselves to the military as an institution and converted it into a partner rather than a menace to their interests. In many instances the prerogatives of officership and the fuero militar were simply additional reinforcements for already established arrangements in what

1. See J. León Helguera, "The Changing Role of the Military in Colombia," pp. 351–57, and Anthony P. Maingot, "Social Structure, Social Status, and Civil-Military Conflict in Urban Colombia, 1810–1858."

amounted to interlocking political, commercial, and military directorates presided over by military governors. The militia experiment was, it is true, short-lived in the highland provinces, but it is significant that the close connection that developed between the aristocracy and the military reform averted the kind of anti-military hostility that lingered in upland Colombia. In Guayaquil the intimate connection between the creole elite and the reformed military endured up to the independence period.

In the Ecuadorian nation that eventually emerged from the territories of the Presidency of Quito, the army became a much stronger force in political affairs than in Colombia. The divergent colonial experiences of these two countries suggest a partial explanation for that contrast. The legal and social foundation for an elitist military tradition was firmly established in Guayaquil by the time of Independence, while no significant anti-militarism had developed elsewhere in the presidency. In addition, Guayaquil became in later years a highly significant part of Ecuador economically and politically, and, presumably, its colonial heritage had a major effect on the emerging national character. Hard and fast conclusions must, however, be avoided until the fate of the colonial officer corps is systematically traced through the independence movement into the republic. Only then will we fully understand the extent of continuity and change in civil-military relations between the Ecuadorian colonial and national periods.

Appendix: Tables

TABLE 1

THE ARMY OF NEW GRANADA IN 1772

REGULARS[b]	
FIXED INFANTRY	
Two companies of Santa Marta	154
Battalion of Cartagena	621
Company of Guayaquil	50
Three companies of Quito	150
Company of Popayán	50
Halberdier viceregal guard	75
Three companies of Maracaibo[a]	231
Three companies of Cumaná (estimated)[a]	231
Three companies of Guayana[a]	231
Company of Margarita Island[a]	50
Total	**1,843**
ARTILLERY	
Royal Corps (Panama)	100
Royal Corps (Cartagena)	100
Company of Cartagena (attached to infantry battalion)	79
Half company of Santa Marta	23
Half company of Guayana[a]	27
Total	**329**

Continued

191

TABLE 1—*Continued*

CAVALRY	
Company of the viceregal guard	75

SPANISH ROTATING INFANTRY	
Battalion of Murcia (Panama)	679
Battalion of Naples (Panama)	679
Battalion of Savoy (Cartagena)	679
Total	2,037
Total regulars	**4,284**

SOURCES: The only available listing for the army at this time is in Francisco Antonio Moreno y Escandón, "Estado del Virreinato de Santafé, Nuevo Reino de Granada . . . 1772," pp. 609–10. Unfortunately, Moreno's survey is far from systematic. For some units he lists authorized strength, for others he lists actual strength; for some he counts officers, for others he does not; and in some cases he appears to have simply guessed. The present writer has attempted to systematize the list as much as possible, basing his entries on authorized strengths, not the force of the moment. These entries do not include company officers and command and staff group personnel which normally averaged about 6 per cent. (Totals for personnel do not include officer counts.) This system is also followed in the other tables in the text. It should also be noted that the small number of men that was placed on salary at various times to escort and protect missionaries is not included in the troop tables of this study. For corroborative and corrective material for the Moreno tabulation, see ANC: MM, vol. 51, fols. 601–2, vol. 64, fols. 677–80, vol. 65, fols. 370–72, vol. 71, fols. 211–14, 587–90, 1041–44, 1066–69, 1087, vol. 81, fol. 962, vol. 85, fols. 230–33, 280–83, vol. 89, fols. 585–96, vol. 90, fols. 948–52, vol. 92, fols. 760–66, vol. 97, fols. 837–42, vol. 99, fols. 57–75, vol. 100, fols. 658–66, vol. 103, fols. 75–88, 104–5, and vol. 105, fols. 481–86; ANC: RO, vol. 53, fol. 188; ANC: GM, vol. 14, fol. 148; and ANE: Pres., vol. 43, fols. 55–56, and vol. 134, fol. 101.

a. These units pertained to the jurisdiction of the Captaincy General of Caracas after 1777.

b. In 1772, the militia consisted merely of numerous unorganized units, with varying totals.

TABLE 2
THE ORGANIZATION OF A VETERAN INFANTRY REGIMENT

Grade	Number in Each Grenadier Company (one per battalion)	Number in Each Fusileer Company (eight per battalion)	Total in the Regiment
Captains	1	1	18
Lieutenants	1	1	18
Second Lieutenants	1	1	18
First Sergeants	1	1	18
Second Sergeants	1	2	34
First Corporals	3	4	70
Second Corporals	3	4	70
Drummers	1	2	34
Soldiers	54	64	1132
Totals	63	77	1358

COMMAND AND STAFF GROUP

FIRST BATTALION	SECOND BATTALION
1 Colonel	1 Lieutenant colonel
1 Sargento mayor	1 Ayudante mayor
1 Ayudante mayor	2 Standard-bearers
2 Standard-bearers	1 Chaplain
1 Chaplain	1 Surgeon
1 Surgeon	1 Corporal, gastador
1 Corporal, gastador	6 Gastadores
6 Gastadores	1 Master armorer
1 Master armorer	2 Fifers
1 Drum major	
2 Fifers	

SOURCES: Adapted from *Ordenanzas de S.M. para el régimen, disciplina, subordinación, y servicio de sus exércitos* . . . . , 1:Trat. I, tit. i, arts 1–6. Each regiment normally contained two battalions.

TABLE 3
UNIT ORGANIZATION UNDER THE REGLAMENTO FOR THE DISCIPLINED
MILITIA OF CUBA, 1769

WHITE INFANTRY BATTALION

Grade	Number in Each Grenadier Company (one per battalion)	Number in Each Fusileer Company (eight per battalion)	Total
Captains	1	1	9
Lieutenants (Vet.)	1	1	9
Second Lieutenants	1	1	9
Sergeants (Vet.)	1	1	9
Sergeants (Vol.)	2	2	18
Drummers (Vet.)	1	1	9
First Corporals (Vet.)	2	2	18
First Corporals (Vol.)	4	4	36
Second Corporals	6	6	54
Soldiers	64	74	656
Total			**800**

COMMAND AND STAFF GROUP

One colonel; one sargento mayor (veteran); one ayudante (veteran); two standard-bearers; one chaplain; one surgeon; one drum major (veteran); one corporal (gastador); six gastadores.

PARDO INFANTRY BATTALION

Grade	Number in Each Grenadier Company	Number in Each Fusileer Company	Total
Captains	1	1	9
Lieutenants	1	1	9
Second Lieutenants	1	1	9
First Sergeants	1	1	9
Second Sergeants	2	2	18
Drummers	1	1	9
First Corporals	6	6	54
Second Corporals	6	6	54
Soldiers	64	74	656
Total		800	**800**

COMMAND AND STAFF GROUP

White: one ayudante mayor (subinspector); four ayudantes; five garzones.
Pardo: one commander; two standard-bearers; one drum major; one corporal (gastador); six gastadores; eight fifers.

Continued

TABLE 3—*Continued*

CAVALRY REGIMENT

Grade	Number in Each Carabineer Company (one per regiment)	Number in Each Cavalry Company (twelve per regiment)[a]	Total
Captains	1	1	13
Lieutenants (Vet.)	1	1	13
Second Lieutenants	1	1	13
Ensigns	1	1	13
Sergeants (Vet.)	1	1	13
Sergeants (Vol.)	1	1	13
Corporals (Vet.)	2	2	26
Corporals (Vol.)	2	2	26
Soldiers	44	44	572
Total			**650**

COMMAND AND STAFF GROUP

One colonel; one lieutenant colonel; one sargento mayor (veteran); one ayudante mayor (veteran); one chaplain; one surgeon; four trumpeters (veteran).

DRAGOON REGIMENT

Grade	Number in Each Foot Company (three per regiment)	Number in Each Mounted Company (three per regiment)	Total
Captains	1	1	6
Lieutenants	1	1	6
Second Lieutenants	1	1	6
Sergeants (Vet.)	1	0	3
Sergeants (Vol.)	2	2	12
Drummers (Vet.)	1	0	3
First Corporals (Vet.)	2	0	6
First Corporals (Vol.)	4	3	21
Second Corporals	6	3	27
Soldiers	84	42	378
Totals	**100**	**50**	**450**

COMMAND AND STAFF GROUP

One colonel; one ayudante mayor (veteran); two standard-bearers; one chaplain; one surgeon.

a. Three cavalry companies comprised a squadron.

TABLE 4
THE ARMY OF NEW GRANADA IN 1779

Regulars	Infantry	Artillery	Mounted
Two companies of Santa Marta	154		
Half company of Santa Marta		25	
Regiment of Cartagena	1,358		
Royal Corps (two companies			
of Cartagena)		200	
(company of Panama)		100	
Battalion of Panama	679		
Parties of light infantry of			
all colors of Chimán			
(Panama)	46		
Company of Guayaquil	100		
Three companies of Quito	225		
Detachment of Popayán	25		
Halberdier viceregal guard	75		
Cavalry viceregal guard			75
Totals	**2,662**	**325**	**75**

Total regulars   **3,062**

Disciplined Militia	Infantry	Artillery	Mounted
Two companies of pardo			
dragoons, Riohacha			252
Battalion of whites, Cartagena	800		
Battalion of pardos, Cartagena	800		
Company of morenos, Cartagena	90		
Company of pardos, Cartagena		100	
Company of morenos, Cartagena		100	
Brigade of pardos, Tolú of the			
partido of Lorica			
(Cartagena)		30	
Two companies of whites, partido			
of Barranquilla (Cartagena)	180		
Four companies of pardos,			
partido of Barranquilla			
(Cartagena)	360		
Four companies of morenos,			
partido of Barranquilla			
(Cartagena)	360		
Six companies of all colors,			
partido of Barranquilla			
(Cartagena)	540		
Company of white cavalry,			
partido of Barranquilla			
(Cartagena)			90
Company of pardo cavalry,			
partido of Barranquilla			
(Cartagena)			90
Five companies of whites, partido			
of Mompós (Cartagena)	450		
Two companies of pardos, partido			
of Mompós (Cartagena)	180		

Continued

TABLE 4—*Continued*

Six companies of all colors, partido of Mompós (Cartagena)	540		
Nine companies of whites, partido of Lorica (Cartagena)	810		
Nineteen companies of all colors, partido of Lorica (Cartagena)	1,710		
Battalion of whites, partido of Natá (Panama)	720		
Battalion of pardos, partido of Natá (Panama)	720		
Battalion of pardos, Panama	720		
Five companies of whites, Panama and Portobelo	300		
Company of morenos, Panama	80		
Four companies of pardos, Panama and Portobelo	308		
Two companies of morenos, Panama and Portobelo		200	
Battalion of whites, Guayaquil	800		
Battalion of pardos, Guayaquil	800		
Regiment of white dragoons, Guayaquil (twelve companies)			600
Five companies of whites, Guayaquil	250		
Company of pardos, Guayaquil	50		
Company of whites, Guayaquil		50	
Two companies of morenos, Guayaquil		100	
Eleven companies of whites, Popayán	1,100		
Company of pardos, Popayán	100		
Two companies all colors, Popayán	200		
Totals	**12,968**	**580**	**1,032**
Total disciplined militia			**14,580**

SOURCES: This table was compiled from reports and other correspondence. See Commander Diego Antonio Nieto to Viceroy Manuel Flores, Cartago, ANC: MM, vol. 52, fols. 332–48; report on the militia of Cartagena, by Governor Juan Pimienta, Cartagena, March 26, 1778, ANC: MM, vol. 40, fols. 152–65; troop review, Guayaquil, by Commander Víctor Salcedo y Somodevilla, October 1779, ANC: MM, vol. 101, fols. 708–14; troop review, Panama, by Governor Ramón de Carvajal, August 1, 1781, ANC: MM, vol. 103, fols. 500–519; troop review, Santa Marta and Riohacha, by Governor Antonio de Narváez y la Torre, August 1784, ANC: MM, vol. 101, fols. 445–46; troop reviews, Panama, by Governor Pedro Carbonell, August 15, 1779, and March 1, 1784, AGI: Panama, legajos 256 and 360. Also see ANC: MM, vol. 89, fol. 547, vol. 90, fols. 600–608, 628–34, 645–62, 1040, vol. 95, fols. 155–58, vol. 106, fols. 885–90, vol. 109, fols. 171–72, vol. 110, fols. 367–75.

TABLE 5
THE MILITIA OF GUAYAQUIL AND QUITO IN 1783

MILITIA OF QUITO AND ITS DEPENDENCIES[a]

Regiment of infantry, Quito	900
Regiment of dragoons, Quito	360
Company of artillery, Quito	50
Battalion of infantry, Riobamba	450
Battalion of infantry, Cuenca	450
Three companies of infantry, Guaranda	150
Two companies of infantry, Ibarra	100
Two companies of infantry, Loja	100
Company of infantry, Ambato	50
Total	**2,610**

MILITIA OF GUAYAQUIL

Battalion of white infantry	585
Battalion of pardo infantry	585
Four companies of white dragoons	240
Company of white artillery	65
Company of pardo artillery	65
Total	**1,540**

SOURCES: This table was adapted from a troop inspection report for the militia of Guayaquil, July 30,1783, and for the militia of Quito, August 17, 1783, ANE: Pres., vol. 194, fols. 51–62.

a. In the immediate postwar period, the militia of Quito underwent additional growth and reorganization. A 450-man battalion of infantry was organized in Guaranda by combining that district's three companies with the one of Ambato and raising five more; the two companies of Ibarra were expanded into a nine-company, 450-man battalion; and the regiment of dragoons in Quito was increased in strength to 450 members. See Caballero y Góngora to J. García de León y Pizarro, Santa Fe, October 13, 1784, ANE: Pres., vol. 205, fols. 132–38; troop inspection report for the militia of Quito, February 10, 1786, ANE: Pres., vol. 234, fols. 154–67.

TABLE 6
THE ARMY OF NEW GRANADA IN 1789

Regulars[a]	Infantry	Artillery	Mounted
Two companies of Santa Marta	154		
Half company of Santa Marta		24	
Regiment of Cartagena	890		
Royal Corps (two companies			
of Cartagena)		200	
(company of Panama)		100	
Battalion of Panama	679		
Parties of light infantry			
of all colors of			
Chimán (Panama)	80		
Detachment of Chagres	46		
Company of pardos of South			
Darién	109		
Company of Guayaquil	100		
Three companies of Quito	225		
Detachment of Popayán	25		
Auxiliary regiment of			
Santa Fe	1,200	100	
Cavalry viceregal guard			34
Totals	**3,508**	**424**	**34**
Total regulars			**3,966**

Disciplined Militia[b]	Infantry	Artillery	Mounted
Regiment of all colors,			
Riohacha (ten companies)	993		
Two companies of pardo			
dragoons, Riohacha			252
Regiment of all colors, Santa			
Marta (ten companies)	993		
Regiment of whites, Cartagena	892		
Battalion of pardos, Cartagena	893		
Regiment of all colors,			
Mompós and the savannahs			
of Tolú (Cartagena)	893		
Two companies of white			
dragoons, Corozal			
(Cartagena)			200
Company of pardos, Cartagena		100	
Company of morenos, Cartagena		100	
Brigade of pardos, Tolú			
(Cartagena)		20	
Regiment of whites, Panama			
and Natá	892		
Battalion of pardos,			
Panama and Natá	893		
Company of pardos, Panama		100	

Continued

TABLE 6—*Continued*

Four-company corps of light infantry, Portobelo and the margins of the Chagres River	360		
Seven-company corps of whites, Veragua and Alange	700		
Regiment of whites, Guayaquil (ten companies)	893	100	
Squadron of white dragoons, Guayaquil			180
Regiment of whites, Quito (ten companies)	892	50	
Regiment of white dragoons, Quito			450
Regiment of whites, Cuenca (ten companies)	893		50
Regiment of all colors, Popayán (ten companies)	993		
Squadron of white dragoons, Popayán			321
Regiment of whites, Santa Fe	892		
Regiment of white cavalry, Santa Fe (twelve companies)			600
Totals	12,072	470	2,053
Total disciplined militia			14,595

SOURCES: This table was adapted from Antonio Caballero y Góngora, "Relación del estado del Nuevo Reino de Granada . . . 1789," in *Relaciones de mando: Memorias presentadas por los gobernantes del Nuevo Reino de Granada*, ed. F. Posada and P. M. Ibáñez, pp. 268–72; Francisco Gil y Lemos, "Gil y Lemos y su memoria sobre el Nuevo Reino de Granada," ed. and introduction by Enrique Sánchez Pedrote, pp. 205–12; inspection report of Subinspector General Anastasio Zejudo, Quito, 1788, ANE: Pres., vol. 249, fols. 218–26; inspection report of Subinspector General Joaquín de Cañaveral, Cartagena, October 1, 1789, now on display in the Quinta de Bolívar, Bogotá; inspection report of Cañaveral, Cartagena, May 1793, ANC: MM, vol. 92, fols. 1019–35. The unit strengths listed by these sources vary somewhat, and the sources themselves are inconsistent. At times company extras were counted as well as command and staff group members; other times they were not. To make the data in this chart consistent with the other tables, it has been necessary to revise these deviations to a common denominator. It might also be noted that Zejudo, in his review and reorganization from Popayán to Panama, deviated from the unit strengths advanced in the Cuban reglamento by frequently organizing 100-man companies within the battalions, with grenadier strength at 92 or 93. Also see ANC: MM, vol. 64, fols. 1035–38, vol. 66, fols. 442–44, vol. 71, fols. 24–54, vol. 100, fols. 199–205, vol. 107, fols. 112–16.

a. The Regiment of the Princess, which departed in 1789, has not been included.

b. At this time many nine- and ten-company militia units were classified as regiments, apparently because they possessed both a colonel and a lieutenant colonel. Also, most battalions and regiments were increased in authorized strength by ten men per company.

TABLE 7
THE RIOHACHA EXPEDITIONARY FORCE

JULY 26, 1777

Location	Regulars[a]	Militia	Totals
Riohacha	56	41	97
Bahía Honda	44	46	90
Pedraza	24	66	90
Sinamaica	36	54	90
Sabana del Valle	90	0	90
Miscellaneous	0	108	108
Totals	**250**	**315**	**565**

JUNE 12, 1789

Units	Riohacha	Pedraza	Sinamaica	Total
Regular artillery companies of Santa Marta and Cartagena	11	4	1	16
Regular infantry companies of Santa Marta	7	0	0	7
Regular infantry regiment of Cartagena	0	78	0	78
Disciplined militia dragoons of Riohacha	47	118	82	247
Disciplined militia infantry regiment of Riohacha	48	0	0	48
Totals	**113**	**200**	**83**	**396**

SOURCES: 1777 figures adapted from the troop inspection report of Governor Ramón García de León y Pizarro, Riohacha, July 26, 1777, ANC: MM, vol. 99, fol. 299. Figures for 1789 adapted from the troop inspection report of Governor Juan Alvarez de Verina, Riohacha, June 12, 1789, ANC: MM, vol. 64, fol. 822.

a. Of these, 200 were from the regiment of Cartagena and 50 from the companies of Santa Marta.

TABLE 8
THE DARIEN EXPEDITIONARY FORCE IN AUGUST 1788

CAIMÁN

REGULARS

Royal Corps of Artillery	6
Total	6

MILITIA

Regiment of whites, Cartagena	53
Regiment of all colors, Mompós	32
Battalion of pardos, Cartagena	83
Total	168
Total strength	174

CAROLINA

REGULARS

Royal Corps of Artillery	23
Regiment of Cartagena	48
Regiment of the Princess	50
Total	121

MILITIA

Volunteers of Carolina[a]	48
Battalion of pardos, Cartagena	48
Regiment of all colors, Mompós	50
Light infantry of Natá[b]	40
First company of Natá[b]	38
Second company of Natá[b]	44
Total	268
Total strength	389

CONCEPCIÓN

REGULARS

Battalion of Panama	19
Total	19

Continued

TABLE 8—*Continued*

MILITIA

Company of whites, Natá	58
Battalion of pardos, Panama	19
Battalion of pardos, Natá	66
Battalion of pardos, Cartagena	26
Company of moreno artillery, Portobelo	8
Total	177

Total strength	**196**

MANDINGA

REGULARS

Royal Corps of Artillery, Panama	3
Battalion of Panama	7
Total	10

MILITIA

First company of whites of Veragua	51
Pardos of Panama	70
Pardos of Natá	33
Battalion of pardos, Cartagena	15
Company of moreno artillery, Panama	31
Total	200

Total strength	**210**

UNITS WHICH SERVED IN DARIEN AT OTHER TIMES

Battalion of whites, Panama and Natá; Separate company of whites, Panama; Separate company of whites, Portobelo; Company of pardo artillery, Cartagena; White dragoons of Lorica; Pardo dragoons of Riohacha; Urban company of Nóvita (Chocó); Urban company of Zitará (Chocó); Volunteers of Mandinga; Company of French Volunteers.

SOURCES: Adapted from the troop inspection report of Commander of the Expedition Antonio deArévalo, Carolina, August 27, 1788, ANC: MM, vol. 120, fols. 414–15. Also see ANC: MM, vol. 122, fols. 31–32, 314–15, 381–82, and troop inspection report, Arévalo, Cartagena, May 8, 1789, AGI: Santa Fe, legajo 573.
a. These were apparently activated colonists.
b. No color was listed for these units.

TABLE 9
THE ARMY OF NEW GRANADA IN 1794

Regulars	Infantry	Artillery	Mounted
Regiment of Cartagena	1,358		
Royal Corps (two companies			
and a brigade of Cartagena)		232	
(company of Panama)		100	
Battalion of Panama	679		
Parties of light infantry			
of all colors of Chimán			
(Panama)	80		
Detachment of Chagres	50		
Company of pardos of South			
Darién	109		
Four-company corps of Quito	308		
Company of Popayán	80		
Auxiliary battalion of Santa Fe	543		
Halberdier viceregal guard	24		
Cavalry viceregal guard			34
Totals	3,231	332	34
Total regulars			**3,597**

Disciplined Militia[a]	Infantry	Artillery	Mounted
Corps of light infantry and			
cavalry, Riohacha[b]	200		200
Regiment of Santa Marta[c]	710	90	
Regiment of Cartagena			
(two battalions)	1,600		
Battalion of pardos,			
Cartagena	800		
Two companies of pardos,			
Cartagena		200	
Squadron of dragoons,			
Corozal (Cartagena)			200
Two companies of San			
Bernardo and San Gerónimo			
(Cartagena)	200		
Regiment of Panama and Natá[c]	800		
Battalion of pardos,			
Panama and Natá	800		
Company of pardos, Panama		100	
Corps of light infantry of			
Portobelo and the margins			
of the Chagres River[b]	400		
Regiment of Guayaquil[c]	710	90	
Squadron of dragoons,			
Guayaquil			200

Continued

TABLE 9—*Continued*

Two companies of			
Jaén de Bracamoros	180		
Two companies of Loja	180		
Two companies of Barbacoas	200		
Totals	**6,780**	**480**	**600**
Total disciplined militia			**7,860**

SOURCES: This table was adapted from *Reglamento para las milicias disciplinadas de infantería y dragones del Nuevo Reyno de Granada, y provincias agregadas a este virreynato;* Joaquín Durán y Díaz, *Estado general de todo el Virreynato de Santa Fe de Bogotá,* pp. 391–408; José de Ezpeleta, "Relación del estado del Nuevo Reino de Granada . . . 1796," in *Relaciones de mando: Memorias presentadas por los gobernantes del Nuevo Reino de Granada,* ed. F. Posada and P. M. Ibáñez, pp. 386–95.

a. Class designations were discontinued for all but pardo units.

b. Twenty-five men of each of these units were also trained in the skills of artillery.

c. These units claimed the status of "regiments," apparently because they possessed both a colonel and a lieutenant colonel; in fact, the reglamento at times refers to them as battalions although in other instances they rate the higher classification.

TABLE 10
THE SOCIAL COMPOSITION OF THE REGULAR ARMY OFFICER CORPS

Year	Infantry, Cartagena						Artillery, Cartagena				Infantry, Santa Marta					
	Total		Senior[a]		Cadets		Total		Senior		Total		Senior		Cadets	
	Sp	Cr	Sp	Cr	Sp	Cr	Sp	Cr	Sp	Cr	Sp	Cr	Sp	Cr	Sp	Cr
1749	28	7	9	2	0	0										
1751																
1763																
1764	27	8	9	1	0	0										
1765	24	8	8	1	0	0										
1766	20	9	8	1	0	0					0	6	0	3	0	0
1767	21	7	9	1	0	0										
1768	20	10	9	1	0	0					0	6	0	2	0	0
1769	20	10	9	1	0	0										
1770	19	10	9	1	0	0										
1771																
1772																
1773																
1774																
1775																
1776							10	0	2	0	0	6	0	2	1	3
1777							9	0	2	0						
1778																
1779																
1780																
1781																
1782																
1783																
1784	24	8	12	1	6	10										
1785	22	8	12	1	7	11										
1786	19	8	11	1	7	10										
1787	17	8	9	1	7	10										
1788																
1789	19	10	7	0	5	11										
1790																
1791	30	28	12	9	5	12										
1792																
1793																
1794	26	25	12	7	6	13										
1795	29	25	13	6	4	15										
1796	29	29	10	9	3	14										
1797	27	30	11	8	3	18										
1798																
1799																
1800	30	29	11	10	3	21										
1801																
1802																
1803	27	30	8	10	3	17										
1804																
1805																
1806																
1807	23	34[b]	7	12												
1808																
1809																

Continued

TABLE 10—*Continued*

	Infantry, Panama						Artillery, Panama				Infantry, Santa Fe					
	Total		Senior[a]		Cadets		Total		Senior		Total		Senior		Cadets	
	Sp	Cr	Sp	Cr	Sp	Cr	Sp	Cr	Sp	Cr	Sp	Cr	Sp	Cr	Sp	Cr
1749																
1751	18	3	6	0	0	0										
1763	16	3	6	0	2	10	3	0	1	0						
1764	17	4	7	1	2	9										
1765	17	4	7	1	6	9	3	0	1	0						
1766																
1767																
1768																
1769																
1770																
1771																
1772																
1773																
1774																
1775																
1776	28	3	10	0	0	0										
1777																
1778																
1779																
1780	22	5	7	2	3	9										
1781																
1782																
1783																
1784																
1785																
1786																
1787											22	12	10	2	5	3
1788	16	10	9	2	1	13					22	11	9	2	5	10
1789	16	10	9	2	2	15					16	6	8	2	5	11
1790																
1791																
1792	17	11	9	1	0	16										
1793											16	6	6	1	3	5
1794	15	13	7	1	0	15					15	7	5	2	3	6
1795																
1796																
1797	13	12	9	2	0	16					14	7	4	3	2	4
1798																
1799							4	0	3	0						
1800	10	17	7	2	0	17					15	9	5	3	2	3
1801																
1802																
1803																
1804																
1805																
1806																
1807	4	26	4	6	0	7c										
1808																
1809											14	5	4	1	3	7

Continued

TABLE 10—*Continued*

	Infantry, Popayán						Infantry, Quito						Infantry, Guayaquil					
	Total		Senior		Cadets		Total		Senior		Cadets		Total		Senior		Cadets	
	Sp	Cr	Sp	Cr	Sp	Cr	Sp	Cr	Sp	Cr	Sp	Cr	Sp	Cr	Sp	Cr	Sp	Cr
1749																		
1751																		
1763																		
1764																		
1765																		
1766																		
1767																		
1768																		
1769																		
1770																		
1771																		
1772																		
1773																		
1774																		
1775																		
1776	2	1	1	0	0	0	4	3	3	0	0	0	2	0	1	0	0	0
1777																		
1778																		
1779																		
1780																		
1781																		
1782																		
1783																		
1784																		
1785																		
1786																		
1787																		
1788																		
1789																		
1790							3	3	2	0	0	7						
1791							3	6	2	1	0	7						
1792	3	0	1	0	2	0												
1793													2	0	1	0	1	0
1794	2	0	0	0	0	0	7	6	3	1	0	6						
1795																		
1796																		
1797	3	0	1	0	0	0	5	6	3	1	1	6						
1798																		
1799							6	6	3	1	1	7						
1800	2	0	0	0	0	0	5	6	2	1	1	7						
1801																		
1802																		
1803																		
1804																		
1805																		
1806																		
1807																		
1808																		
1809																		

Continued

TABLE 10—*Continued*

Sources: This table was constructed from service records found in AGS: GM, legajos 7280–82; AGI: Santa Fe, legajos 940–41, 944, 1010, 1156; AGI: Quito, legajo 573; AGI: Panama, legajos 356–57, 360; ANC: MM, vols. 13–14, vol. 45, fols. 347–52, 503–13, vol. 65, fols. 405–20, 528–38, vol. 79, fols. 188–92, vol. 90, fols. 32–33, 105–27, 909–33, vol. 94, fols. 445–504, vol. 97, fols. 413–30, 514–28, vol. 98, fols. 502–4, vol. 107, fols. 189–92, vol. 109, fols. 351–71, vol. 110, fols. 28–48, vol. 142, fols. 452–519.

a. "Senior" includes officers of the rank of captain and above.

b. One captain and two lieutenants are unaccounted for.

c. Seven cadets are unaccounted for.

TABLE 11
THE ARMY OF NEW GRANADA IN 1799

Regulars[a]	Infantry	Artillery	Mounted
Regiment of Cartagena	1,358		
Royal Corps (two companies			
and a brigade of Cartagena)		232	
(company of Panama)		100	
Battalion of Panama	679		
Parties of light infantry of all			
colors of Chimán (Panama)	80		
Detachment of Chagres	29		
Company of pardos of South			
Darién	109		
Four-company corps of Quito	308		
Company of Popayán	80		
Auxiliary battalion of Santa Fe	543		
Halberdier viceregal guard	24		
Cavalry viceregal guard			34
Totals	**3,210**	**332**	**34**
Total regulars			**3,576**

Disciplined Militia	Infantry	Artillery	Mounted
Corps of light infantry and			
cavalry, Riohacha[b]	200		200
Regiment of Santa Marta	710	90	
Regiment of Valledupar			
(Santa Marta)	400		200
Regiment of Cartagena			
(two battalions)	1,600		
Battalion of pardos, Cartagena	800		
Two companies of pardos,			
Cartagena		200	
Squadron of dragoons, Corozal			
(Cartagena)			200
Two companies of San			
Bernardo and San Gerónimo			
(Cartagena)	200		
Regiment of Panama and Natá	800		
Battalion of pardos, Panama			
and Natá	800		
Company of pardos, Panama		100	
Corps of light infantry of			
Portobelo and the margins			
of the Chagres River[b]	400		
Regiment of Guayaquil	710	90	
Squadron of dragoons, Guayaquil			200
Two companies of Jaén			
de Bracamoros	180		

Continued

TABLE 11—*Continued*

Two companies of Loja	180		
Two companies of Barbacoas	200		
Totals	7,180	480	800
Total disciplined militia			8,460

Sources: This table was adapted from *Estado militar de España;* Pedro Mendinueta, "Relación del estado del Nuevo Reino de Granada . . . 1803," in *Relaciones de mando: Memorias presentadas por los gobernantes del Nuevo Reino de Granada,* ed. F. Posada and P.M. Ibáñez, pp. 532–52. At this time there was also an independent troop detachment for the Governorship of Mainas to protect the boundary commission from savage Indians. Formerly, detachments from Quito had discharged this duty, but by the end of the century transportation difficulties led to the emergence of a separate body of roughly seventy-seven troops in that jurisdiction. These troops were not organized into a formal unit, however, and, therefore, are not included in this table. See José Ezpeleta, "Relación del estado del Nuevo Reino de Granada . . . 1796," in *Relaciones de mando,* pp. 391–92; expediente on the garrison of Quito, 1793–98, AGS: GM, legajo 7070.

a. This table does not include some 400 men from the Regiment of the Queen who arrived in early 1799.

b. Twenty-five men from these units were to be trained also in artillery skills.

TABLE 12
THE SOCIAL COMPOSITION OF THE DISCIPLINED MILITIA OFFICER CORPS

	White and All-Colored Infantry, Cartagena[a]								Pardo Infantry, Cartagena		Dragoons, Corozal (Cartagena)							
	Volunteers						Vets.		Veterans		Volunteers						Vets.	
	Total		Senior		Cadets						Total		Senior		Cadets			
	Sp	Cr	Sp	Cr	Sp	Cr	Sp	Cr	Sp	Cr	Sp	Cr	Sp	Cr	Sp	Cr	Sp	Cr
1776	10	5	6	1	3	7	25	4	3	1								
1777																		
1778																		
1779																		
1780																		
1781																		
1782																		
1783																		
1784																		
1785	24	15	15	3	0	3	4	0	2	1	4	2	2	0	0	1	0	0
1786																		
1787																		
1788																		
1789																		
1790	11	4	6	1	0	1	4	0										
1791																		
1792																		
1793																		
1794																		
1795																		
1796																		
1797	10	29	7	9	0	2	8	1	3	2	3	8	2	1	0	1	2	0
1798																		
1799																		
1800	7	28	6	8	1	4	5	3	2	2	3	6	2	2	0	1	1	0
1801										2	3	4	6	2	1	0	0	1	0
1802																		
1803	11	39	6	11	1	4	6	2										
1804																		
1805																		
1806																		
1807									0	2								
1808																		
1809																		

Continued

TABLE 12—*Continued*

	All-Colored Infantry, Santa Marta						Vets.		Dragoons of Valledupar (Santa Marta)						Vets.	
	Volunteers								Volunteers							
	Total		Senior		Cadets				Total		Senior		Cadets			
	Sp	Cr	Sp	Cr	Sp	Cr	Sp	Cr	Sp	Cr	Sp	Cr	Sp	Cr	Sp	Cr
1776																
1777																
1778																
1779																
1780																
1781																
1782																
1783																
1784																
1785																
1786																
1787																
1788	5	24	2	9	0	1	1	2								
1789																
1790																
1791																
1792																
1793																
1794																
1795																
1796																
1797	7	17	2	9	0	2	2	2								
1798																
1799																
1800	8	19	2	9	0	3	3	1	1	23	0	7	0	2	2	0
1801																
1802																
1803																
1804																
1805																
1806										1	21	0	8	0	2	2	0
1807																
1808																
1809	4	15	2	6	0	1	2	1								

Continued

TABLE 12—*Continued*

	Cazadores, Riohacha[b]						Vets.		White Infantry, Panama						Vets.	
	Volunteers								Volunteers							
	Total		Senior		Cadets				Total		Senior		Cadets			
	Sp	Cr	Sp	Cr	Sp	Cr	Sp	Cr	Sp	Cr	Sp	Cr	Sp	Cr	Sp	Cr
1776																
1777																
1778																
1779																
1780									4	15	3	6	0	0	11	0
1781																
1782																
1783																
1784									12	4	7	6	0	0	8	0
1785																
1786																
1787																
1788																
1789																
1790																
1791																
1792																
1793																
1794																
1795																
1796																
1797	1	2	1	0	0	1	2	0	5	19	3	7	0	1	4	0
1798																
1799																
1800	0	6	0	2	0	2	2	0	6	23	3	6	0	0	2	1
1801																
1802																
1803																
1804																
1805																
1806									5	20	2	5	0	0	3	1
1807																
1808																
1809	0	3	0	1	0	3	2	0								

Continued

TABLE 12—*Continued*

	Pardo Infantry, Panama Veterans		Cazadores, Portobelo[b]						White Infantry, Barbacoas			
			Volunteers				Vets.		Volunteers			
			Total		Senior				Total		Senior	
	Sp	Cr	Sp	Cr	Sp	Cr	Sp	Cr	Sp	Cr	Sp	Cr
1776	10	0										
1777												
1778												
1779												
1780												
1781												
1782												
1783												
1784	9	0	1	3	0	2	2	0				
1785												
1786												
1787												
1788												
1789												
1790												
1791												
1792												
1793												
1794												
1795												
1796												
1797	5	0	2	4	0	2	2	0	1	4	0	1
1798												
1799												
1800	1	0	1	3	0	1	1	0	0	4	0	1
1801	2	2										
1802												
1803												
1804												
1805												
1806			2	2	0	1	0	0				
1807												
1808												
1809												

Continued

TABLE 12—*Continued*

	White Infantry, Guayaquil								Dragoons, Guayaquil								Infantry, Jaén			
	Volunteers						Vets.		Volunteers						Vets.		Volunteers			
	Total		Senior		Cadets				Total		Senior		Cadets				Total		Senior	
	Sp	Cr	Sp	Cr	Sp	Cr	Sp	Cr	Sp	Cr	Sp	Cr	Sp	Cr	Sp	Cr	Sp	Cr	Sp	Cr
1776																				
1777																				
1778																				
1779																				
1780																				
1781																				
1782																				
1783																				
1784																				
1785																				
1786																				
1787																				
1788									1	12	1	2	0	1	0	0				
1789																				
1790																				
1791																				
1792																				
1793																				
1794																				
1795																				
1796																				
1797	4	24	2	8	0	6	3	0	1	10	0	3	0	4	2	0				
1798																				
1799																				
1800	4	22	2	7	0	7	4	0	0	12	0	3	0	3	1	0				
1801																				
1802	4	22	3	7	0	7	4	0	0	13	0	4	0	2	1[c]	0				
1803																				
1804																				
1805																	0	4	0	1
1806																				
1807																				
1808																				
1809																				

SOURCES: This table was constructed from service records found in AGS: GM, legajos 7280–82; AGI: Santa Fe, legajos 946, 1156; AGI: Panama, legajo 360; ANC: MM, vol. 13, fols. 126–32, 242–314, vol. 14, fols. 74–80, vol. 21, fols. 791–830, 914–31, vol. 26, fols. 692–739, 869–1011, vol. 27, fols. 202–59, 672–719, vol. 36, fols. 694–97, vol. 38, fols. 328–40, vol. 40, fols. 1–47, vol. 41, fols. 797–99, vol. 45, fols. 173–79, 459–94, 674–99, 903–4, vol. 46, fols. 160–228, vol. 47, fols. 10–34, vol. 75, fols. 42–50, vol. 97, fols. 79–124; and ANC: Virreyes, vol. 18, fols. 227–36.

a. The data for 1776 are only for the six companies of the city of Cartagena; those for 1790 include only the regiment of whites.

b. The data include only the white companies for these localities. It should also be noted that the companies of Portobelo had not been converted to cazadores in 1784, although for the sake of convenience they are entered in that column.

c. One veteran advisor is unaccounted for.

TABLE 13
THE ARMY OF NEW GRANADA IN 1806

Regulars	Infantry	Artillery	Mounted
Regiment of Cartagena	1,358		
Royal Corps (three companies			
of Cartagena)		315	
(company of Panama)		150	
Battalion of Panama	679		
Parties of light infantry of all			
colors of Chimán (Panama)	82		
Detachment of Chagres	29		
Company of pardos of			
South Darién	109		
Two companies of Quito	154		
Company of Popayán	96		
Auxiliary battalion of Santa Fe	543		
Halberdier viceregal guard	24		
Cavalry viceregal guard			34
Totals	**3,074**	**465**	**34**
Total regulars			**3,573**

Disciplined Militia[a]	Infantry	Artillery	Mounted
Corps of light infantry and			
cavalry, Riohacha	200		200
Company of pardos, Riohacha		70	
Regiment of Santa Marta	710	90	
Company of pardos, Santa Marta		70	
Regiment of Valledupar			
(Santa Marta)	400		200
Regiment of Cartagena			
(two battalions)	1,600		
Battalion of pardos, Cartagena	800		
Two companies of pardos,			
Cartagena		200	
Company of pardos, Tolú			
(Cartagena)		70	
Squadron of dragoons, Corozal			
(Cartagena)			200
Two companies of San			
Bernardo and San Gerónimo	200		
Regiment of Panama and Natá	800		
Battalion of pardos, Panama			
and Natá	800		
Company of pardos, Panama		100	
Corps of light infantry of			
Portobelo and the margins			
of the Chagres River	400		
Company of pardos, Portobelo		70	
Two companies of			
Jaén de Bracamoros	180		

Continued

TABLE 13—*Continued*

Two companies of Loja	180		
Two companies of Barbacoas	200		
Totals	6,470	670	600
Total disciplined militia			**7,740**

SOURCES: This table was adapted from Antonio José García, *Kalendario manual y guía de forasteros en Santa Fe de Bogotá, capital del Nuevo Reyno de Granada para el año de 1806*, pp. 334–46; report of Subinspector General Anastasio Zejudo, Cartagena, 1805, ANC: MM, vol. 43, fols. 976–94. These sources also contain listings for the urban militia remaining from the endeavors of Viceroy Mendinueta. They were as follows: Veragua, an 800-man infantry battalion; Mompós, a four-company corps of light infantry totaling 480; Las Tablas (Cartagena), one 50-man infantry company; and Barranca and Mahates (Cartagena), three 60-man companies of dragoons.

a. Guayaquil is not included in these reports because it was transferred to the jurisdiction of the Viceroyalty of Peru in 1803 for military matters.

Bibliography

Archives

Archivo Central del Cauca (ACC)
    Cabildos
    Gobiernos
    Militares

Archivo General de Indias (AGI)
    Audiencia de Panama
    Audiencia de Quito
    Audiencia de Santa Fe
    Audiencia de Santo Domingo
    Estado
    Indiferente General

Archivo General de Simancas (AGS)
    Guerra Moderna (GM)

Archivo Nacional de Colombia (ANC)
    Cabildos
    Competencias
    Guerra y Marina (GM)
    Milicia y Marina (MM)
    Reales Ordenes (RO)
    Virreyes

Archivo Nacional de Ecuador (ANE)
    Presidencia (Pres.)

Printed documents and contemporary works

Alsedo y Herrera, Dionisio. *Compendio histórico de la provincia . . . de Guayaquil. . . .* Madrid, 1741.
————. *Descripción geográfica de la Real Audiencia de Quito.* Madrid, 1915.
Amat y Junient, Manuel de. *Memoria de gobierno.* Edited by Vicente Rodríguez Casado and Florentino Pérez Embid. Seville, 1947.
Arrázola, Roberto, comp. *Documentos para la historia de Cartagena.* 3 vols. Cartagena, 1963–65.
————. *Historial de Cartagena.* Cartagena, 1961.
Blanco, José Félix, and Ramón Azpurua, comps. *Documentos para la historia de la vida pública del Libertador. . . .* 14 vols. Caracas, 1875–78.
Cabrer, Carlos Francisco, ed. "Proyecto de defensa militar de Bogotá (1797)." *Boletín de historia y antigüedades* 2 (December 1903): 230–32.
Caro, Francisco Javier. *Diario de la secretaría del Virreynato de Santa Fe de Bogotá. No comprehende más que doce días. Pero no importa, que por la uña se conoce el león; por la jaula el páxaro, y por la hebra se saca el ovillo.* Edited with introduction by Francisco Viñals. Madrid, 1904.
Colón y Larriátegui Ximénez de Embún, Félix. *Juzgados militares de España y sus Indias. . . .* 2d ed. 4 vols. Madrid, 1786–96.
Cuervo, Antonio B., comp. *Colección de documentos inéditos sobre la geografía y la historia de Colombia.* 3 vols. Bogotá, 1891–93.
Durán y Díaz, Joaquín. *Estado general de todo el Virreynato de Santa Fe de Bogotá, 1794.* Santa Fe de Bogotá, 1794.
Estado militar de España. Madrid, 1799.
Flores y Caamaño, Alfredo, ed. *Relación inédita de la ciudad y la provincia de Guayaquil.* Antiguallas históricas de la colonia, vol. 2. Quito, 1925.
García de la Guardia, Antonio Josef. *Kalendario manual y guía de forasteros en Santa Fe de Bogotá, capital del Nuevo Reino de Granada para el año de 1806.* Santa Fe de Bogotá, 1806.
Gil y Lemos, Francisco. "Gil y Lemos y su memoria sobre el Nuevo Reino de Granada." Edited with introduction by Enrique Sánchez Pedrote, in *Anuario de estudios americanos* 8 (1951): 169–212.
Humboldt, Alexander von, and Aimé Bonpland. *Personal Narrative of Travels to the Equinoctial Region of America during the Years 1799–1804.* 3 vols. London, 1852–53.
Jaramillo, Gabriel Giraldo, ed. *Relaciones de mando de los virreyes de la Nueva Granada: Memorias económicas.* Bogotá, 1954.
Juan, Jorge, and Antonio de Ulloa. *Noticias secretas de América (siglo XVIII).* 2 vols. Madrid, 1918.
————. *A Voyage to South America.* Translated by John Adams. New York, 1964.
King, James Ferguson, ed. "Admiral Vernon at Portobelo: 1739." *Hispanic American Historical Review* 23 (May 1943): 258–82.
————. "The Case of José Ponciano de Ayarza: A Document on *Gracias al Sacar.*" *Hispanic American Historical Review* 31 (November 1951): 640–47.
Konetzke, Richard, comp. *Colección de documentos para la historia de la formación social de Hispanoamérica, 1493–1810.* 3 vols. Madrid, 1953–62.
Moreno y Escandón, Francisco Antonio. "Estado del Virreinato de Santafé, Nuevo Reino de Granada . . . 1772." *Boletín de historia y antigüedades* 23 (September–October 1936): 547–616.
Narváez y la Torre, Antonio de. "Relación, o informe de la provincia de Santa Marta y Río Hacha . . . ." In *Escritos de dos economistas coloniales,* edited by Sergio Elías Ortiz. Bogotá, 1965.
Ordenanzas de S. M. para el régimen, disciplina, subordinación, y servicio de sus ejércitos. . . . 2 vols. Madrid, 1768.
"Pacificación general de los Indios del Darién, celebrada el 21 de julio, 1787." *Boletín de historia y antigüedades* 13 (June 1920): 197–202.
Palacios de la Vega, Joseph. *Diario del viaje entre los Indios y Negros de la provincia de Cartagena en el Nuevo Reino de Granada, 1787–1788.* Edited by Gerardo Reichel-Dolmatoff. Bogotá, 1955.
Pérez Sarmiento, José Manuel, and Luis Martínez Delgado, comps. *Causas célebres a los precursores. . . .* 2 vols. Biblioteca de Historia Nacional, vols. 59–60. Bogotá, 1939.

Posada, E., and P. M. Ibáñez, eds. *Relaciones de mando: Memorias presentadas por los gobernantes del Nuevo Reino de Granada.* Biblioteca de Historia Nacional, vol. 8. Bogotá, 1910.

Real declaración sobre puntos esenciales de la ordenanza de milicias provinciales de España, que ínterin se regla la formal, que corresponde a estos cuerpos, se debe observar como tal en todas sus partes. Madrid, 1767.

Reclus, Eliseo. *Viaje a la Sierra Nevada de Santa Marta.* Biblioteca Popular de Cultura Colombiana, vol. 112. Bogotá, 1947.

Reglamento para la guarnición de la plaza de Cartagena de Indias, castillos y fuertes de su jurisdicción. Madrid, 1736.

Reglamento para las milicias de infantería de la Provincia de Yucatán, y Campeche. . . . Madrid, 1778.

Reglamento para las milicias de infantería y caballería de la isla de Cuba, aprobado por S. M. Madrid, 1769.

Reglamento para las milicias disciplinadas de infantería y dragones del Nuevo Reyno de Granada, y provincias agregadas a este virreynato. Madrid, 1794.

Reglamento que El Rey ha mandado expedir para el nuevo pie y establecimiento de los Regimientos de Infantería de Toledo y Vitoria. Aranjuez, 1791.

Royal cédula, "sobre las formas y facultades con que don Sebastián de Eslava ha de erigir y servir el Virreinato del Nuevo Reino de Granada." *Ximénez de Quesada* 4 (August 1968): 241–49.

Silvestre, Francisco. *Descripción del Reyno de Santa Fe de Bogotá, escrita en 1789.* Biblioteca Popular de Cultura Colombiana, vol. 121. Bogotá, 1950.

Vargas, Pedro Fermín de. *Pensamientos políticos y memoria sobre la población del Nuevo Reino de Granada.* Biblioteca de Cultura Popular Colombiana, vol. 53. Bogotá, 1944.

Vernaza, Cornelio Escipión, comp. *Recopilación de documentos oficiales de la época colonial, con un apéndice relativo a la independencia de Guayaquil.* . . . Guayaquil, 1894.

Zamora y Coronado, José María, comp. *Biblioteca de legislación ultramarina en forma de diccionario alfabético.* . . . 6 vols. Madrid, 1844–46.

Articles

Aiton, Arthur S. "Spanish Colonial Reorganization under the Family Compact." *Hispanic American Historical Review* 12 (August 1932): 269–80.

Archer, Christon I. "The Key to the Kingdom: The Defense of Veracruz, 1780–1810." *The Americas* 27 (April 1971): 426–49.

———. "The Deportation of Barbarian Indians from the Internal Provinces of New Spain: 1789–1810." *The Americas* 29 (January 1973): 376–85.

———. "To Serve the King: Military Recruitment in Late Colonial Mexico." *Hispanic American Historical Review* 55 (May 1975): 226–50.

Barbier, Jacques A. "Elite and Cadres in Bourbon Chile." *Hispanic American Historical Review* 52 (August 1972): 416–35.

Brading, D. A. "Government and Elite in Late Colonial Mexico." *Hispanic American Historical Review* 53 (August 1973): 389–414.

Burkholder, Mark A. "From Creole to Peninsular: The Transformation of the Audiencia of Lima." *Hispanic American Historical Review* 52 (August 1972): 395–415.

Burkholder, Mark A., and David S. Chandler. "Creole Appointments and the Sale of Audiencia Positions in the Spanish Empire under the Early Bourbons, 1701–1750." *Journal of Latin American Studies* 4 (November 1972): 187–206.

Campbell, Leon G. "A Colonial Establishment: Creole Domination of the Audiencia of Lima during the Late Eighteenth Century." *Hispanic American Historical Review* 52 (February 1972): 1–20.

———. "The Changing Racial and Administrative Structure of the Peruvian Military under the Later Bourbons." *The Americas* 32 (July 1975): 117–33.

———. "The Army of Peru and the Túpac Amaru Revolt, 1780–1783." *Hispanic American Historical Review* 56 (February 1976): 31–57.

Comadrán Ruiz, Jorge. "En torno al problema del Indio en el Río de la Plata." *Anuario de estudios americanos* 12 (1955): 39–74.

Diggs, Irene. "Color in Colonial Spanish America." *Journal of Negro History* 38 (October 1953): 403–27.

Dusenberry, William. "Discrimination Aspects of Legislation in Colonial Mexico." *Journal of Negro History* 33 (July 1948): 284–302.

Frankl, Victor. "La estructura barroca del pensamiento político, histórico y económico del Arzobispo-Virrey de Nueva Granada Caballero y Góngora." *Bolívar* (Bogotá), no. 5 (1951): 805–73.

————. "La filosofía social tomista del Arzobispo-Virrey Caballero y Góngora y la de los Comuneros Colombianos." *Bolívar* (Bogotá), no. 14 (1952): 595–626.

Frías, R. "La expedición botánica al Nuevo Reino de Granada." *Universidad Nacional de Colombia* 5 (1946): 113–78.

Gilmore, Robert L. "The Imperial Crisis, Rebellion and the Viceroy: Nueva Granada in 1809." *Hispanic American Historical Review* 40 (February 1960): 1–24.

Hanke, Lewis. "A Modest Proposal for a Moratorium on Grand Generalizations: Some Thoughts on the Black Legend." *Hispanic American Historical Review* 51 (February 1971): 112–27.

Harrison, John P. "The Evolution of the Colombian Tobacco Trade, to 1875." *Hispanic American Historical Review* 32 (May 1952): 163–74.

Helguera, J. León. "The Changing Role of the Military in Colombia." *Journal of Inter-American Studies* 3 (July 1961): 351–58.

Hernández de Alba, Guillermo. "Sir Edward Vernon y don Blas de Lezo." *Boletín de historia y antigüedades* 28 (1941): 468–73.

Jaramillo Uribe, Jaime. "Mestizaje y diferenciación social en el Nuevo Reino de Granada en la segunda mitad del siglo XVIII." *Anuario colombiano de historia social y de la cultura* 2 (1965): 21–48.

King, James Ferguson. "Negro History in Continental Spanish America." *Journal of Negro History* 29 (January 1944): 7–23.

————. "Negro Slavery in New Granada." In *Greater America: Essays in Honor of Herbert Eugene Bolton*. Berkeley and Los Angeles, 1945, pp. 295–318.

Klein, Herbert S. "The Colored Militia of Cuba: 1568–1868." *Caribbean Studies* 6 (July 1966): 17–27.

Konetzke, Richard. "Estado y sociedad en las Indias." *Anuario de estudios americanos* 3 (1951): 33–58.

————. "La formación de la nobleza en Indias." *Anuario de estudios americanos* 3 (1951): 329–57.

————. "Ideas políticas del Virrey Francisco Gil de Taboada." *Mar del sur* 7 (March–April 1952): 44–55.

Kuethe, Allan J. "Un interesante caso de tolerancia religiosa en la época colonial." *Boletín de historia y antigüedades* 53 (January–February–March 1966): 153–59.

————. "The Pacification Campaign on the Riohacha Frontier, 1772–1779." *Hispanic American Historical Review* 50 (August 1970): 467–81.

————. "The Status of the Free Pardo in the Disciplined Militia of New Granada." *Journal of Negro History* 56 (April 1971): 105–17.

————. "La batalla de Cartagena de 1741: Nuevas perspectivas." *Historiografía y bibliografía americanistas* 18 (Seville, 1974): 19–38.

Lanning, John Tate. "Legitimacy and Limpieza de Sangre in the Practice of Medicine in the Spanish Empire." *Jahrbuch für Geschichte von Staat: Wirlschaft und Gesellschaft Lateinamerikas* 4 (Cologne, Germany, 1967): 37–60.

León Borja, Dora, and Ádám Szászdi Nagy. "El comercio del cacao de Guayaquil." *Revista de historia de América*, nos. 57–58 (1964): 1–50.

Love, Edgar F. "Negro Resistance to Spanish Rule in Colonial Mexico." *Journal of Negro History* 52 (April 1967): 89–103.

Luengo Muñoz, Manuel. "Génesis de las expediciones militares al Darién en 1785–86." *Anuario de estudios americanos* 18 (1961): 333–416.

Lynch, John. "British Policy and Spanish America, 1783–1808." *Journal of Latin American Studies* 1 (May 1969): 1–30.

Maingot, Anthony P. "Social Structure, Social Status, and Civil-Military Conflict in Urban Colombia, 1810–1858." *Nineteenth-Century Cities: Essays in the New Urban History*. Edited by Stephen Thernstrom and Richard Sennett. New Haven and London, 1969, pp. 297–355.

Marzahl, Peter. "Creoles and Government: The Cabildo of Popayán." *Hispanic American Historical Review* 54 (November 1974): 636–56.

McAlister, Lyle N. "The Reorganization of the Army of New Spain, 1763–1766." *Hispanic American Historical Review* 33 (February 1953): 1–32.

———. "Social Structure and Social Change in New Spain." *Hispanic American Historical Review* 43 (August 1963): 349–70.

Morner, Magnus. "Aspectos sociorraciales del proceso de poblamiento en la Audiencia de Quito durante los siglos XVI y XVII." In *Homenaje a don José María de la Peña y Cámara.* Madrid, 1969.

Muñoz Pérez, J. "La publicación del reglamento de comercio libre de Indias, de 1778." *Anuario de estudios americanos* 4 (1947): 615–64.

Nowell, Charles E. "The Defense of Cartagena." *Hispanic American Historical Review* 42 (November 1962): 477–501.

O'Dogherty, Angel. "La matrícula de mar en el reinado de Carlos III." *Anuario de estudios americanos* 9 (1952): 347–70.

Ots Capdequí, José María. "El indio en el Nuevo Reino de Granada durante la etapa histórica de la dominación española." *Revista de Indias* 17 (January–March 1957): 11–57.

Pacheco, Juan Manuel. "La expulsión de la Compañía de Jesús del Nuevo Reino de Granada en 1767." *Ximénez de Quesada* 4 (January 1968): 53–63.

———. "La Universidad de San José de Popayán." *Boletín de historia y antigüedades* 58 (July–September 1971): 453–61.

Palacio Atard, Vicente. "Areche y Guirior: Observaciones sobre el fracaso de una visita al Perú." *Anuario de estudios americanos* 3 (1946): 271–376.

Pérez Ayala, José Manuel. "Aspectos desconocidos de la vida del Virrey don Manuel de Guirior, co-fundador de la Biblioteca Nacional de Bogotá." *Boletín de historia y antigüedades* 43 (1956): 156–82.

Phelan, John Leddy. "El auge y la caída de los criollos en la Audiencia de Nueva Granada, 1700–1781." *Boletín de historia y antigüedades* 59 (November–December 1972): 597–618.

———. "La trayectoria enigmática de Manuel García Olano durante la revolución comunera." *Boletín de historia y antigüedades* 61 (April–June 1974): 157–85.

Quintero Guzmán, Miguel W. "Valencia: Una ilustre familia Cartagueña." *Boletín de historia y antigüedades* 58 (October–December 1971): 673–78.

Ramsey, Russell W. "The Defeat of Admiral Vernon at Cartagena in 1741." *Southern Quarterly* 1 (July 1963): 332–55.

Restrepo Canal, Carlos. "El sitio de Cartagena por el Almirante Vernon." *Boletín de historia y antigüedades* 28 (1941): 447–67.

Restrepo Posada, José, and Bernardo Sanz de Santamaría. "Genealogías 163 Gutiérrez." *Boletín de historia y antigüedades* 59 (April–June 1972): 297–304.

Restrepo Sáenz, José María. "Los secretarios del virreinato." *Boletín de historia y antigüedades* 33 (January–February 1946): 52–59.

———. "Gobernadores de Cartagena en el siglo XVIII." *Boletín de historia y antigüedades* 35 (1948): 57–61.

Riaño, Camilo. "Las milicias del '20 de julio'; Origen del ejército nacional." *Revista de las fuerzas armadas* (Colombia) 2 (October 1960): 91–106.

Rivas, Raimundo. "El Marqués de San Jorge." *Boletín de historia y antigüedades* 6 (May 1911): 721–50.

Sánchez Pedrote, Enrique. "La idea del poder en dos virreyes neogranadinos." *Estudios americanos* 11 (May 1956): 405–16.

Sharp, William F. "The Profitability of Slavery in the Colombian Chocó, 1680–1810." *Hispanic American Historical Review* 55 (August 1975): 468–95.

Smith, Robert C. "Requena and the Japura: Some Eighteenth-Century Watercolors of the Amazon and Other Rivers." *The Americas* 3 (July 1946): 31–65.

Smith, Robert S. "The Consulado in Santa Fe de Bogotá." *Hispanic American Historical Review* 45 (August 1965): 442–51.

Smith, T. Lynn. "The Racial Composition of the Population of Colombia." *Journal of Inter-American Studies* 8 (April 1966): 212–35.

Tanzi, Héctor José. "La justicia militar en el derecho indiano." *Anuario de estudios americanos* 26 (1969): 175–277.
———. "La justicia naval militar en el período hispano." *Revista de historia de América*, nos. 67–68 (1969): 65–102.
Tapson, Alfred J. "Indian Warfare on the Pampa during the Colonial Period." *Hispanic American Historical Review* 42 (February 1962): 1–28.
Torres Ramírez, Bibiano. "Alejandro O'Reilly en Cuba." *Anuario de estudios americanos* 24 (1967): 1357–88.
Torres Reyes, Ricardo. "El Mariscal O'Reilly y las defensas de San Juan, 1765–1777." *Historia* (Puerto Rico) 4 (April 1954): 3–36.
Vigness, David M. "Don Hugo Oconor and New Spain's Northeastern Frontier, 1764–1776." *Journal of the West* 6 (January 1967): 27–40.
Whitaker, Arthur P. "The Elhuyar Mining Missions and the Enlightenment." *Hispanic American Historical Review* 31 (November 1951): 557–85.

Books

Aguirre Beltrán, Gonzalo. *La población negra de México, 1519–1810*. Mexico, 1946.
Alcácer, Antonio de. *Las misiones capuchinas en el Nuevo Reino de Granada, hoy Colombia (1648–1820)*. Bogotá, 1959.
Arboleda, Gustavo. *Historia de Cali desde los orígines de la ciudad hasta la expiración del período colonial*. 3 vols. Cali, 1956.
———. *Diccionario biográfico y genealógico del antiguo departamento del Cauca*. Bogotá, 1962.
Arboleda Llorente, José María. *Popayán a través del arte y de la historia*. Popayán, 1966.
Arcila Farías, Eduardo. *Comercio entre Venezuela y México en los siglos XVII y XVIII*. Mexico, 1950.
Arnade, Charles W. *The Emergence of the Republic of Bolivia*. Gainesville, Fla., 1957.
Bagú, Sergio. *Estructura social de la colonia: Ensayo de historia comparada de América Latina*. Buenos Aires, 1952.
Bannon, John Francis. *The Spanish Borderlands Frontier, 1513–1821*. New York, 1970.
Becker, Jerónimo, and José María Rivas Groot. *El Nuevo Reino de Granada en el siglo XVIII*. Madrid, 1921.
Benedetti, Carlos. *Historia de Colombia*. Lima, 1887.
Beneyto Pérez, Juan. *Historia social de España y de Hispanoamérica*. Madrid, 1961.
Beverina, Juan. *El virreinato de las provincias del Río de la Plata: Su organización militar*. Buenos Aires, 1935.
Blossom, Thomas. *Nariño: Hero of Colombian Independence*. Tucson, Ariz., 1967.
Brading, D. A. *Miners and Merchants in Bourbon Mexico, 1763–1810*. London and New York, 1971.
Briceño, Manuel. *Los Comuneros: Historia de la insurrección de 1781*. Bogotá, 1880.
Cárdenas Acosta, Pablo E. *El movimiento comunal de 1781 en el Nuevo Reino de Granada*. 2 vols. Biblioteca de Historia Nacional, vols. 96–97. Bogotá, 1960.
Castillo, Abel-Romeo. *Los gobernadores de Guayaquil del siglo XVIII*. Madrid, 1931.
Colmenares, Germán. *Las haciendas de los Jesuitas en el Nuevo Reino de Granada: siglo XVIII*. Bogotá, 1969.
———. *Historia económica y social de Colombia, 1537–1719*. Bogotá, 1973.
Dousdebes, Pedro Julio. *Cartagena de Indias, plaza fuerte*. Bogotá, 1948.
Escalante, Aquiles. *El negro en Colombia*. Bogotá, 1964.
Farriss, N. M. *Crown and Clergy in Colonial Mexico, 1759–1821*. London, 1968.
Fisher, J. R. *Government and Society in Colonial Peru: The Intendant System, 1784–1814*. London, 1970.
Fisher, Lillian Estelle. *The Last Inca Revolt, 1780–1783*. Norman, Okla., 1966.
Floyd, Troy S. *The Anglo-Spanish Struggle for Mosquitia*. Albuquerque, 1967.
Franklin, John Hope. *From Slavery to Freedom: A History of Negro Americans*. 3d ed. New York, 1967.
García Vásquez, Demetrio. *Revaluaciones históricas para la ciudad de Santiago de Cali*. 3 vols. Cali, 1951–60.
Garrido Conde, María Teresa. *La primera creación del Virreinato de Nueva Granada (1717–1723)*. Seville, 1965.

Gómez Hoyos, Rafael. *La revolución granadina de 1810: Ideario de una generación y de una época, 1781–1821.* 2 vols. Bogotá, 1962.

González Suárez, Federico. *Historia general de la República de Ecuador.* 7 vols. Quito, 1890–1901.

Grases, Pedro. *La conspiración de Gual y España y el ideario de la independencia.* Caracas, 1949.

Groot, José Manuel. *Historia eclesiástica y civil de Nueva Granada.* 3d ed. 5 vols. Bogotá, 1953.

Guzmán, José Alejandro. *Títulos nobiliarios en el Ecuador.* Madrid, 1957.

Hamnett, Brian R. *Politics and Trade in Southern Mexico, 1750–1821.* New York and London, 1971.

Haring, Clarence H. *The Spanish Empire in America.* 2d ed. New York, 1963.

Henao, Jesús María, and Gerardo Arrubla. *Historia de Colombia.* . . . 2 vols. Bogotá, 1929.

Herr, Richard. *The Eighteenth-Century Revolution in Spain.* Princeton, N.J., 1958.

Holmes, Jack D. L. *Honor and Fidelity: The Louisiana Infantry Regiment and the Louisiana Militia Companies, 1766–1821.* Birmingham, Ala., 1965.

Humphreys, R. A., and John Lynch, eds. *The Origins of the Latin American Revolutions, 1808–1826.* New York, 1965.

Ibáñez, Pedro M. *Crónicas de Bogotá.* 2d ed. 3 vols. Biblioteca de Historia Nacional, vols. 10–12. Bogotá, 1908–23.

León, Nicolás. *Las castas del México colonial o Nueva España.* Mexico, 1924.

Lewin, Boleslao. *La insurrección de Túpac Amaru.* 2d ed. Buenos Aires, 1967.

Liévano Aguirre, Indalecio. *Los grandes conflictos sociales y económicos de nuestra historia.* 4 vols. Bogotá, n.d.

Lynch, John. *Spanish Colonial Administration, 1782–1810: The Intendant System in the Viceroyalty of Río de la Plata.* London, 1958.

Marco Dorta, Enrique. *Cartagena de Indias: Puerto y plaza fuerte.* Cartagena, 1960.

Marroquín, L. *Precursores.* Bogotá, 1913.

Martínez Delgado, Luis, ed. *Popayán, ciudad prócera.* Biblioteca Eduardo Santos, vol. 16. Bogotá, 1959.

——. *Historia extensa de Colombia.* 25 vols. Bogotá, 1965–.

McAlister, Lyle N. *The "Fuero Militar" in New Spain, 1764–1800.* Gainesville, Fla., 1957.

Medina, José Toribio. *Historia del tribunal del Santo Oficio de la Inquisición de Cartagena de Indias.* Santiago de Chile, 1899.

Moore, John Preston. *The Cabildo in Perú under the Bourbons: A Study in the Decline and Resurgence of Local Government in the Audiencia of Lima, 1700–1824.* Durham, N.C., 1966.

Morner, Magnus, ed. *The Expulsion of the Jesuits from Latin America.* New York, 1965.

Navarro García, Luis. *Intendencias de Indias.* Seville, 1959.

Nieto Arteta, Luis Eduardo. *Economía y cultura en la historia de Colombia.* 2d ed. Bogotá, 1962.

Olano, Antonio. *Popayán en la colonia: Bosquejo histórico de la gobernación y la ciudad de Popayán en los siglos XVII y XVIII.* Popayán 1910.

Ortiz, Sergio Elías. *Crónicas de la ciudad de Sant Joan de Pasto.* Pasto, 1948.

——. *Agustín Agualongo y su tiempo.* Biblioteca Eduardo Santos, vol. 15. Bogotá, 1958.

Ospina Vásquez, Luis. *Industria y protección en Colombia, 1810–1930.* Medellín, 1955.

Ots Capdequí, José María. *Instituciones de gobierno del Nuevo Reino de Granada durante el siglo XVIII.* Bogotá, 1950.

——. *Las instituciones del Nuevo Reino de Granada al tiempo de la independencia.* Madrid, 1958.

Palmer, R. R. *The Age of Democratic Revolution: A Political History of Europe and America, 1760–1800.* 2 vols. Princeton, N.J., 1959–64.

Pardo Umaña, Camilo. *Haciendas de la sabana: Su historia, sus leyendas y tradiciones.* Bogotá, 1946.

Pérez Aparicio, Josefina. *Pérdida de la Isla de Trinidad.* Seville, 1966.

Pérez Ayala, José Manuel. *Antonio Caballero y Góngora, virrey y arzobispo de Santa Fe, 1723–96.* Bogotá, 1951.

Phelan, John Leddy. *The Kingdom of Quito in the Seventeenth Century: Bureaucratic Politics in the Spanish Empire.* Madison, Wis., 1967.

Plaza, José Antonio de. *Memorias para la historia de la Nueva Granada desde su descubrimiento hasta el 20 de julio de 1810.* Bogotá, 1850.

Porras Troconis, G. *Cartagena hispánica: 1533–1810.* Bogotá, 1954.

Priestley, Herbert Ingram. *José de Gálvez: Visitor-General of New Spain (1765–1771).* Berkeley, Calif., 1916.

Restrepo, José Manuel. *Historia de la revolución de la República de Colombia en la América meridional.* 8 vols. Biblioteca Popular de Cultura Colombiana, vol. 9. Bogotá, 1942–50.

Restrepo, Vicente. *Estudio sobre las minas de oro y plata de Colombia.* Bogotá, 1952.

Restrepo Sáenz, José María. *Biografías de los mandatarios y ministros de la Real Audiencia (1671–1819).* Biblioteca de Historia Nacional, vol. 84. Bogotá, 1952.

Restrepo Tirado, Ernesto. *Gobernantes del Nuevo Reyno de Granada durante el siglo XVIII.* Buenos Aires, 1934.

Reyes, Oscar Efrén. *Breve historia general del Ecuador.* 3 vols. Quito, 1967.

Rivas, Raimundo. *El andante caballero don Antonio Nariño: La juventud (1765–1803).* Biblioteca de Historia Nacional, vol. 50. Bogotá, 1938.

Rodríguez Casado, Vicente. *La política y los políticos en el reinado de Carlos III.* Madrid, 1962.

Rosenblat, Angel. *La población indígena y el mestizaje en América.* 2 vols. Buenos Aires, 1954.

Safford, Frank. *The Idea of the Practical: Colombia's Struggle to Form a Technical Elite.* Austin and London, 1976.

Scarpetta, Leonidas, and Saturnino Vergara. *Diccionario biográfico de los campeones de la libertad de Nueva Granada, Venezuela, Ecuador i Perú, que comprende sus servicios, hazañas i virtudes.* Bogotá, 1879.

Shafer, R. J. *The Economic Societies in the Spanish World (1763–1821).* Syracuse, N.Y., 1958.

Smith, T. Lynn. *Colombia: Social Structure and the Process of Development.* Gainesville, Fla., 1967.

Thomas, Alfred B. *Teodoro de Croix and the Northern Frontier of New Spain, 1776–1783.* Norman, Okla., 1941.

Tisnes, Roberto María. *Movimientos pre-independientes grancolombianos.* Biblioteca Eduardo Santos, vol. 27. Bogotá, 1962.

Torres Ramírez, Bibiano. *Alejandro O'Reilly en las Indias.* Seville, 1969.

Van Middeldyk, R. A. *The History of Puerto Rico.* New York and London, 1910.

Vargas Ugarte, Rubén. *Historia del Perú: Virreinato (siglo XVIII).* Buenos Aires, 1957.

Vicens Vives, Jaime. *Historia de España y América.* 4 vols. Barcelona, 1961.

West, Robert C. *Colonial Placer Mining in Colombia.* Baton Rouge, La., 1952.

Whitaker, Arthur P., ed. *Latin America and the Enlightenment.* 2d ed. Ithaca, N. Y., 1961.

Williams, Eric. *History of the People of Trinidad and Tobago.* New York, 1964.

Ybot León, Antonio. *La arteria histórica del Nuevo Reino de Granada (Cartagena-Santa Fe, 1538–1798).* Bogotá, 1952.

Dissertations

Campbell, Leon G. "The Military Reform in the Viceroyalty of Peru, 1762–1800." Ph.D. dissertation, University of Florida, 1970.

Fleener, Charles J. "The Expulsion of the Jesuits from the Viceroyalty of New Granada, 1767." Ph.D. dissertation, University of Florida, 1969.

Hamerly, Michael T. "A Social and Economic History of the City and District of Guayaquil during the Late Colonial and Independence Periods." Ph.D. dissertation, University of Florida, 1970.

Leonard, David Phelps. "The Comunero Rebellion of New Granada in 1781. . . ." Ph.D. dissertation, University of Michigan, 1951.

Sharp, William Frederick. "Forsaken but for Gold: An Economic Study of Slavery and Mining in the Colombian Chocó, 1680–1810." Ph.D. dissertation, University of North Carolina, 1970.

Index

LATIN AMERICAN MONOGRAPHS—SECOND SERIES